Primary 1A Preface

Singapore Math® **Intensive Practice** is a series of 12 books written to provide challenging supplementary material for Singapore's Primary Mathematics.

The primary objective of this series of books is to help students generate greater interest in mathematics and gain more confidence in solving mathematical problems. To achieve this, special features are incorporated in the series.

SPECIAL FEATURES

Topical Review

Enables students of mixed abilities to be exposed to a good variety of questions which are of varying levels of difficulty so as to help them develop a better understanding of mathematical concepts and their applications.

Mid-Year or End-Of-Year Review

Provides students with a good review that summarizes the topics learned in Primary Mathematics.

Take the Challenge!

Deepens students' mathematical concepts and helps develop their mathematical reasoning and higher-order thinking skills as they practice their problem-solving strategies.

More Challenging Problems

Stimulate students' interest through challenging and thought-provoking problems which encourage them to think critically and creatively as they apply their knowledge and experience in solving these problems.

Why this Series?

Students will find this series of books a good complement and supplement to the Primary Mathematics textbooks and workbooks. The comprehensive coverage certainly makes this series a valuable resource for teachers, parents and tutors.

It is hoped that the special features in this series of books will inspire and spur young people to achieve better mathematical competency and greater mathematics problem-solving skills.

Published by
Singapore Math Inc
404 Beavercreek Road #225
Oregon City, OR 97045
U.S.A.
E-mail: customerservice@singaporemath.com
www.singaporemath.com

First published 2004
Reprinted 2005, 2006, 2007, 2009, 2010, 2011, 2012

Singapore Math® Intensive Practice 1A (U.S. edition)

ISBN 978-1-932906-00-4

Printed in Singapore

Our special thanks to Jenny Hoerst for her assistance in editing the U.S. edition of Singapore Math® Intensive Practice.

Primary 1A

Contents

Topic 1: Numbers to 10

1. Count the number of fruits in each box and match it to the correct basket.

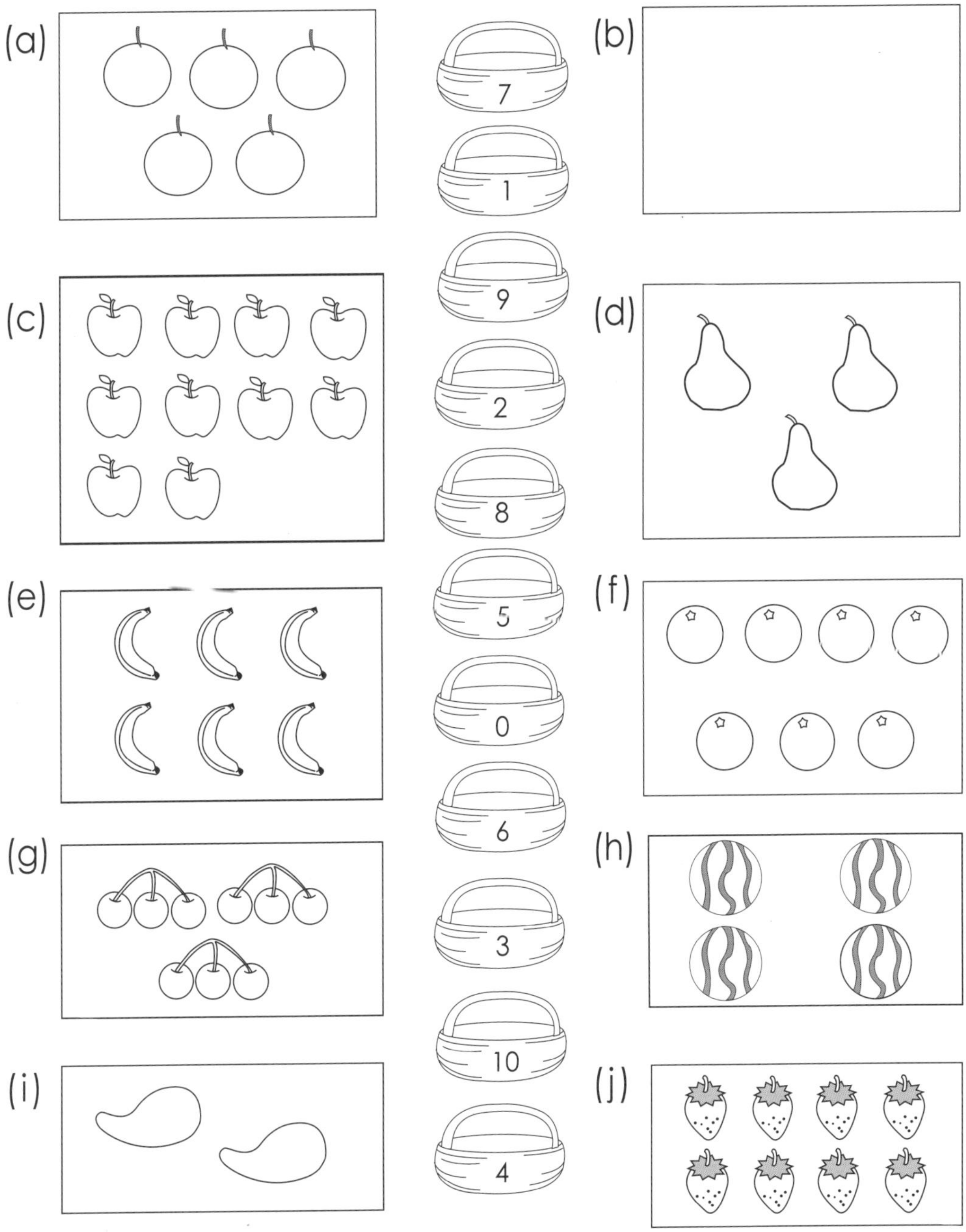

(a) (b)

Baskets: 7, 1, 9, 2, 8, 5, 0, 6, 3, 10, 4

(c) (d)

(e) (f)

(g) (h)

(i) (j)

2. Follow the path, counting from 0 to 10. Pick up the balloons together with the numbers. Then, complete the word puzzle at the bottom of the page.

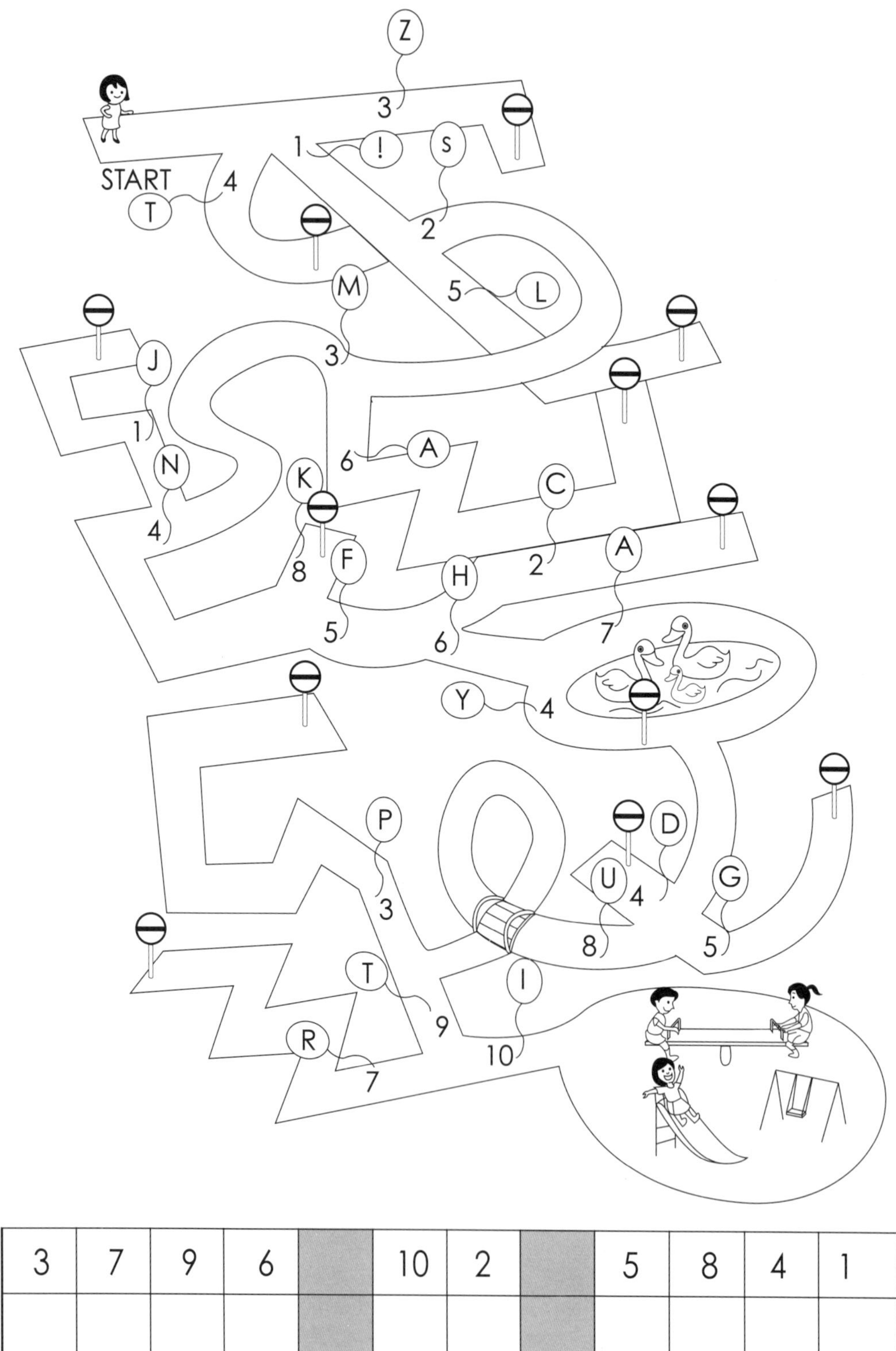

3	7	9	6		10	2		5	8	4	1

3. Look at the picture. Count and put the correct number in the boxes below.

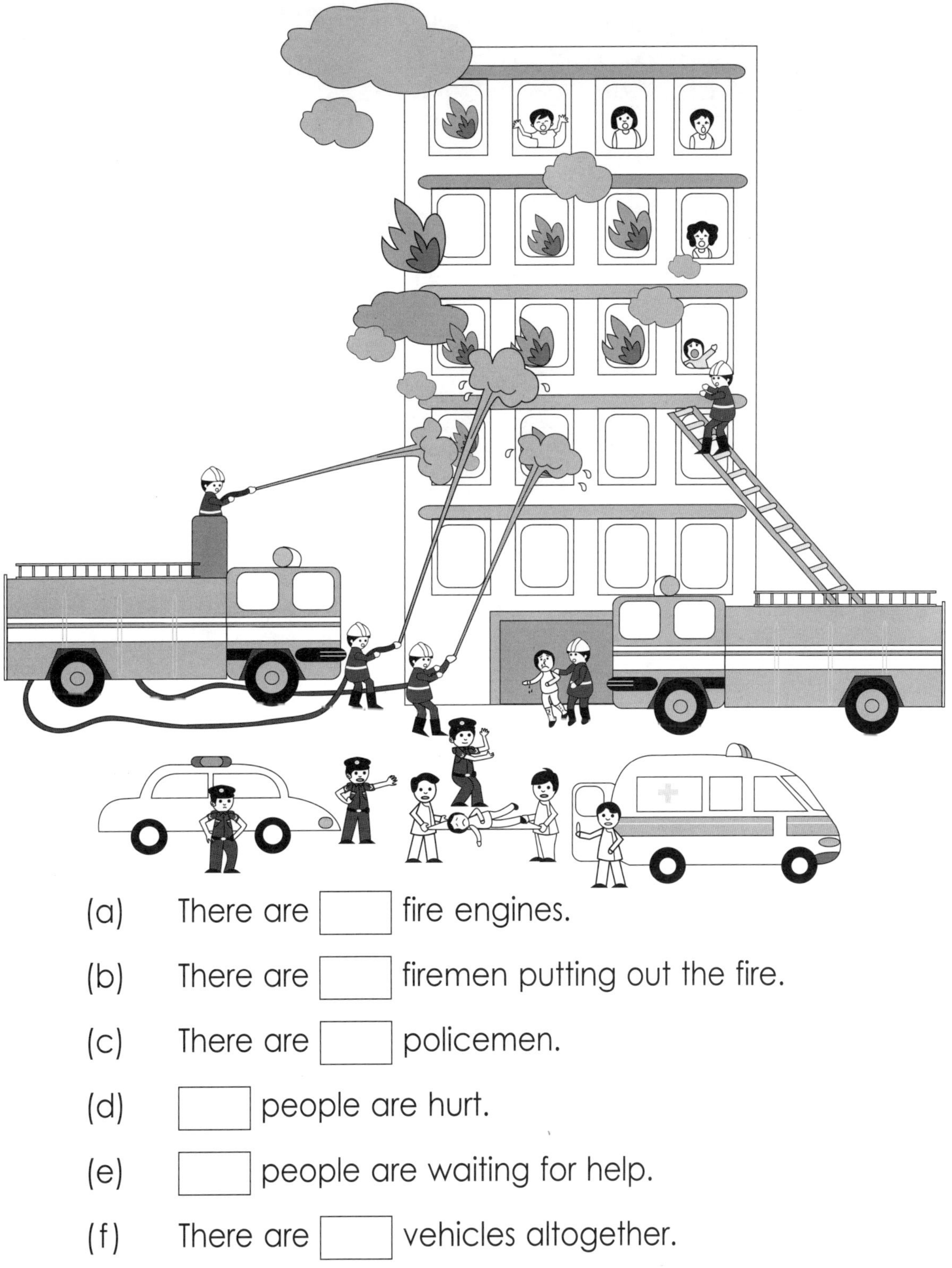

(a) There are ☐ fire engines.

(b) There are ☐ firemen putting out the fire.

(c) There are ☐ policemen.

(d) ☐ people are hurt.

(e) ☐ people are waiting for help.

(f) There are ☐ vehicles altogether.

4. Color the correct number of animals as stated in each box.

(a)

(b)

(c)

(d)

5. Count and write the correct number in words in each star.

(a)

(b)

(c)

(d)

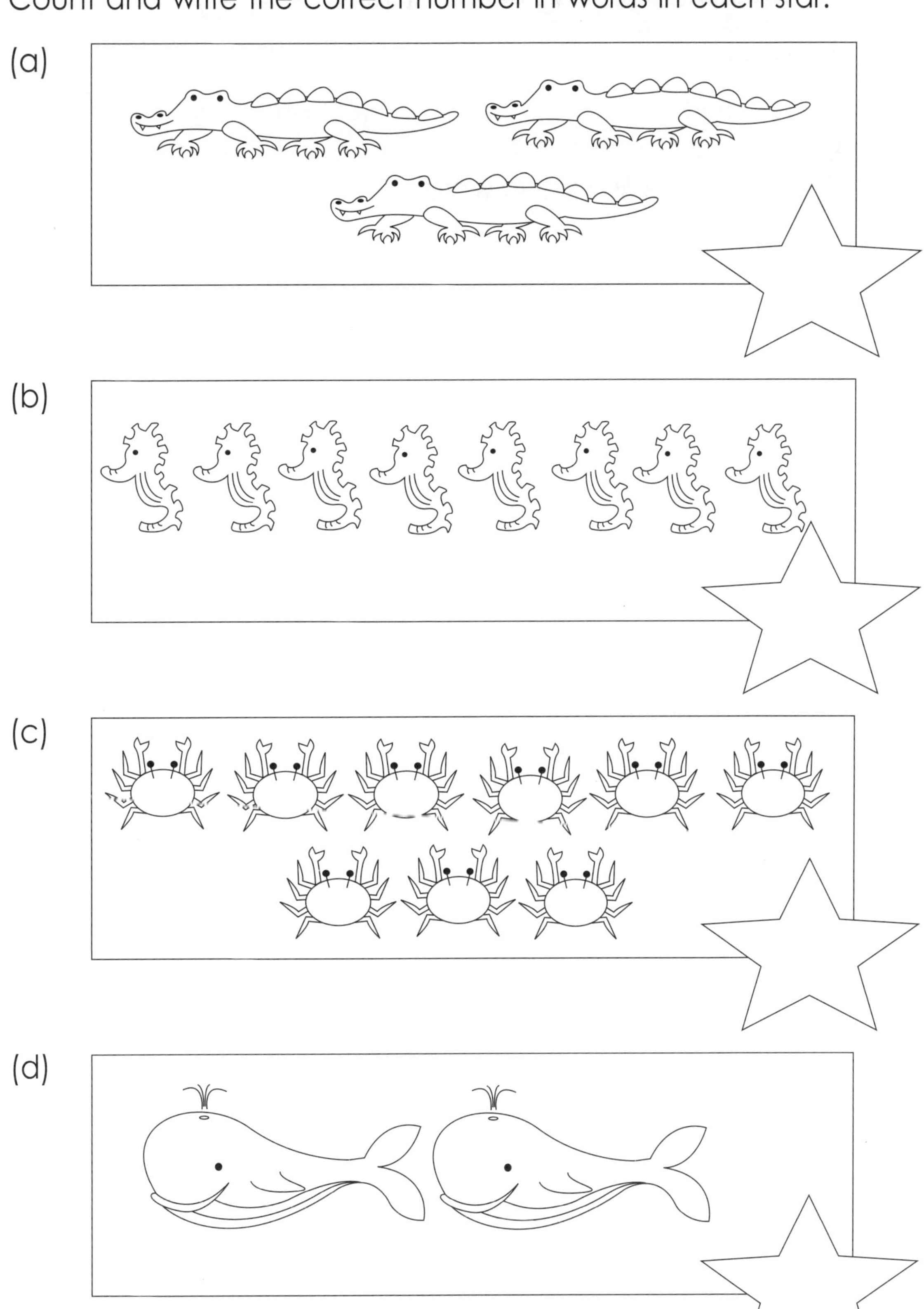

6. Write the following in numerals.

(a) six ☐ (b) three ☐

(c) two ☐ (d) one ☐

7. Write the following in words.

(a) 4 ☐ (b) 5 ☐

(c) 7 ☐ (d) 10 ☐

(e) 0 ☐

8. Fill in the boxes with the correct answers in words. Then, find these words in the puzzle and circle them.
Clues:

(a) ☐ is between 5 and 7.

(b) ☐ comes immediately after 2.

(c) There is a fairy tale called "Snow White and the ☐ Dwarfs".

(d) A car has ☐ wheels.

(e) A hand has ☐ fingers.

(f) You have ☐ nose.

(g) ☐ comes after 8 and before 10.

(h) I have ☐ toes altogether.

(i) ☐ comes before 1.

(j) A spider has ☐ legs.

(k) A sandwich is made up of at least ☐ slices of bread.

N	B	A	W	T	W	O	C
I	O	H	V	P	S	N	H
N	X	T	H	R	E	E	N
E	R	S	J	I	V	I	S
D	F	I	V	E	E	G	K
Y	G	X	T	E	N	H	B
Q	Z	E	R	O	M	T	Y
Z	U	N	I	F	O	U	R

9. Check (✓) the set with the largest number.

(a)

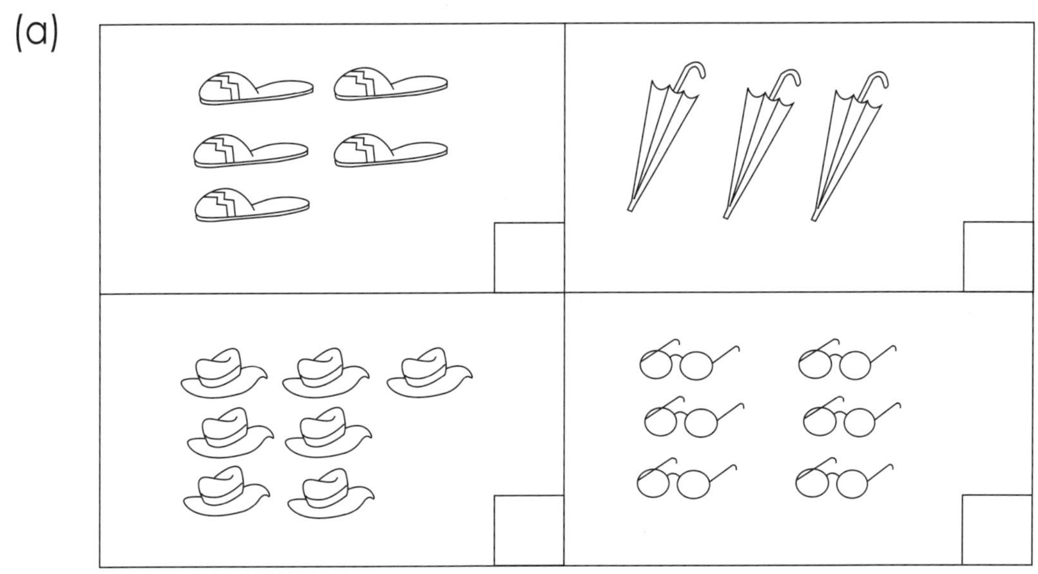

(b)

(c)

(d)

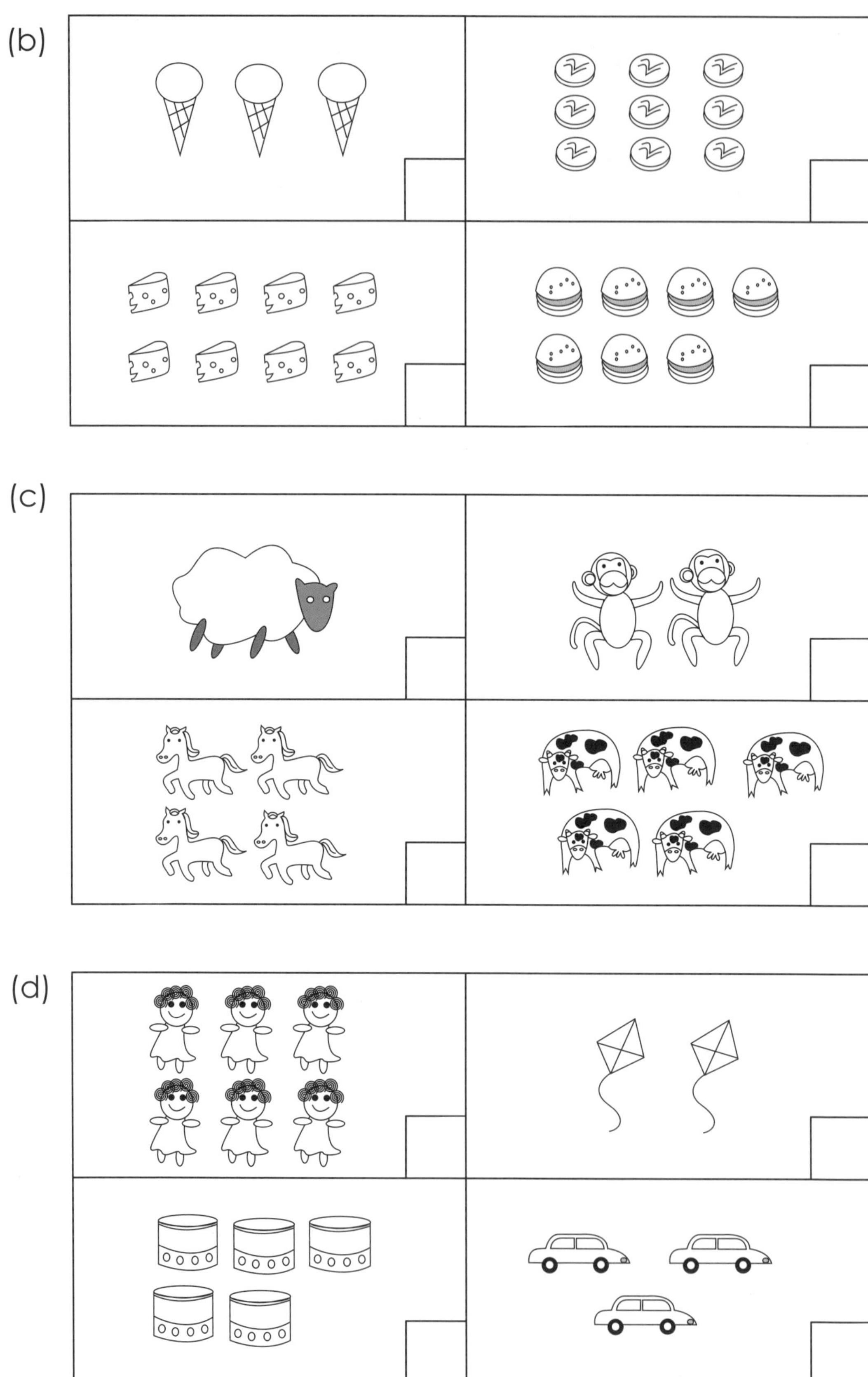

WORD PROBLEMS

1. How many people are in line?

There are ☐ people in line.

2. Samuel is having a birthday party. How many guests are there at the party?

There are ☐ guests at the party.

3. This is a park. How many children are there in the park?

There are ☐ children in the park.

4. Mother hangs clothes on the pole to dry. How many shirts and pairs of shorts are there?

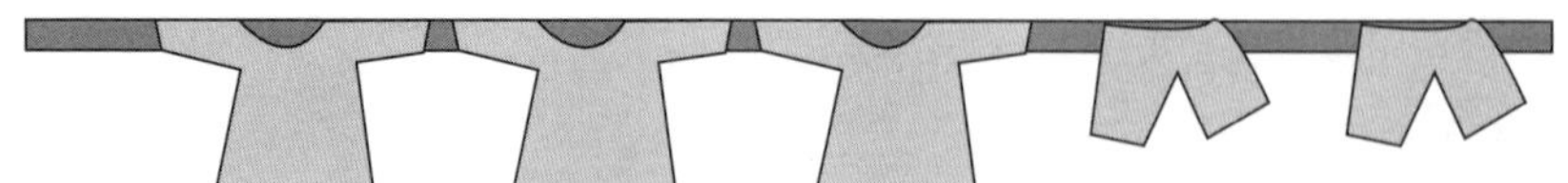

There are ☐ shirts and ☐ pairs of shorts on the pole.

5. Look at the picture. Who has more pets?

☐ has more pets.

6. Look at the picture. Which plate has more candy?

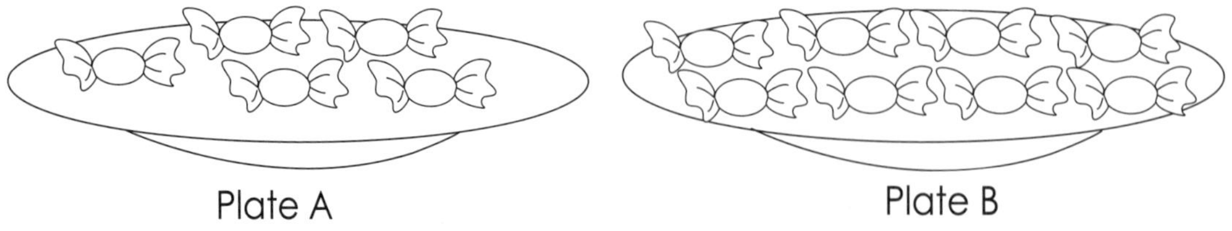

Plate ☐ has more candy.

7. Look at the picture. Which field has more frogs?

Field [ ] has more frogs.

8. Look at the picture. Who picked more strawberries?

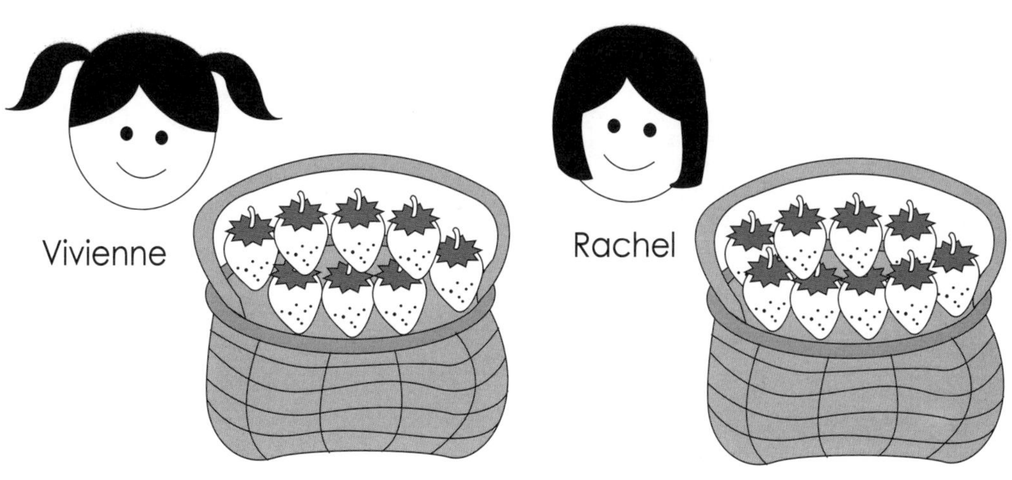

[ ] picked more strawberries.

Take the Challenge!

1. Look at the picture. Ben and Nancy baked some cakes. Who baked more cakes?

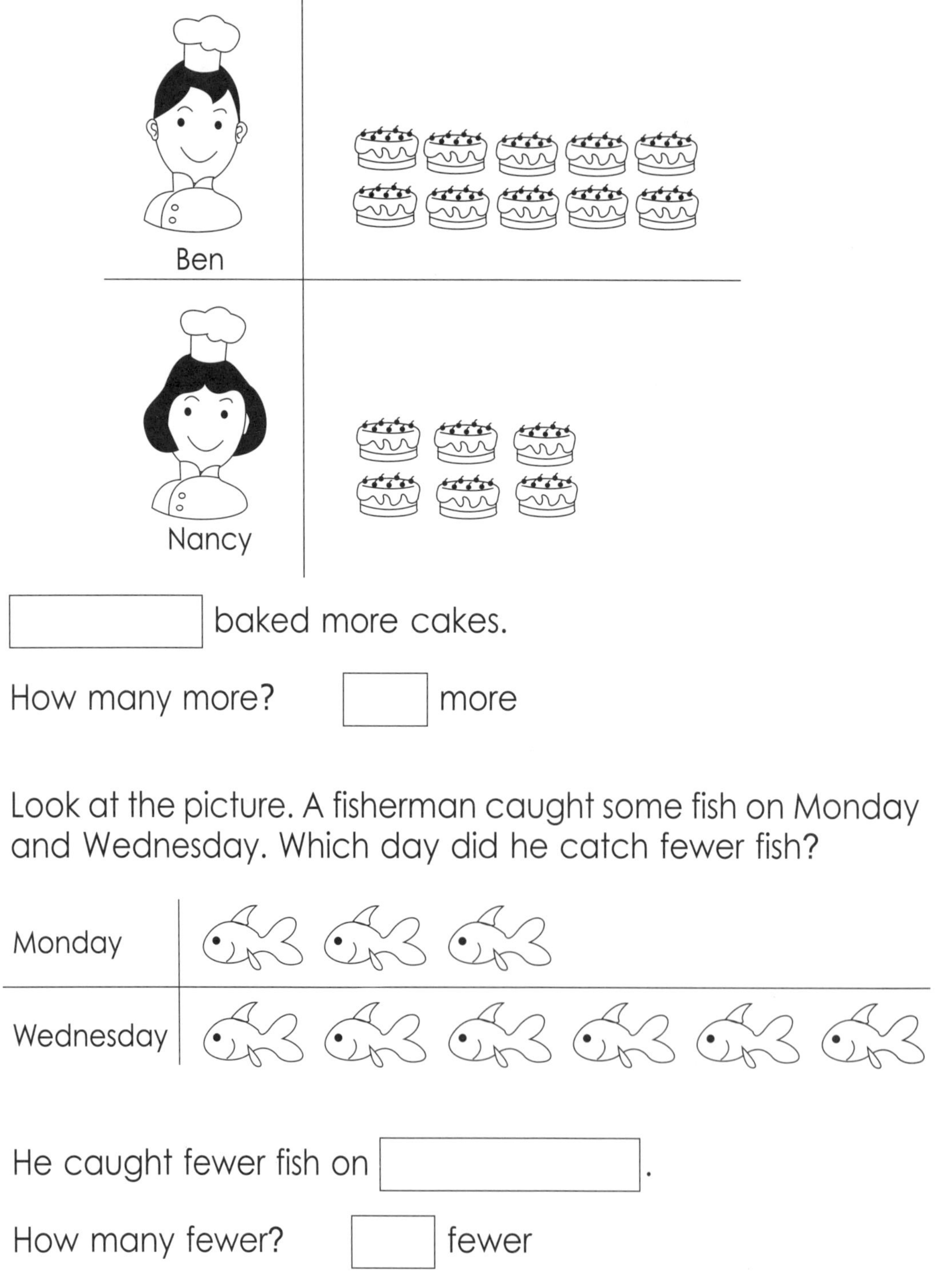

[ ] baked more cakes.

How many more? [ ] more

2. Look at the picture. A fisherman caught some fish on Monday and Wednesday. Which day did he catch fewer fish?

He caught fewer fish on [ ].

How many fewer? [ ] fewer

3. Complete each pattern by filling in the correct numbers.

(a)

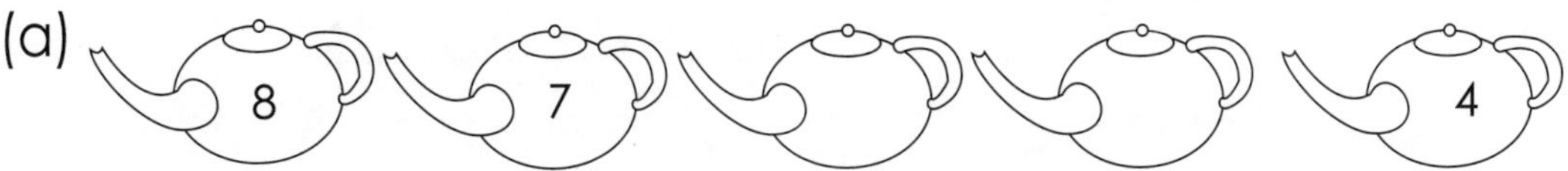

(b)

(c)

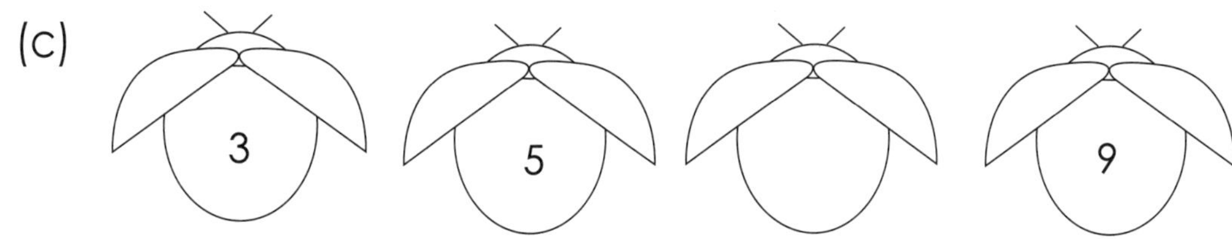

Topic 2: Number Bonds

1. Look at the number bonds. Circle the pictures to show the parts.

(a) 5 → 1, 4

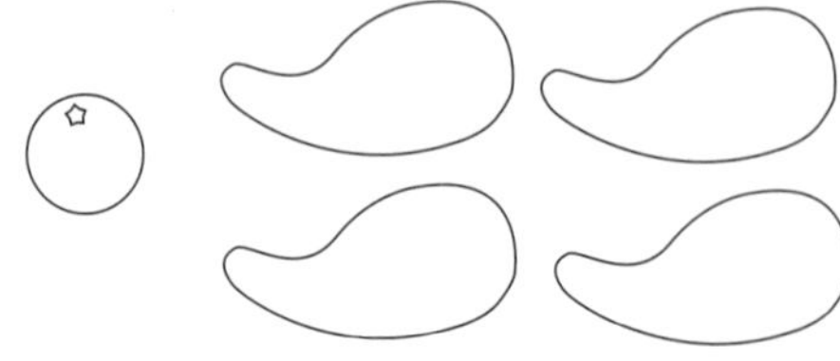

(b) 7 → 5, 2

(c) 8 → 5, 3

(d) 6 → 4, 2

(e)

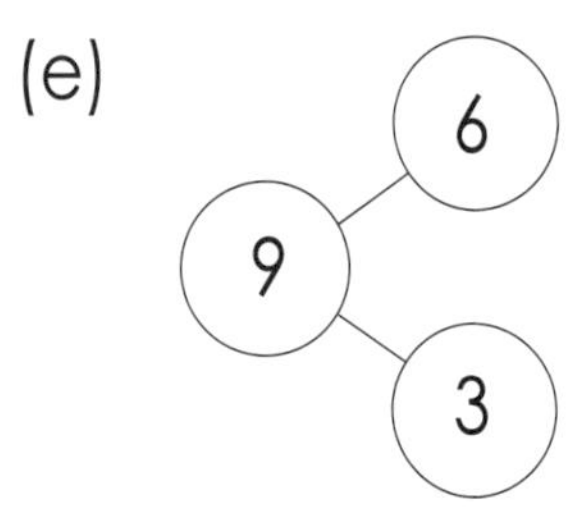

2. Fill in the missing numbers to complete the number bonds.

(a)

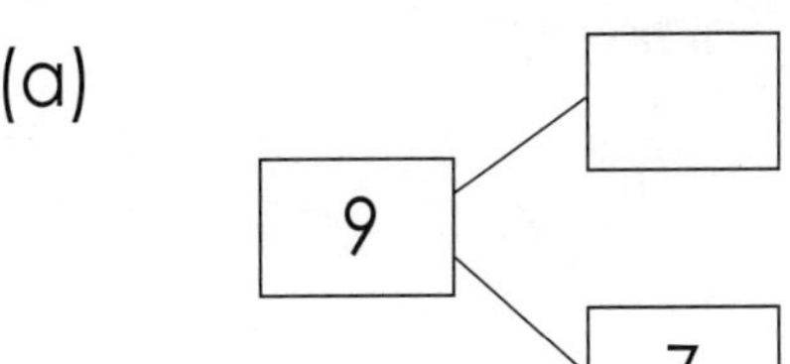

(b)

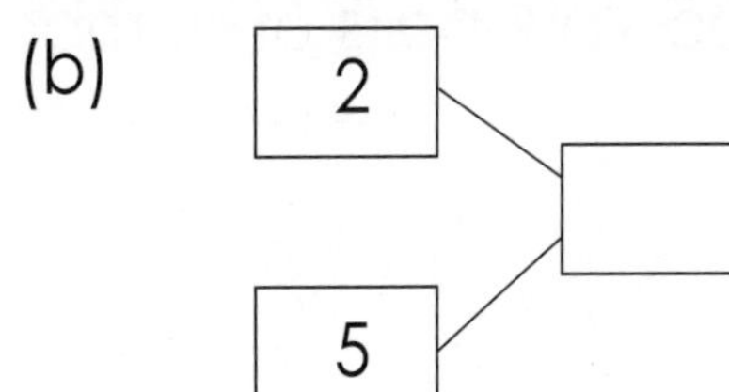

(c)

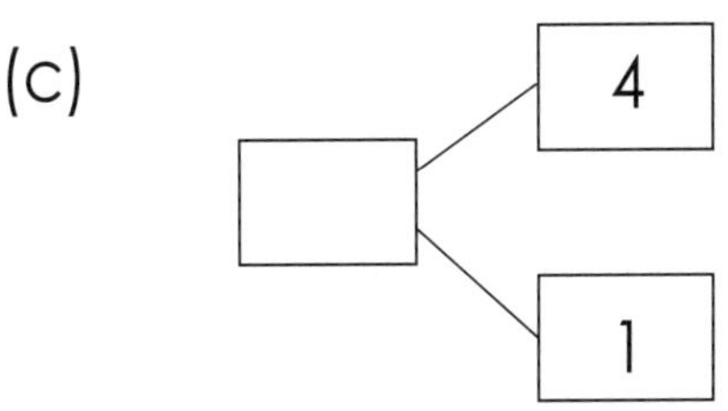

(d)

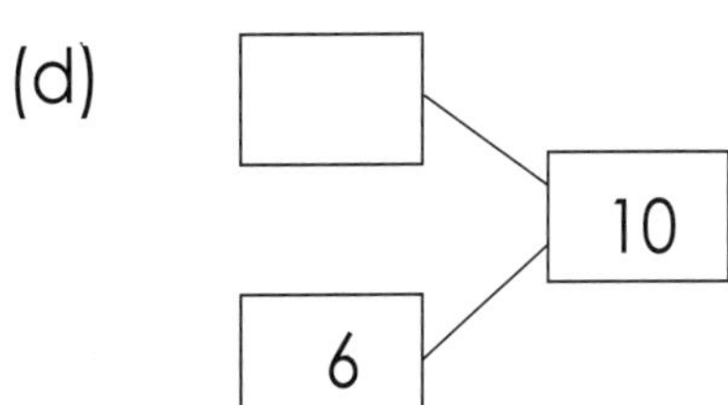

(e)

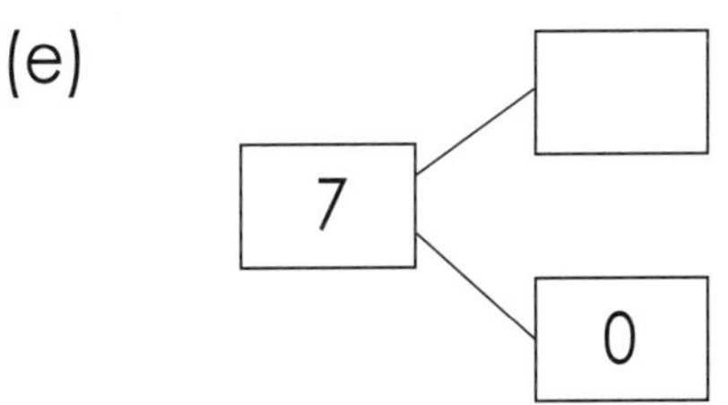

(f)

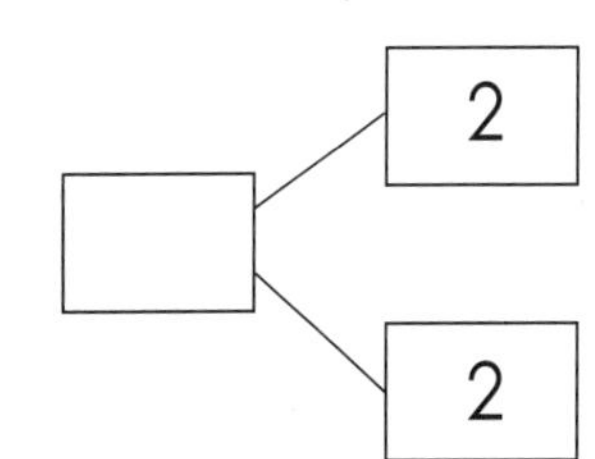

(g)

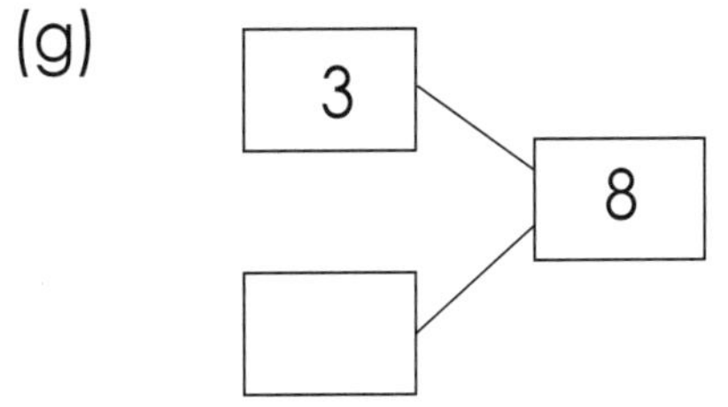

(h)

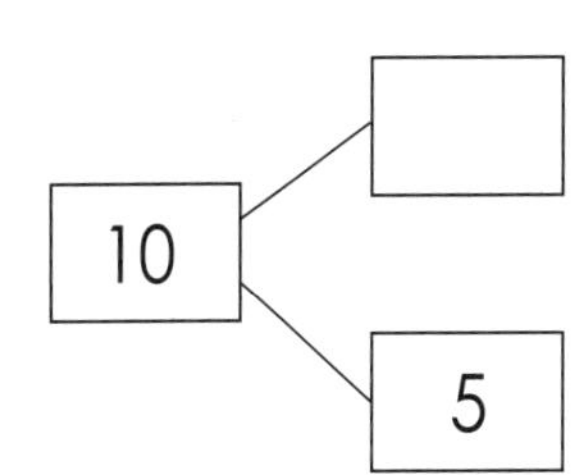

(i)

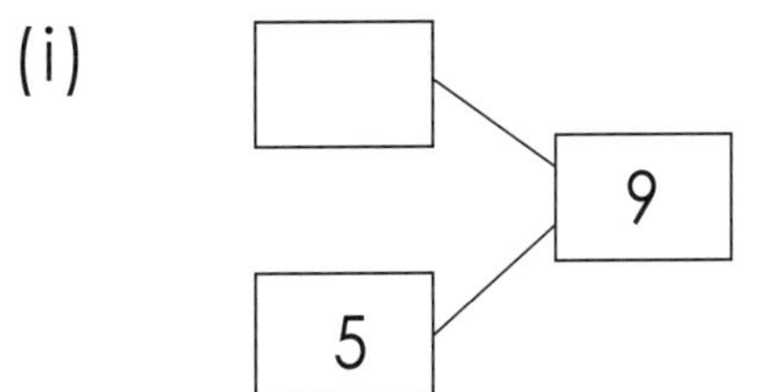

(j)

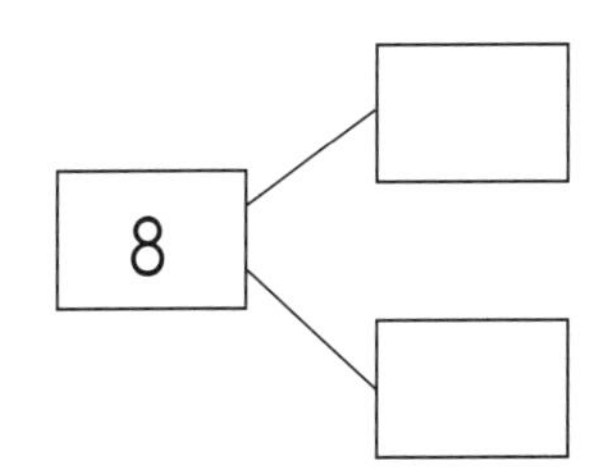

3. Count and write the correct number in each box. Then, join all possible pairs of numbers that make up 9.

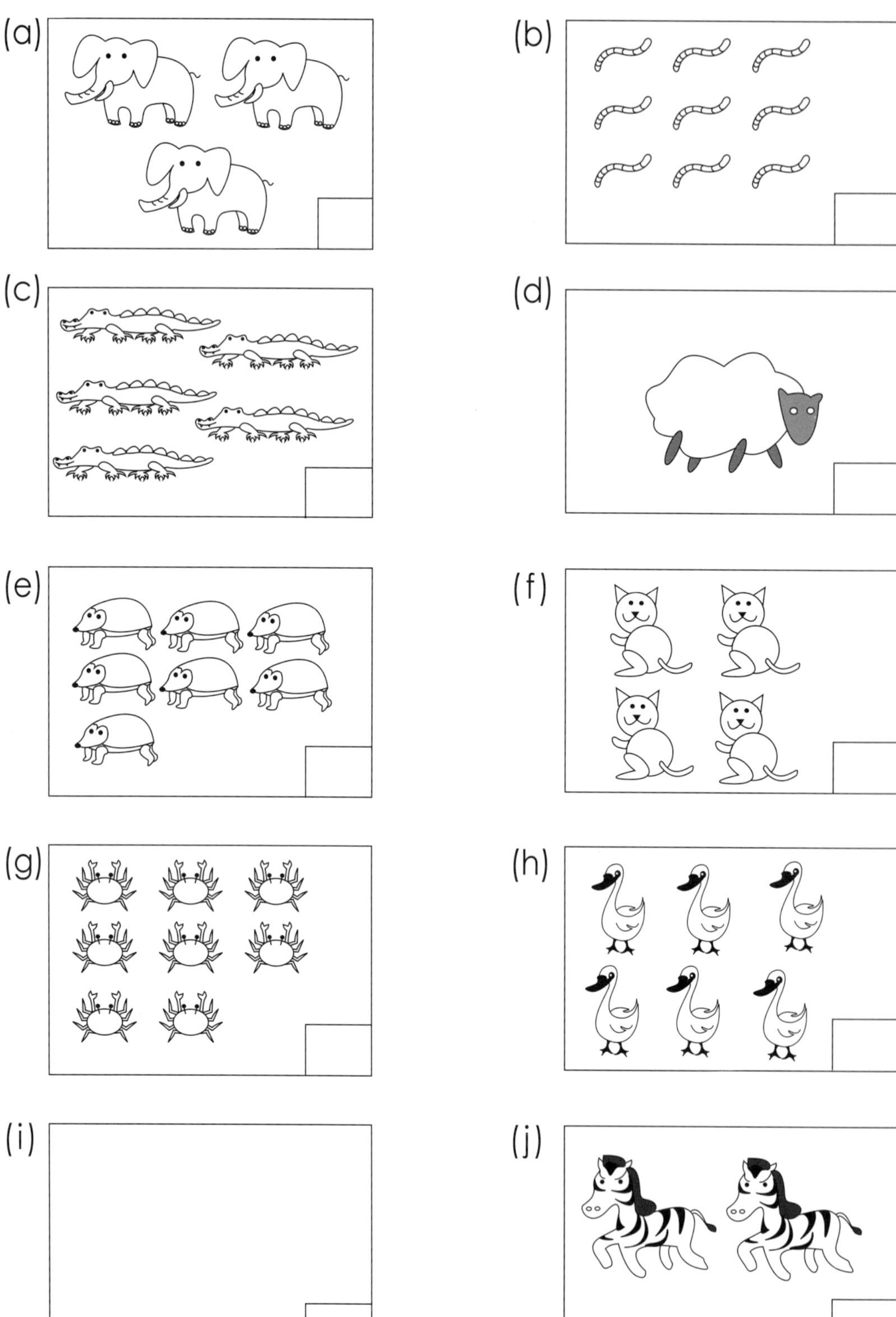

4. Draw and fill in the missing numbers for the number bonds.

(a)

(b)

(c)

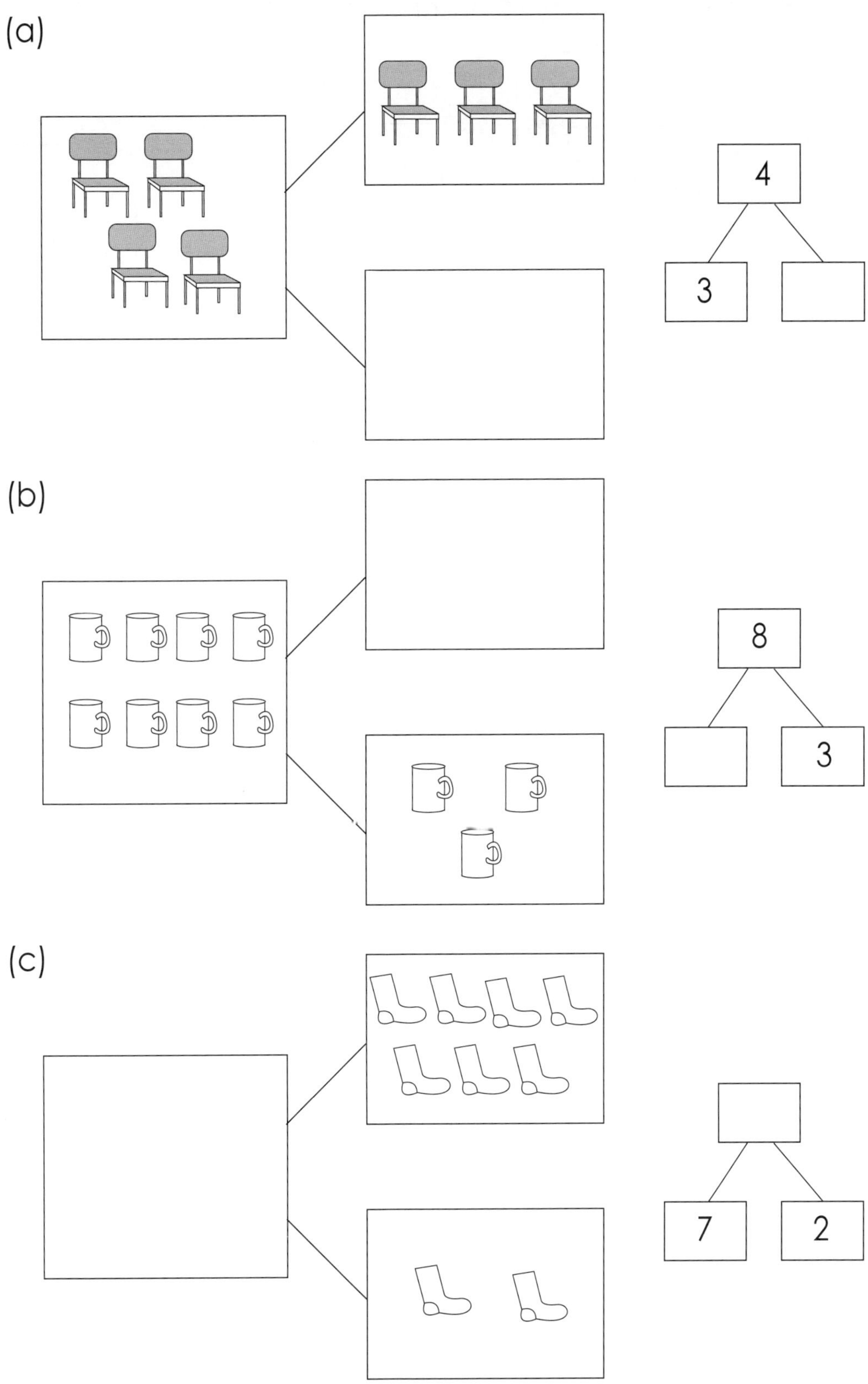

(d)

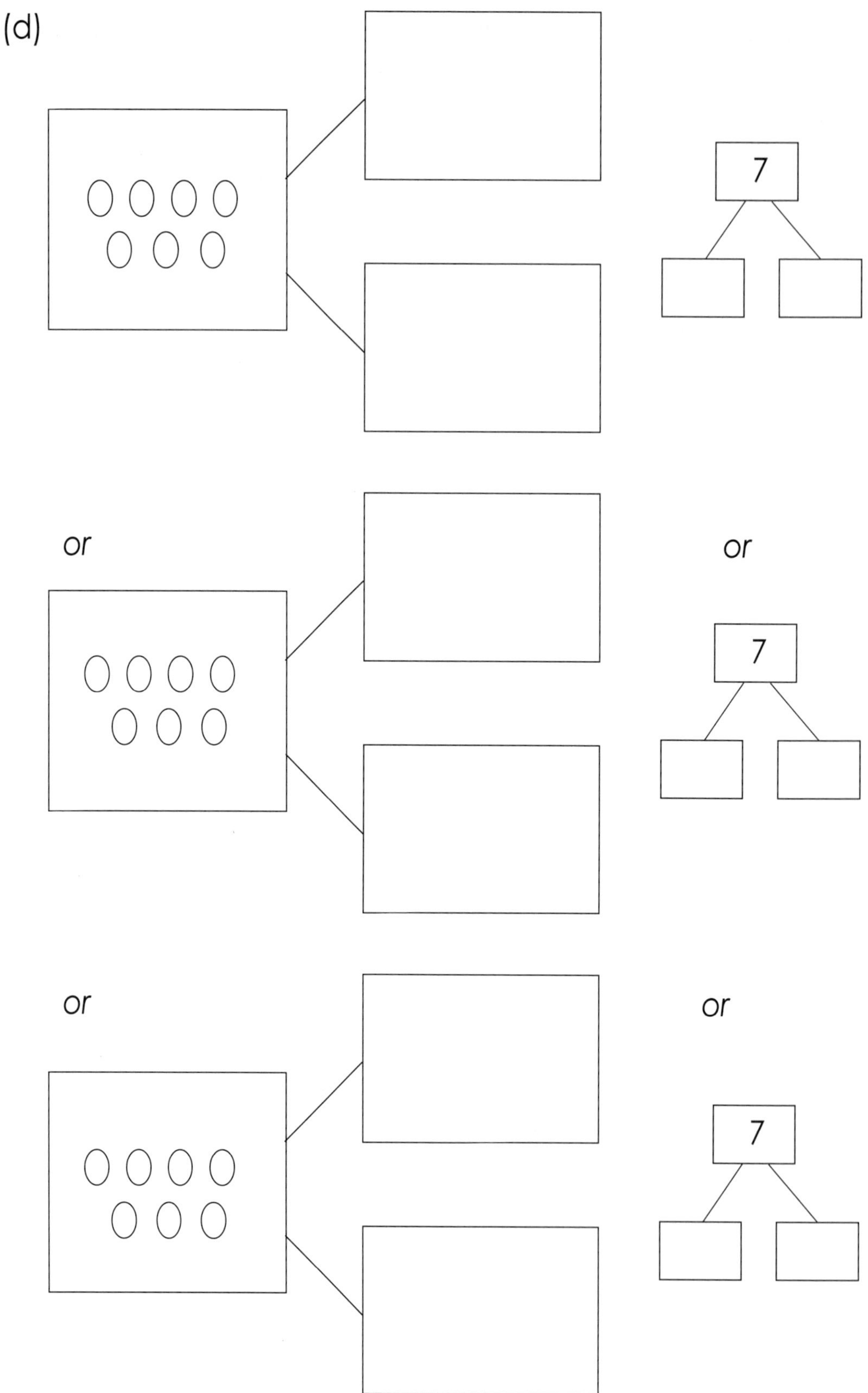

5. Color more seashells to make up the given number on the left. Then, complete the number bonds.

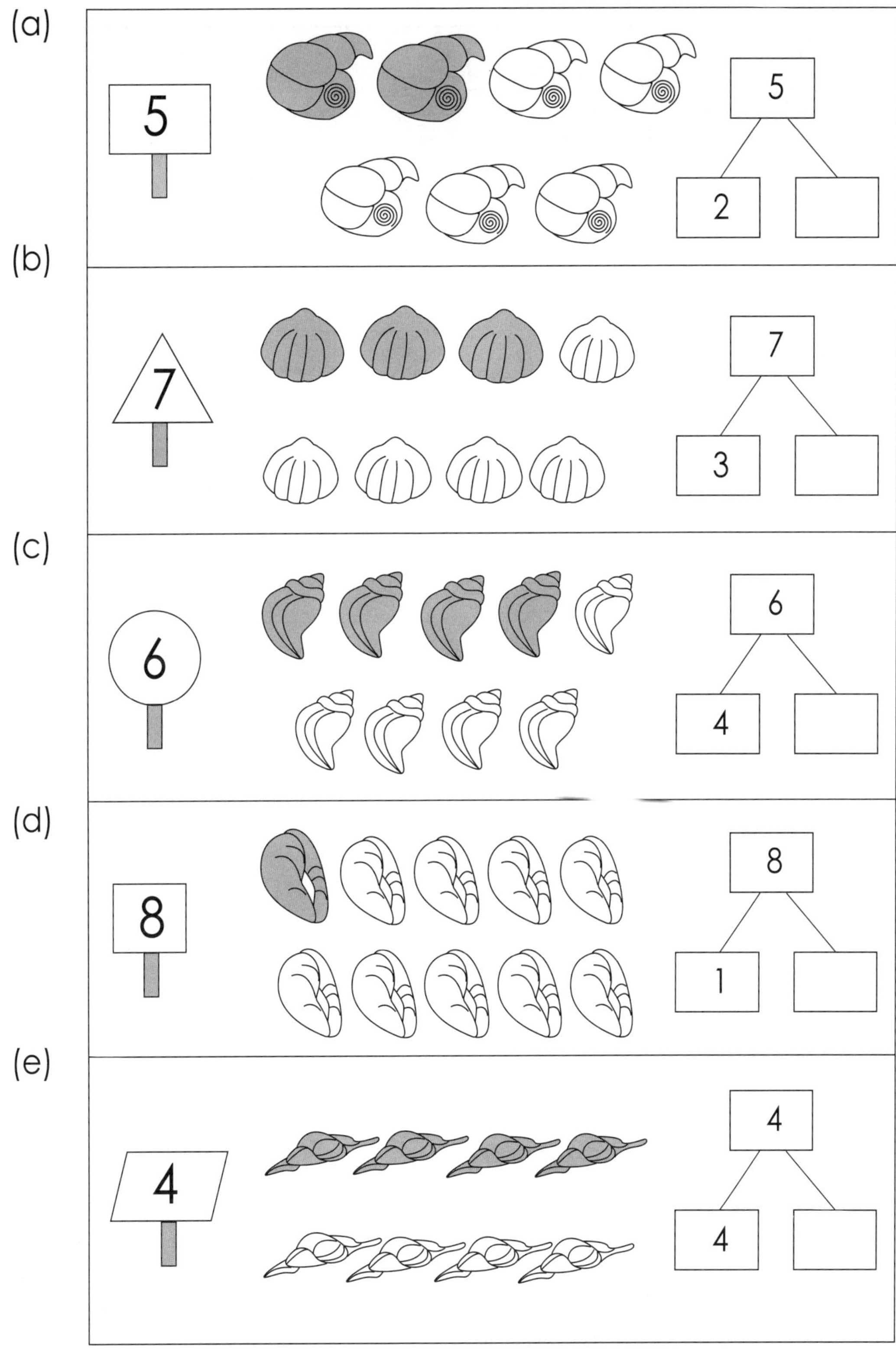

6. Draw more of the same picture to make up the number in each box.

(a)

(b)

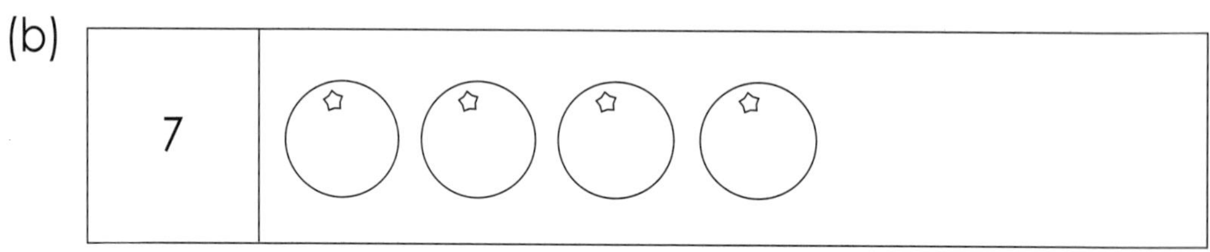

(c)

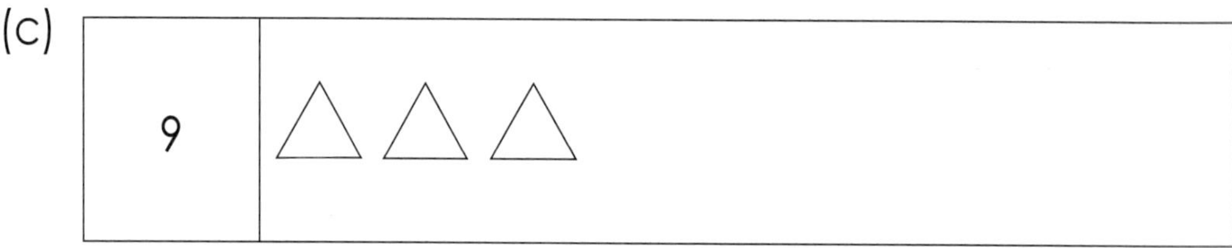

(d)

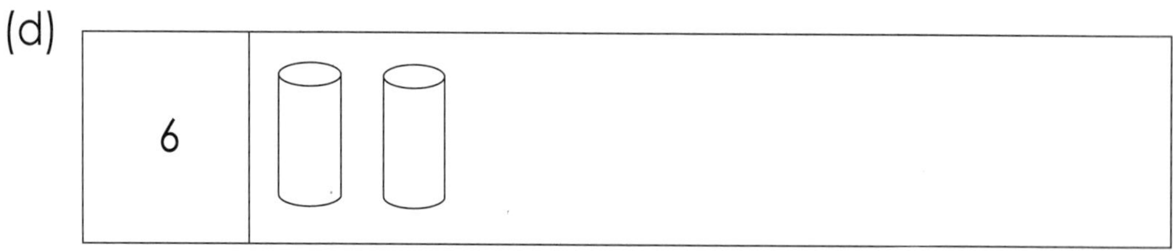

(e)

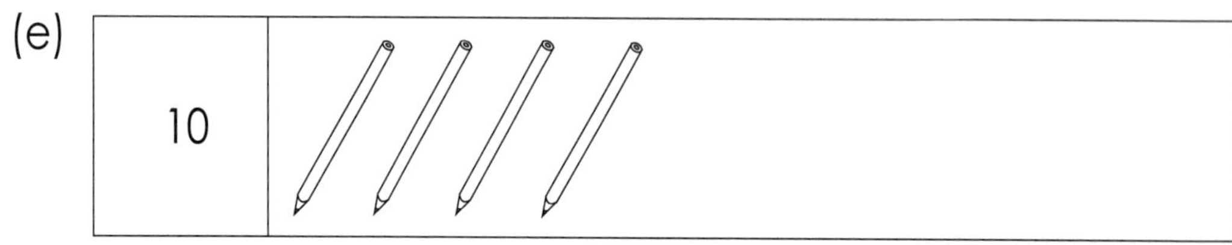

7. Fill in the missing numbers.

(a) 2 and ☐ make 5.

(b) 4 and ☐ make 7.

(c) 2 and ☐ make 8.

(d) 6 and ☐ make 9.

(e) 1 and ☐ make 6.

(f) ☐ and 4 make 4.

(g) ☐ and 2 make 3.

8. Can you think of 6 possible ways to make 10? List them below.

(a) ☐ and ☐ make 10.

(b) ☐ and ☐ make 10.

(c) ☐ and ☐ make 10.

(d) ☐ and ☐ make 10.

(e) ☐ and ☐ make 10.

(f) ☐ and ☐ make 10.

WORD PROBLEMS

1. Five monkeys are playing on a tree. Two more join in the fun. How many monkeys are there on the tree?

5 and 2 make ☐

There are ☐ monkeys on the tree.

2. Two girls are swimming in a pool. Three boys join in. How many children are there in the pool?

2 and 3 make ☐

There are ☐ children in the pool.

3. Karen ate 2 slices of cake. Joe came along and ate 2 slices of cake. How many slices of cake were eaten?

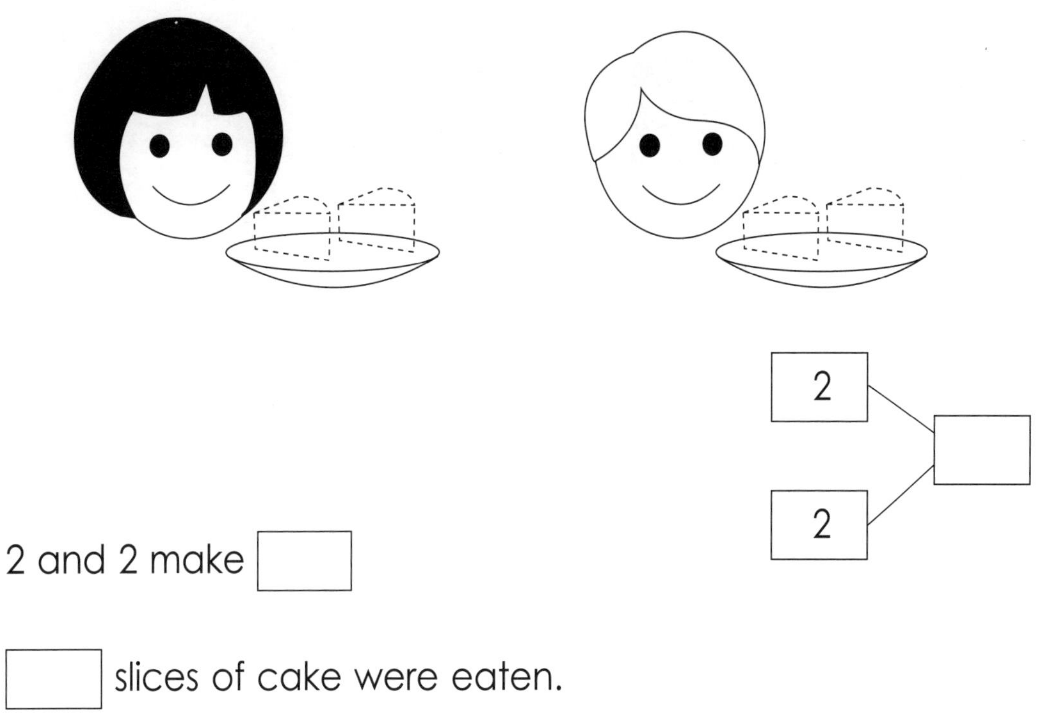

2 and 2 make ☐

☐ slices of cake were eaten.

4. Three spiders are dancing. Another spider joins in. After a while, 4 more spiders come along. How many dancing spiders are there altogether?

3 and 1 and 4 make ☐

There are ☐ dancing spiders altogether.

5. A team of 4 people is climbing a hill. A boy and another team of 5 people join in. How many people are climbing the hill now?

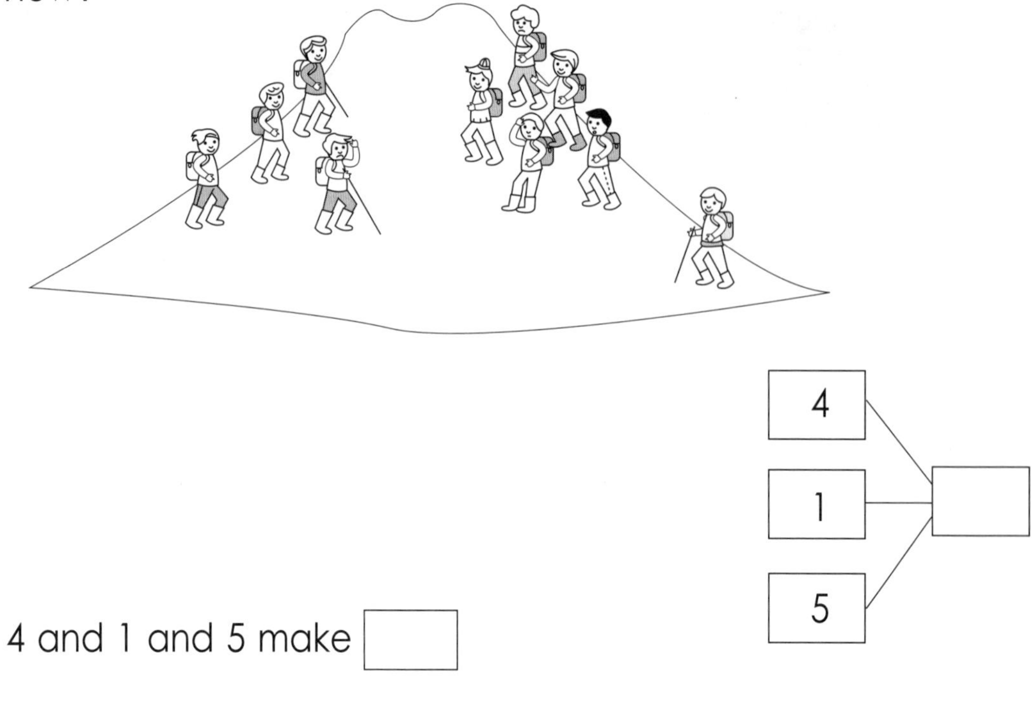

4	
1	☐
5	

4 and 1 and 5 make ☐

☐ people are climbing the hill now.

Take the Challenge!

1. Fill in the missing numbers to complete the number bonds.

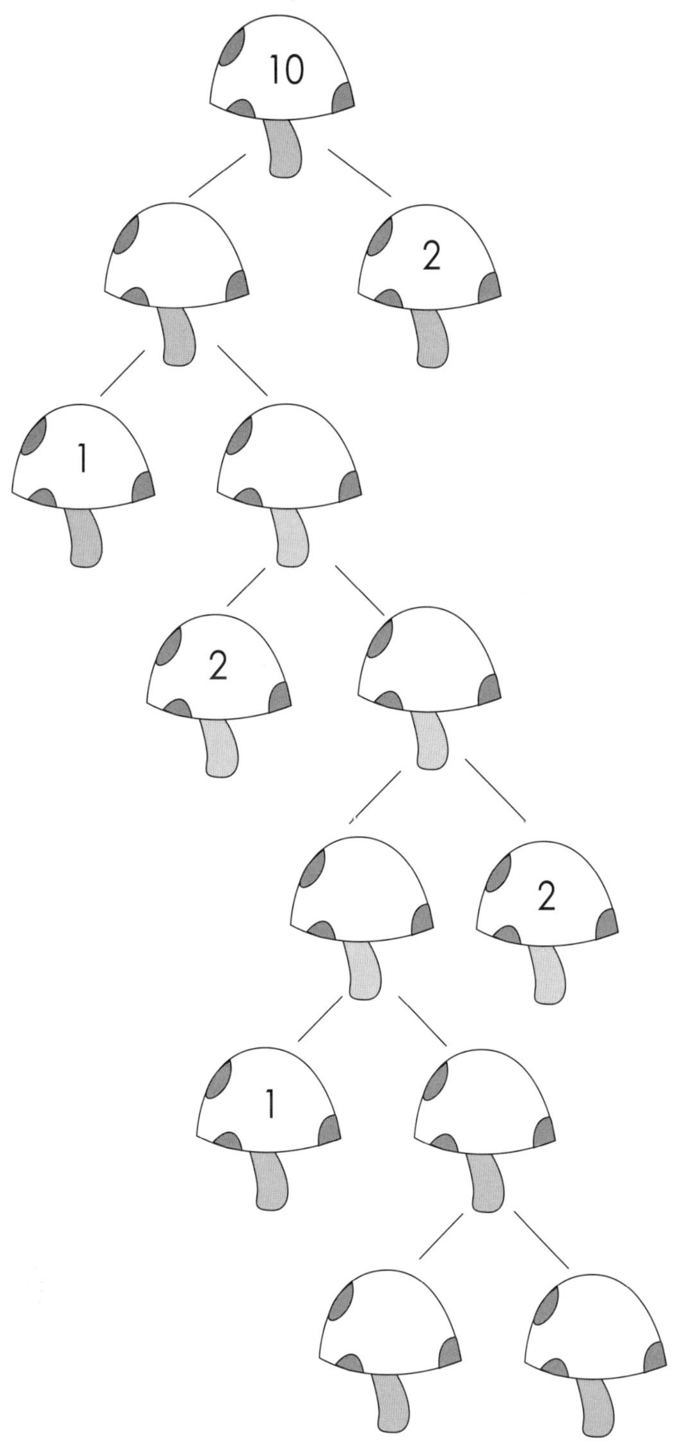

2. Fill in the missing numbers to complete the number bonds.

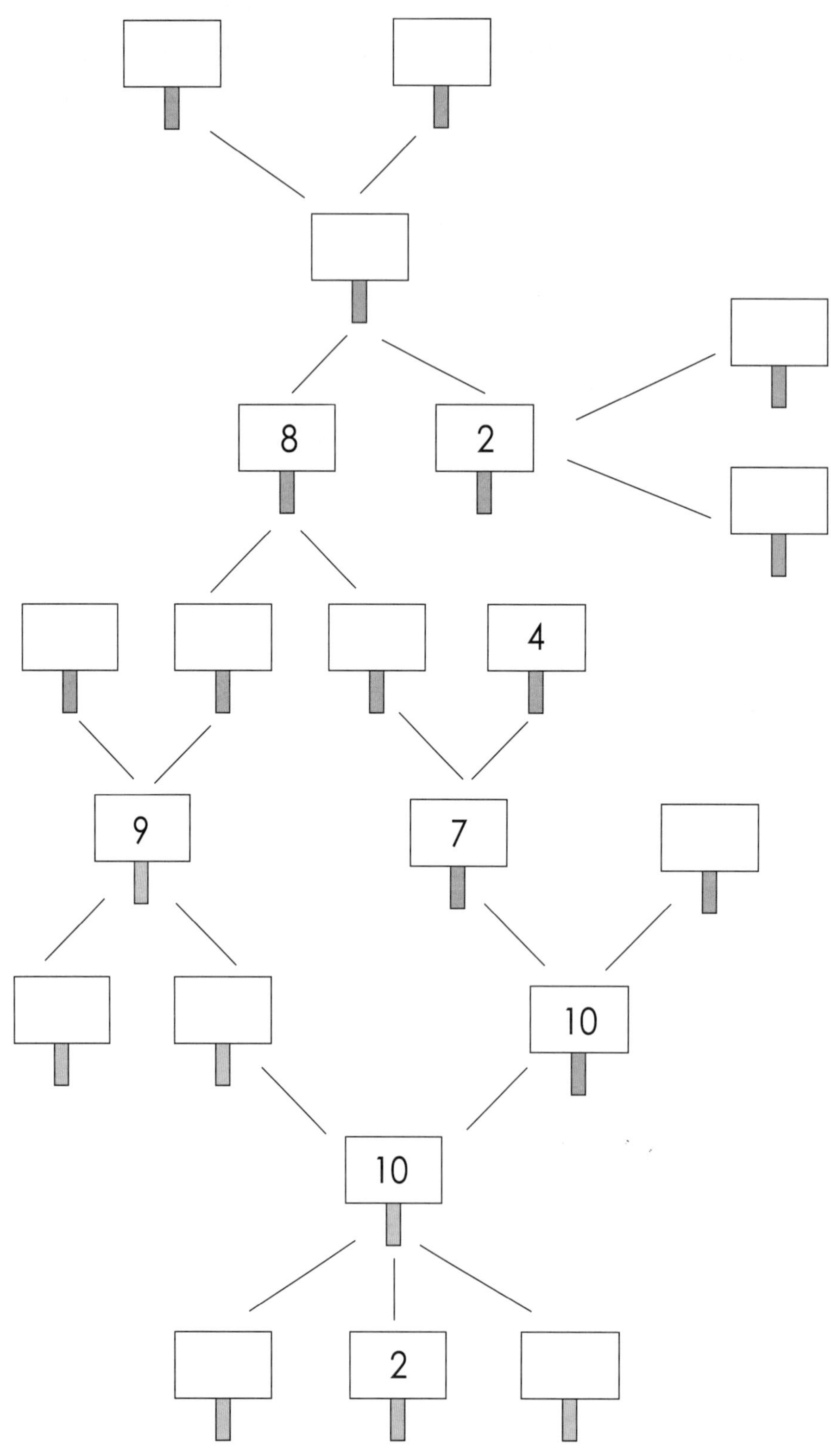

Topic 3: Addition Within 10

1. Complete the number sentence.

(a)   + 

☐ + 3 = ☐

(b)  + 

1 + ☐ = ☐

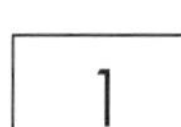 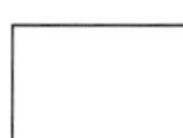 

(c)  + 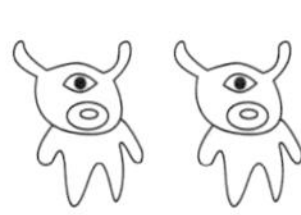

☐ + 2 = ☐

(d)  + 

5 + ☐ = ☐

(e) + 

☐ + 8 = ☐

2. Match the following correctly and fill in the missing numbers.

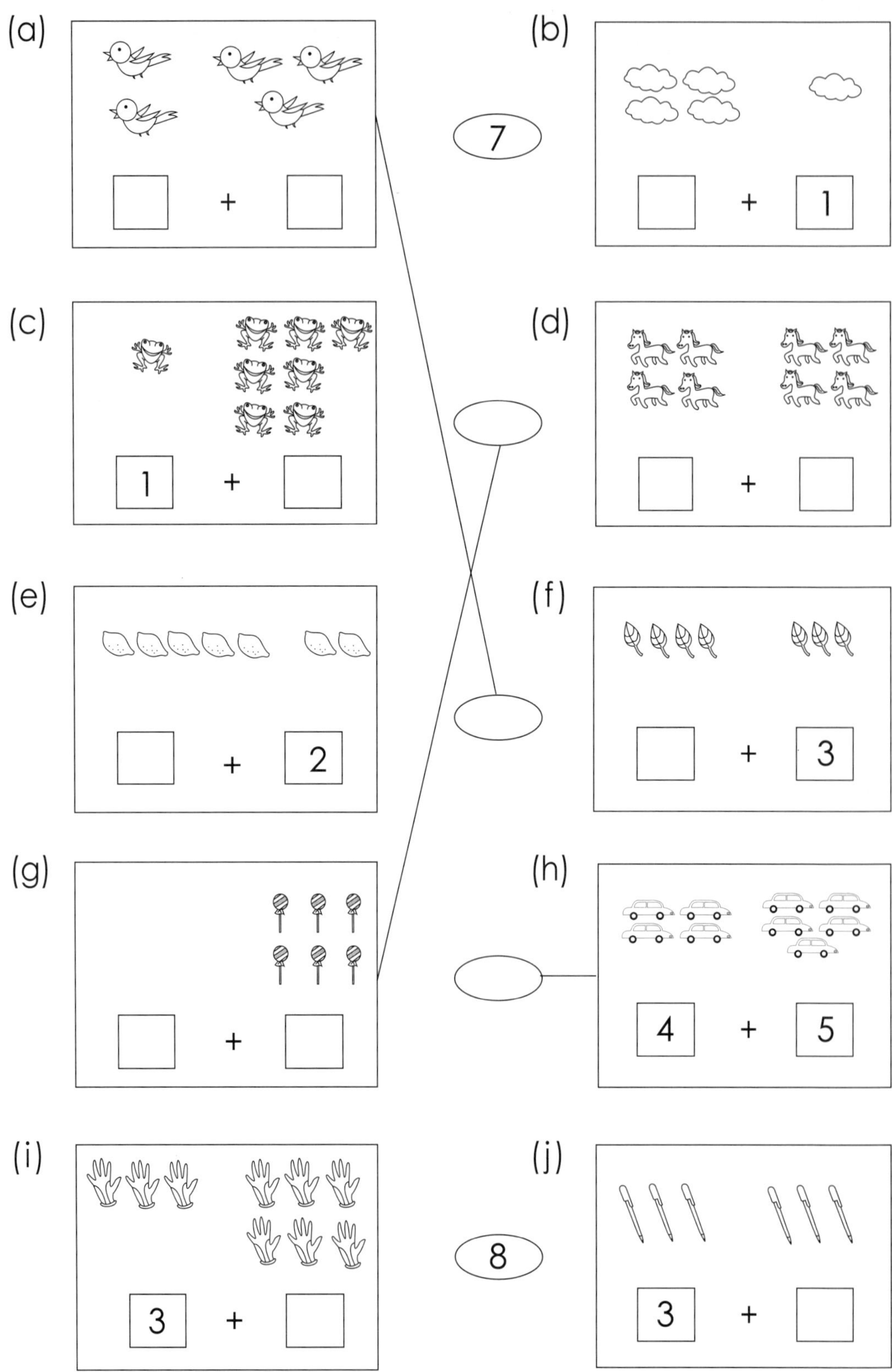

3. Add correctly by 'counting on'.

Example: 4 + 3 = <u>7</u>
Count 3 ones from 4: 5, 6, <u>7</u>

(a) 3 + 5 = ____ (b) 9 + 1 = ____

(c) 4 + 2 = ____ (d) 5 + 4 = ____

(e) 6 + 1 = ____ (f) 3 + 2 = ____

(g) 0 + 8 = ____ (h) 7 + 3 = ____

4. Complete the number bonds and number sentences.

(a)

3

5

3 + 5 = ____

5 + 3 = ____

(b)

4 3

4 + 3 = ____

3 + 4 = ____

(c)

2

3

2 + 3 = ____

3 + 2 = ____

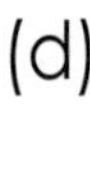

(d)

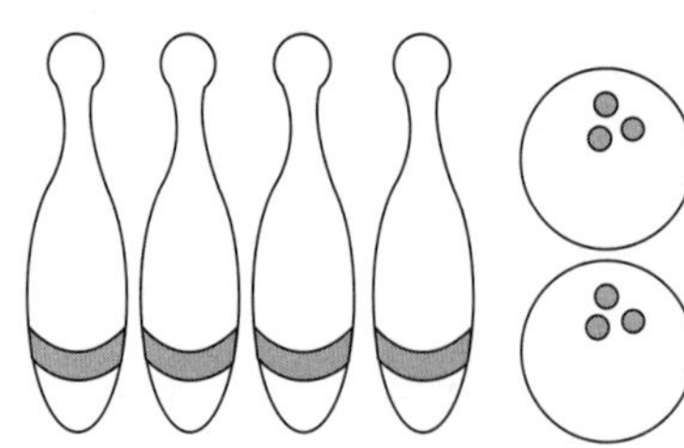

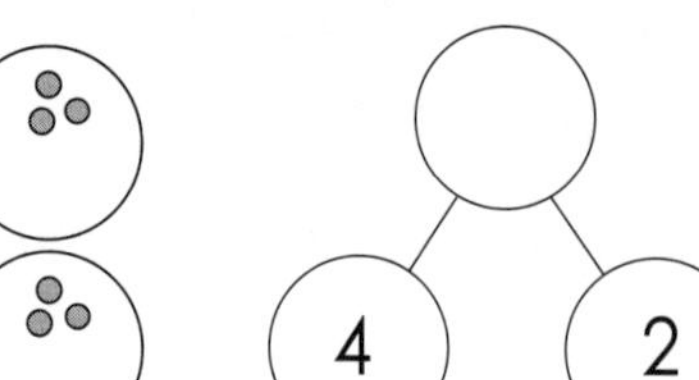

4 + 2 = ☐

2 + 4 = ☐

(e)

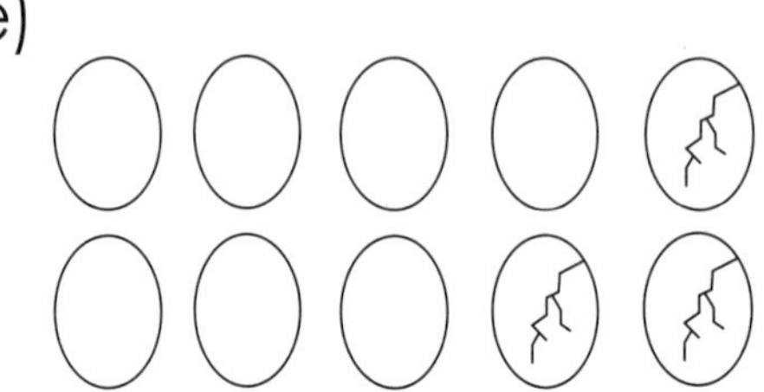

3

7 + 3 = ☐

3 + 7 = ☐

(f)

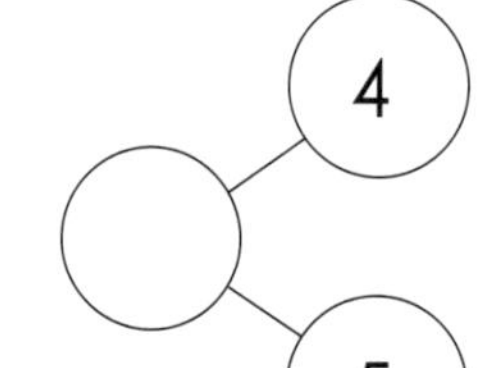

5

4 + 5 = ☐

5 + 4 = ☐

(g)

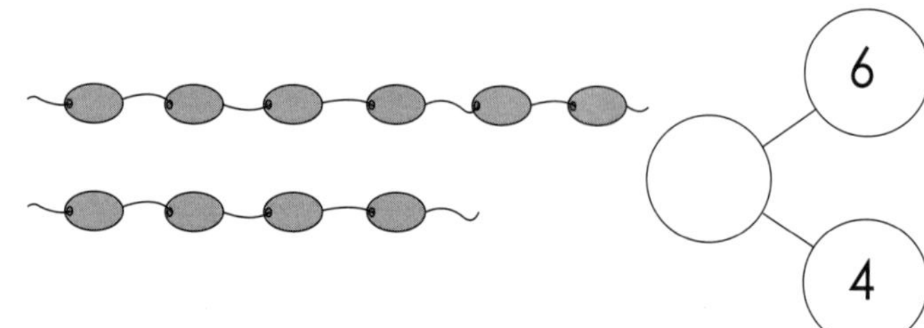

6 + 4 = ☐

4 + 6 = ☐

5. Look at the pictures. Complete the addition stories and addition sentences.

(a)

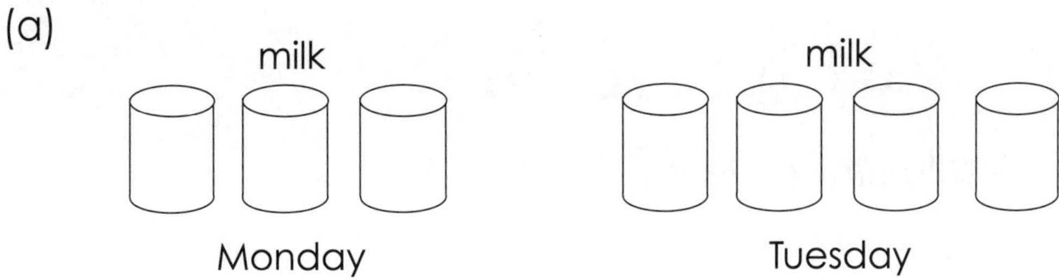

I drank ________ glasses of milk on Monday.

I drank ________ glasses of milk on Tuesday.

☐ + ☐ = ☐

I drank ________ glasses of milk altogether on both days.

(b)

________ boys are swimming.

________ boys are sitting on the beach.

☐ + ☐ = ☐

There are ________ boys altogether.

(c) 

Mommy gave me ________ toy cars for Christmas.

Daddy gave me ________ toy robots for Christmas.

☐ + ☐ = ☐

I received ________ toys for Christmas altogether.

6. Use the numbers and signs in each box to form a correct number sentence.

(a) | 4, =, 1, +, 5 | ____________________

(b) | 7, 2, =, 5, + | ____________________

(c) | 9, 0, +, =, 9 | ____________________

(d) | 6, =, 10, +, 4 | ____________________

(e) | 3, +, =, 8, 5 | ____________________

7. Fill in the missing numbers.

(a) 1 + ________ = 6

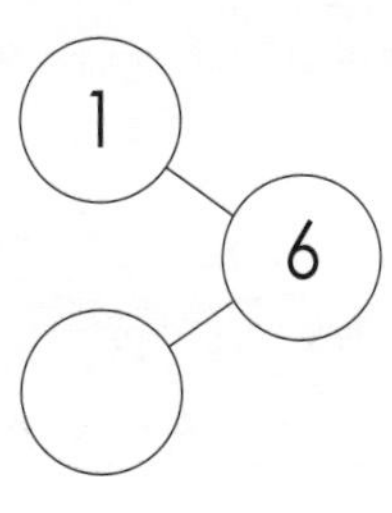

(b) 3 + ________ = 9

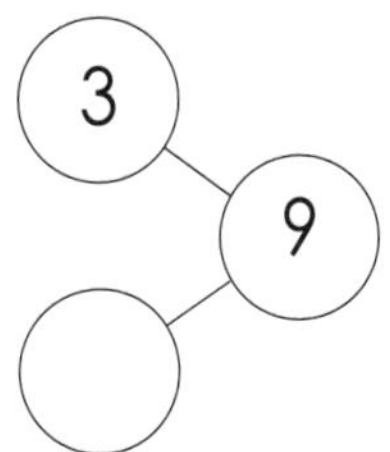

(c) 6 + ________ = 10

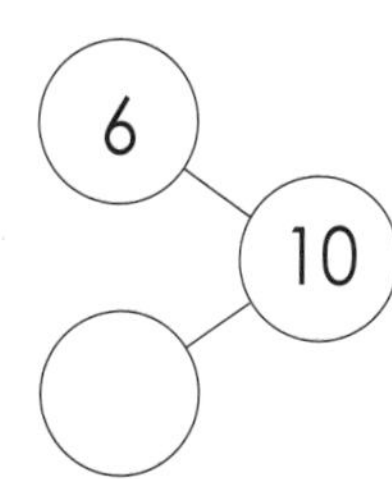

(d) ________ + 3 = 7

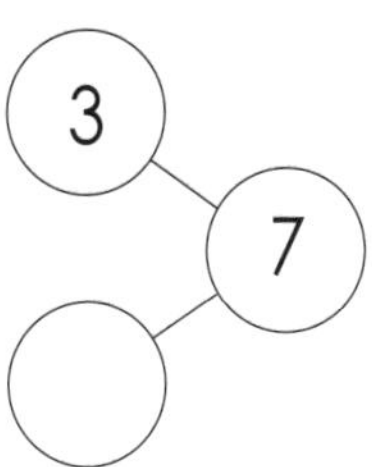

(e) 5 + ________ = 8

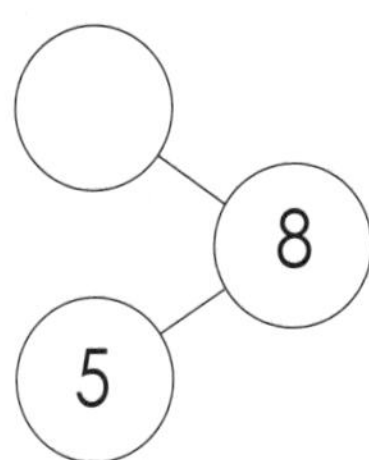

(f) 10 + ________ = 10

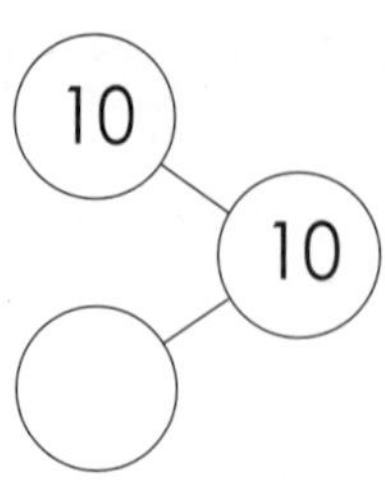

(g) 8 + ________ = 9

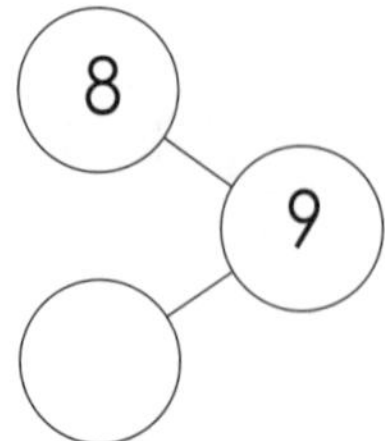

(h) 4 + ________ = 5

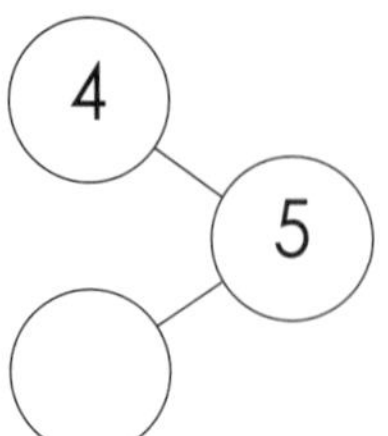

8. Use the given numbers to form correct number sentences. Each number can be used more than once. Some questions can have more than one answer.

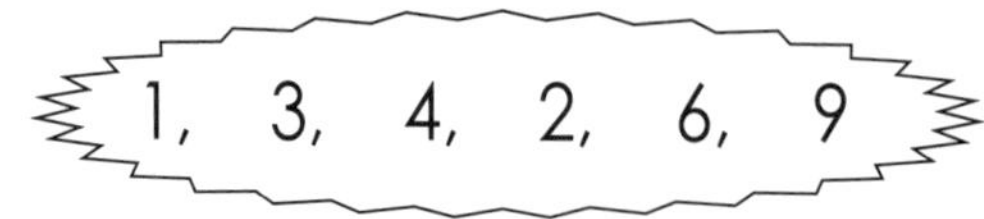

(a) △ + △ = 10

(b) △ + 4 = 7

(c) 5 + △ = 9

(d) 3 + △ = 7 + 2

(e) △ + 4 = △

(f) △ + △ = 8

(g) △ + 3 = 6

9. Fill in the blanks.

(a) 1 more than 5 is ________ .

1 + 5 = ________

(b) 1 more than 8 is ________ .

1 + 8 = ________

(c) 2 more than 3 is ________ .

2 + 3 = ________

(d) ________ is 1 more than 9.

________ = 1 + 9

(e) ________ is 4 more than 4.

________ = 4 + 4

(f) 5 more than 3 is ________ .

5 + 3 = ________

(g) ________ is 2 more than 1 + 4.

(h) ________ is 3 more than 2 + 3.

(i) ________ is 1 more than 6 + 3.

WORD PROBLEMS

1. Sandy found 4 seashells on the beach. May found 2 seashells. How many seashells did they find altogether?

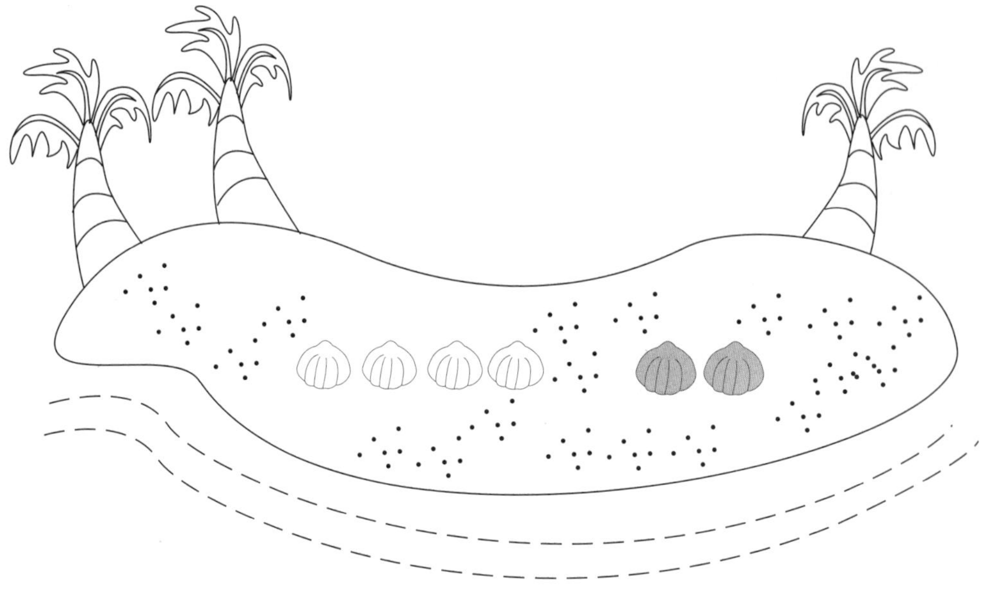

They found ☐ + ☐ = ☐ seashells altogether.

2. Lisa has 4 pearls. How many more pearls must she buy to make a necklace of 10 pearls?

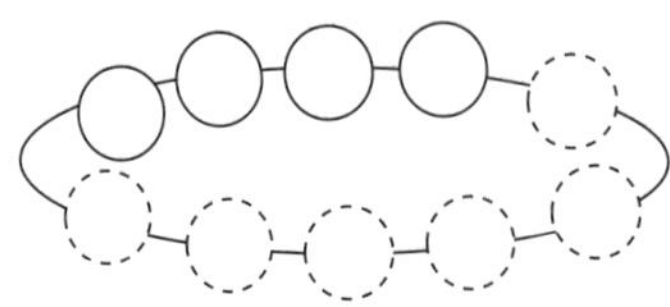

She must buy ☐ more pearls.

3. There are 2 kittens, 3 monkeys and 4 squirrels playing around a tree. How many animals are there altogether?

There are ☐ + ☐ + ☐ = ☐ animals altogether.

4. Paul has 3 balls. Peter has 2 more balls than Paul. How many balls does Peter have?

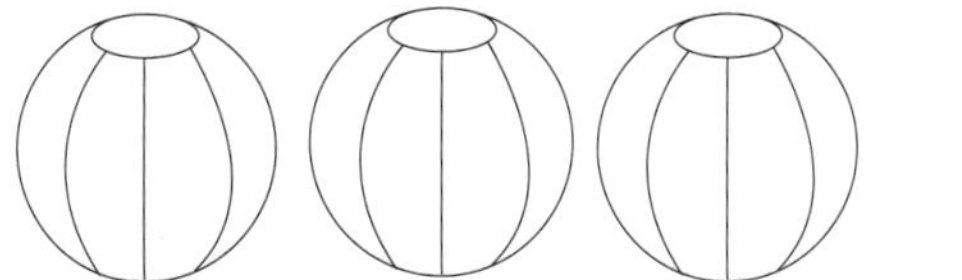

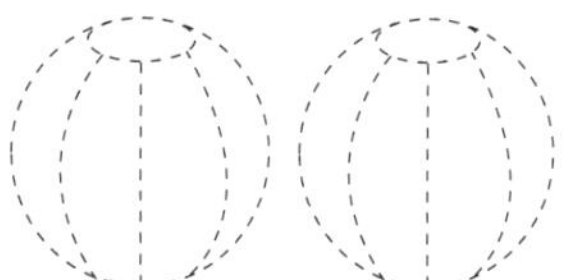

Peter has ☐ + ☐ = ☐ balls.

5. A shopkeeper sold 3 cakes. He sold a few more before he closed for the day. He sold 9 cakes altogether that day. How many more cakes did he sell before he closed for the day?

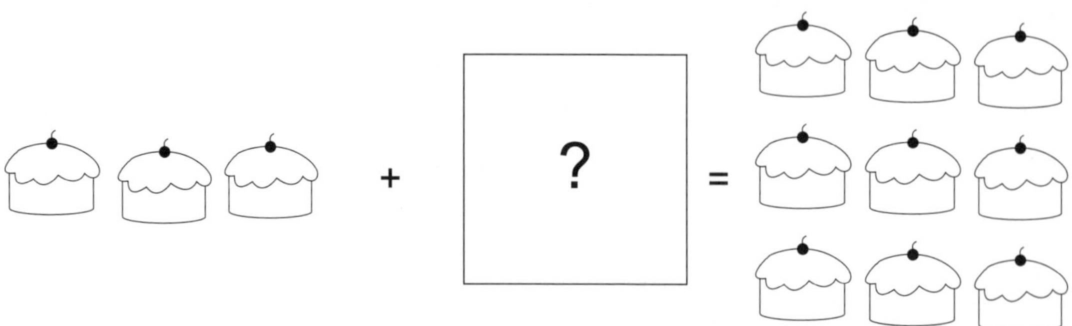

The shopkeeper sold ☐ more cakes before he closed for the day.

6. Kathlyn gave 3 stickers to Alice and 2 to Mabel. She has 4 stickers left now. How many stickers did she have at first?

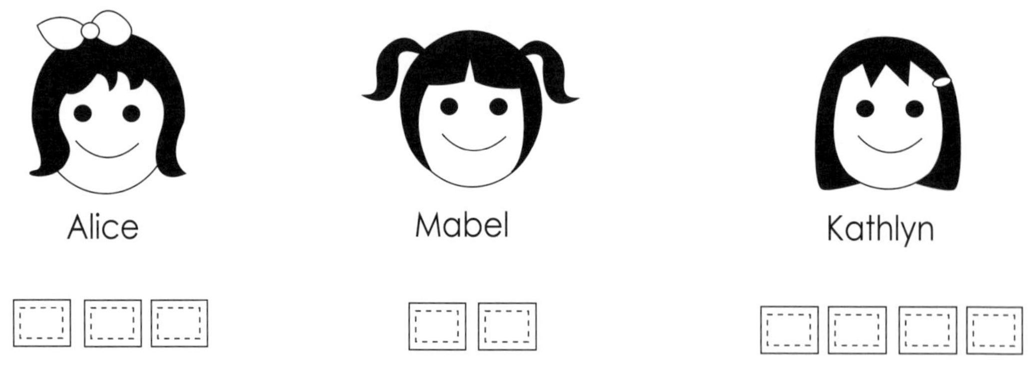

Kathlyn had ☐ + ☐ + ☐ = ☐ stickers at first.

Take the Challenge!

1. If flower = 1, triangle = 2 and moon = 3, fill in the boxes with the correct numbers.

   (a) triangle + flower = ☐

   (b) flower + moon = ☐

   (c) moon + triangle = ☐

   (d) moon + moon = ☐

   (e) flower + moon = ☐ + triangle

   (f) flower + ☐ = moon

   (g) flower + ☐ = triangle

2. If candy = 2, heart = 3, cherries = 4 and star = 5, draw the correct picture in the box to complete each addition sentence.

   (a) ☐ + candy = cherries

   (b) ☐ + ☐ = star

   (c) ☐ + cherries = star + ☐

   (d) ☐ + heart = ☐ + candy

3. This is a train line.

Happy Village → Spy Land → Moon Place → Funland → Gorge → Mini Land → Sunshine Village

(a) I am in Happy Village. Where will I be 3 stops later?

I will be in ______.

(b) How many stops away is Sunshine Village from Happy Village?

Sunshine Village is ___ stops away from Happy Village.

Topic 4: Subtraction Within 10

1. Cross out (×) the number of objects to be subtracted and fill in the missing numbers.

(a)

5 – 2 = ☐

(b)

☐ – 5 = ☐

(c)

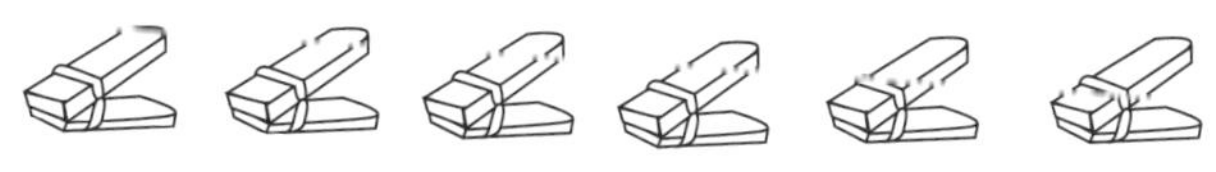

☐ – 3 = ☐

(d)

☐ – 4 = ☐

(e)

☐ – 3 = ☐

2. Subtract by 'counting backwards'. Use the number line to help you.

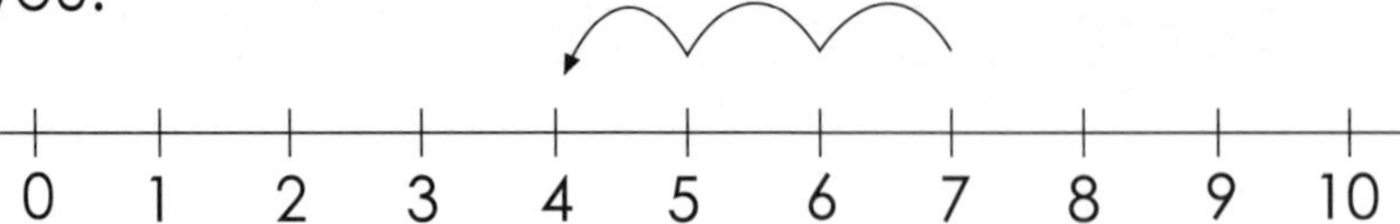

Example: $7 - 3 = \underline{4}$
Begin with 7 and count 3 ones backwards: 6, 5, <u>4</u>

(a) $5 - 2 =$ ______ (b) $9 - 5 =$ ______

(c) $8 - 4 =$ ______ (d) $4 - 0 =$ ______

(e) $7 - 6 =$ ______ (f) $6 - 1 =$ ______

(g) $10 - 3 =$ ______ (h) $3 - 3 =$ ______

3. Look at the pictures. Complete the subtraction stories and subtraction sentences.

(a)

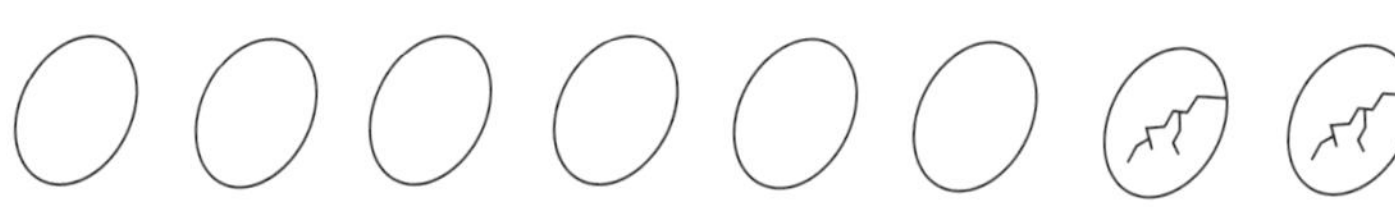

Ann bought 8 eggs.

She broke ______ of them.

☐ – ☐ = ☐

She had ______ eggs left.

(b)

Mother baked 7 cupcakes.

She ate ______ of them.

☐ – ☐ = ☐

There were ______ cupcakes left.

(c)

vanilla ice-cream cones | chocolate ice-cream cones

A man sold 6 ice-cream cones.

________ of them were vanilla ice-cream cones.

The rest were chocolate ice-cream cones.

☐ – ☐ = ☐

He sold ________ chocolate ice-cream cone(s).

(d)

Tom was holding 6 balloons.

The wind blew ________ balloon(s) away.

☐ – ☐ = ☐

Tom has ________ balloons now.

4. Use number bonds to help you subtract. Fill in the missing numbers.

(a) 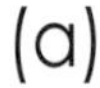

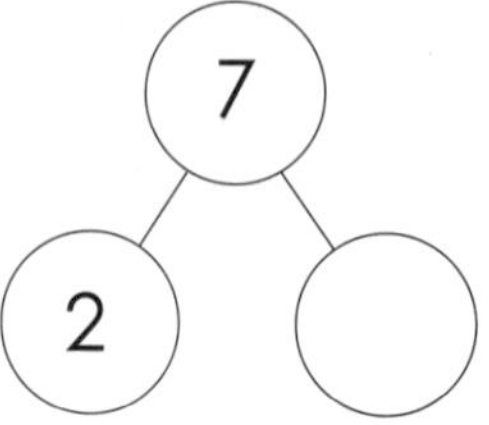

7 – 2 = ☐

7 – ☐ = 2

(b)

9 – 4 = ☐

9 – ☐ = 4

(c)

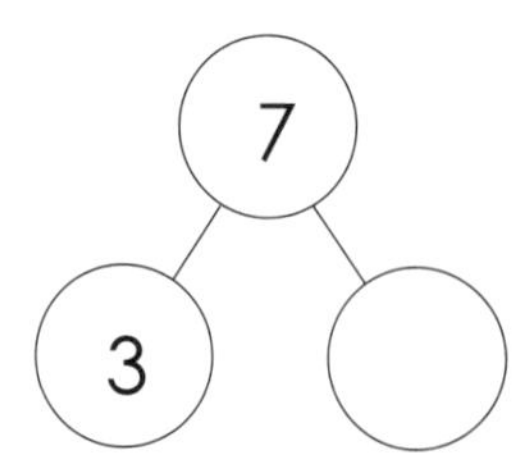

7 – 3 = ☐

7 – ☐ = 3

5. Fill in the missing numbers.

(a) 8 – 1 = ________

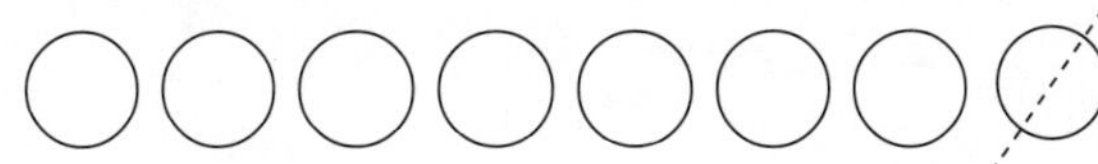

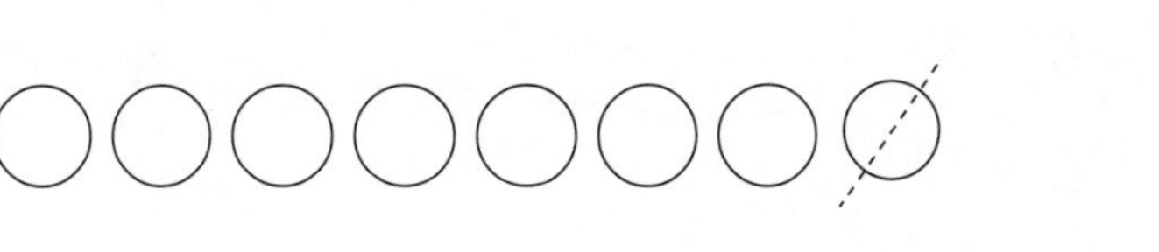

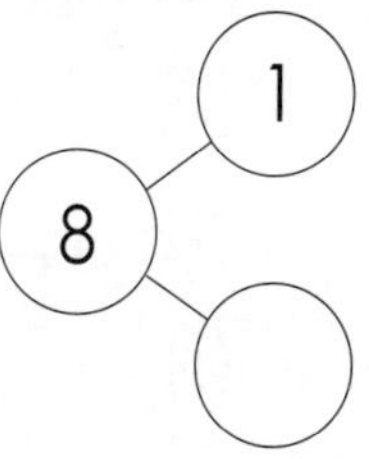

(b) 5 – 4 = ________

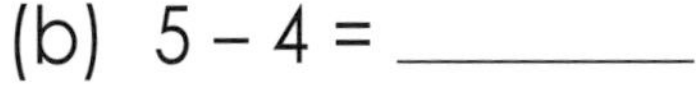

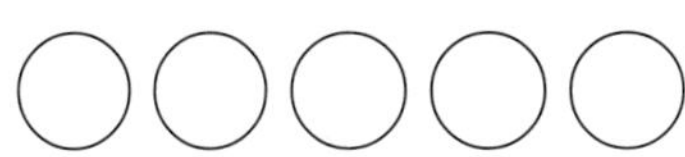

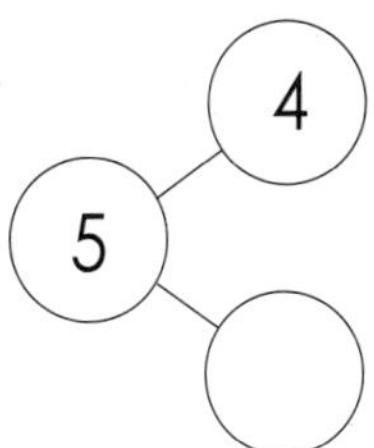

(c) 10 – ________ = 8

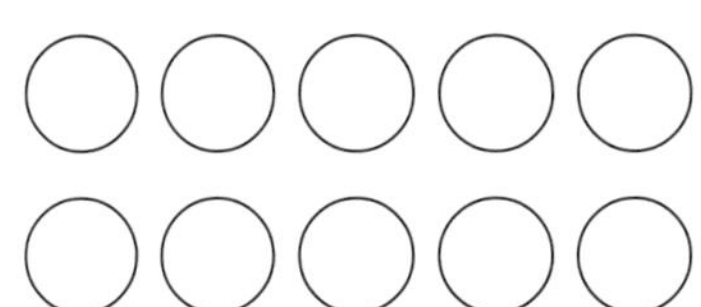

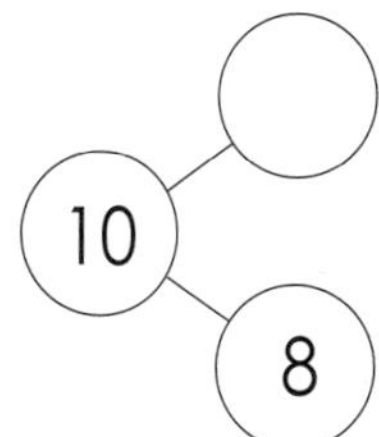

(d) 9 – ________ = 3

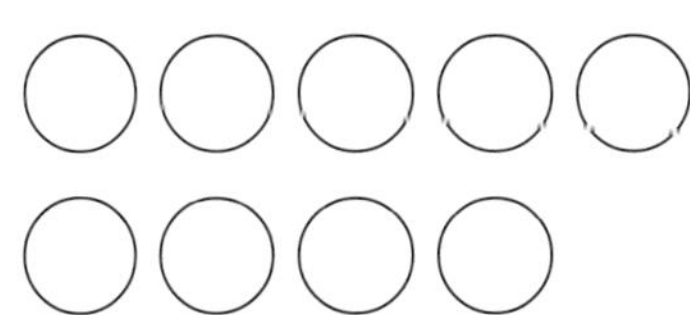

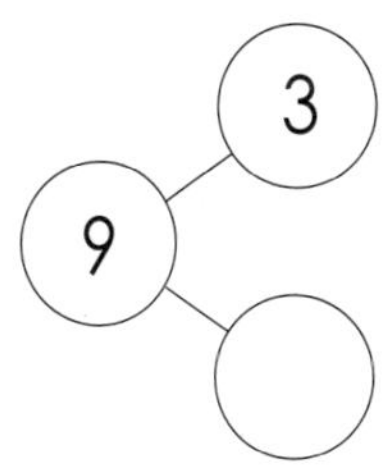

(e) ________ – 1 = 3

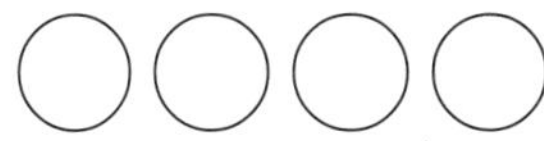

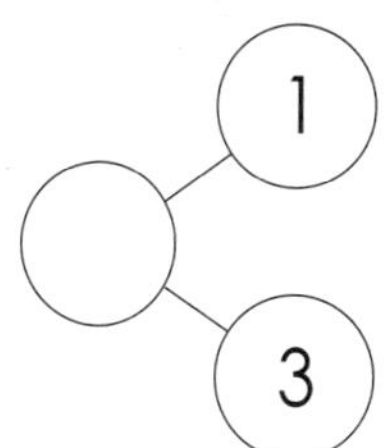

(f) ________ – 4 = 6

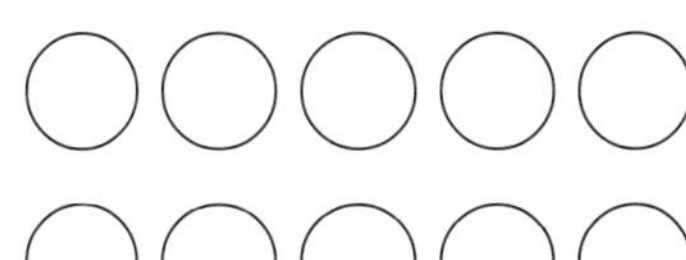

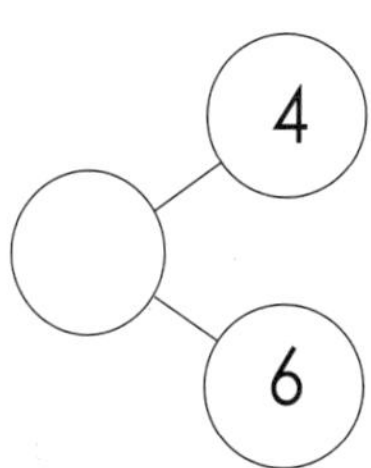

(g) 7 – ________ = 4

(h) 6 – ________ = 1

(i) ________ – 5 = 3

(j) ________ – 0 = 10

6. Use this number line to help you work out the answers.

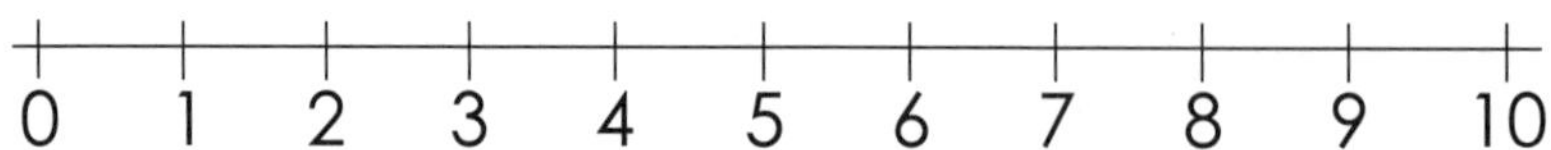

(a) 1 less than 4 is ________.

(b) 1 less than 9 is ________.

(c) 1 less than 6 is ________.

(d) 2 less than 5 is ________.

(e) 2 less than 8 is ________.

(f) 3 less than 7 is ________.

(g) 3 less than 9 is ________.

(h) 4 less than 10 is ________.

(i) Subtract 5 from 10. We get ________.

(j) Subtract 6 from 8. We get ________.

(k) ________ less than 9 is 3.

(l) ________ less than 7 is 5.

(m) 4 is 3 less than ________.

(n) 7 is 3 less than________.

7. Do the subtractions on the house. Match the answers with the colors. Then, color the house.

1:	Orange	2:	Green	3:	Yellow
4:	Red	5:	Gray	6:	Brown
7:	Blue				

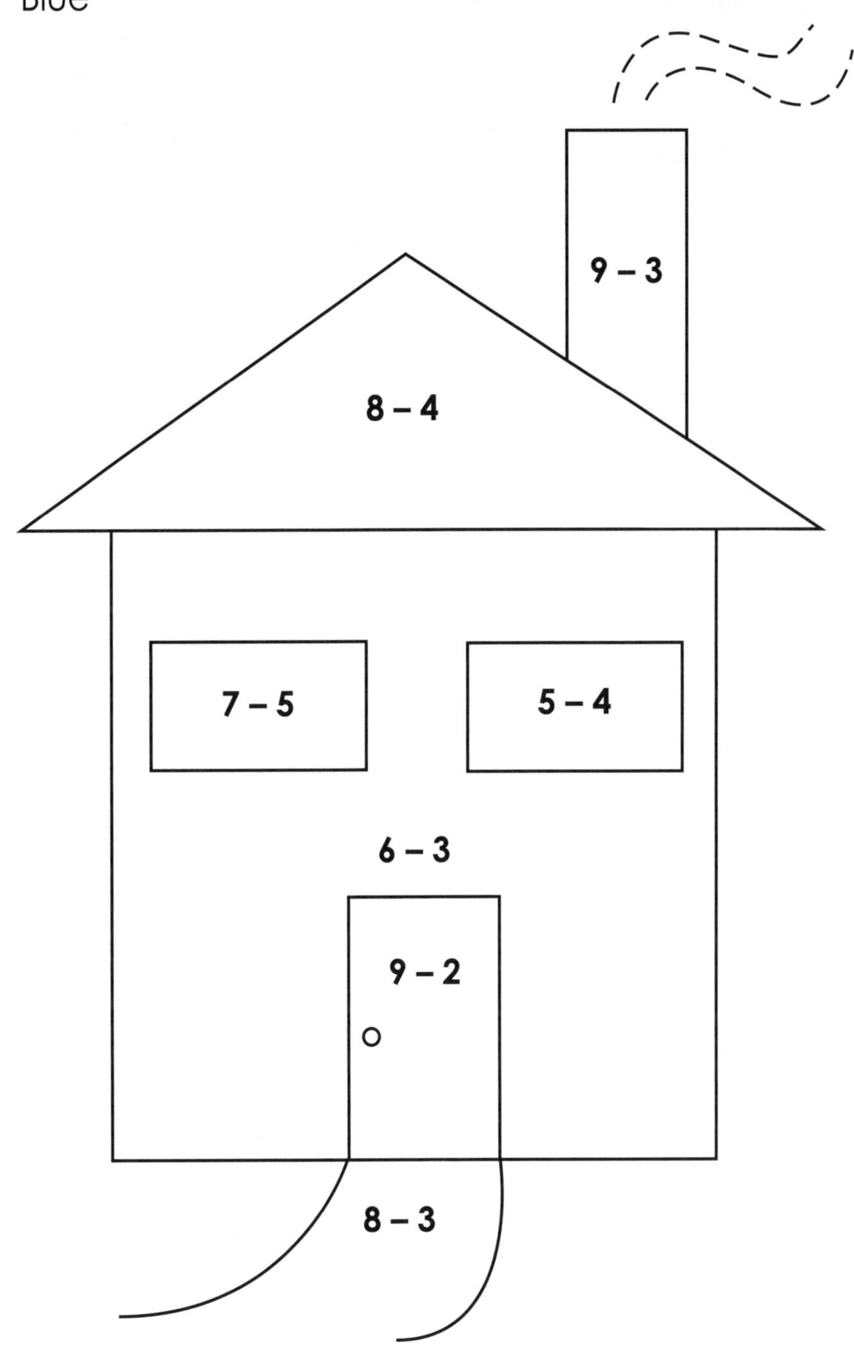

8. Guess the correct number.

9. Check (✓) the correct statements and cross out (×) the wrong statements.

(a) 3 is 10 less than 7. ( )

(b) 5 less than 8 is 3. ( )

(c) Subtract 2 from 6; we get 4. ( )

(d) 2 is 5 less than 8. ( )

(e) 7 less than itself is equal to 1. ( )

(f) Take 4 away from 7; we have 3. ( )

(g) 6 less than 8 is more than 2 less than 5. ( )

(h) 4 less than 5 is less than 7 less than 9. ( )

(i) 8 less than 10 is equal to 6 less than 9. ( )

(j) 10 less than 10 is the same as 5 less than 5. ( )

10. Fill in the missing numbers.

(a) $\square - 2 = 3$

(b) $\square - 7 = 3 = 5 - \square$

(c) $4 - \square = 3 = \square - 4$

(d) $\square - 5 = 6 - \square = 4$

(e) $\square - 3 = 9 - 2 = 7$

(f) $8 - \square = 7 - 5 = \square$

(g) $\square - 3 = 3 - \square = 2$

WORD PROBLEMS

1. Mom bought 7 bars of chocolate. Wendy ate 3 of them. How many bars of chocolate were left?

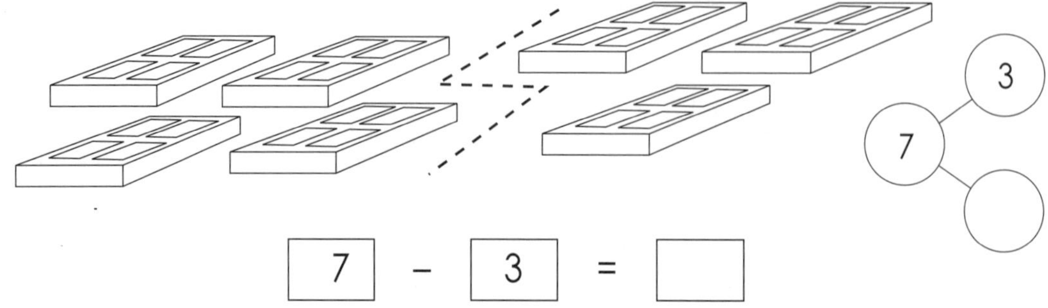

There were ________ bars of chocolate left.

2. Samantha has 10 pieces of candy. She gives each of her 4 sisters 1 piece of candy. How many pieces of candy does she have left?

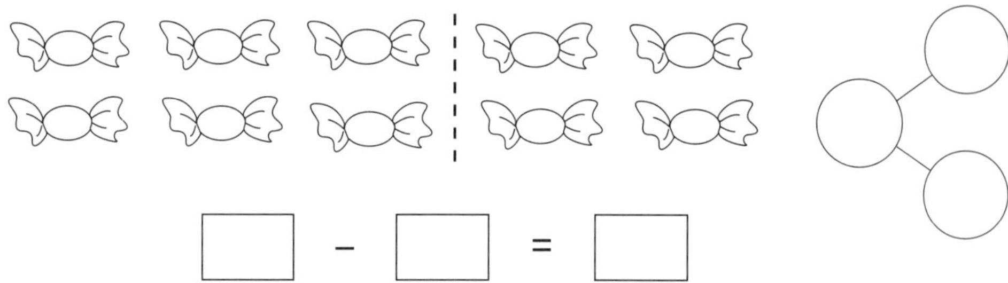

She has ________ pieces of candy left.

3. There were 6 children in a room. Kim and Sara went swimming. After a while, Mary went bowling and Bernice went bike riding. How many children were left in the room?

________ children were left in the room.

4. There are 2 bunches of 4 bananas each on a banana tree. A hungry monkey climbs up the tree and eats 5 bananas. How many bananas are left on the tree?

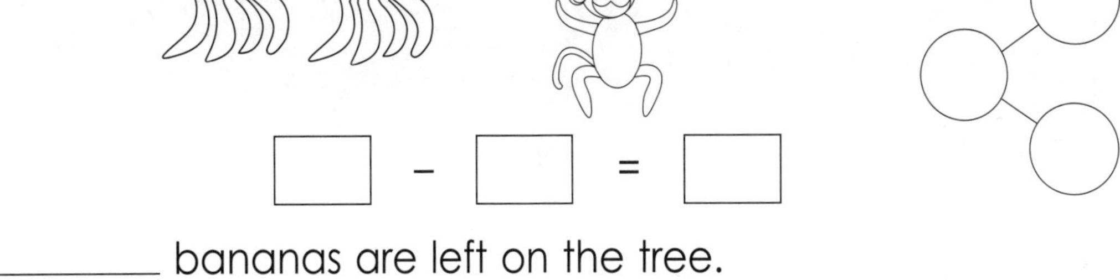

☐ – ☐ = ☐

________ bananas are left on the tree.

5. There are 9 children in the park. Four of them are girls. How many boys are there?

☐ ○ ☐ = ☐

There are ________ boys.

6. Shelby and Karen have 8 hair bands altogether. If Shelby has 6 hair bands, how many hair bands does Karen have?

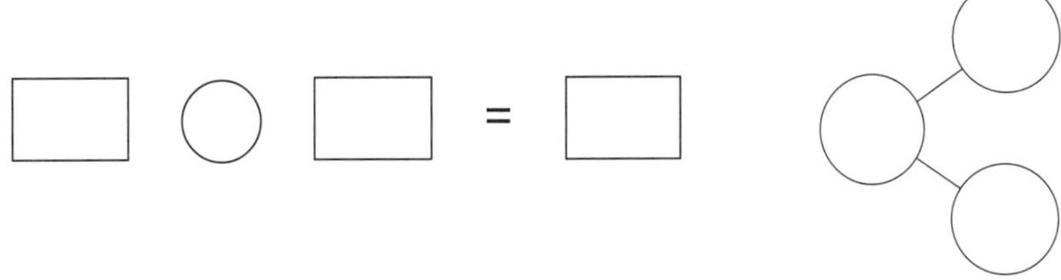

Karen has ________ hair bands.

7. Patrick has 10 erasers. His brother has 3 fewer erasers than him. How many erasers does his brother have?

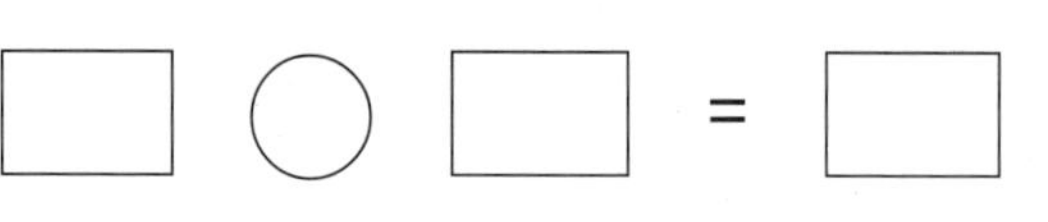

His brother has ________ erasers.

8. There are 9 pieces of candy altogether. Some are placed in the jar. Three are placed outside the jar. How many pieces of candy are there in the jar?

There are ________ pieces of candy in the jar.

Take the Challenge!

1. ◎ + ⬡ = 10

   ⬡ – ◎ = 2

   What are the numbers ◎ and ⬡?

   ◎ = ________ ⬡ = ________

2. Fill in the missing numbers. The first one has been done for you.

(a) (b)

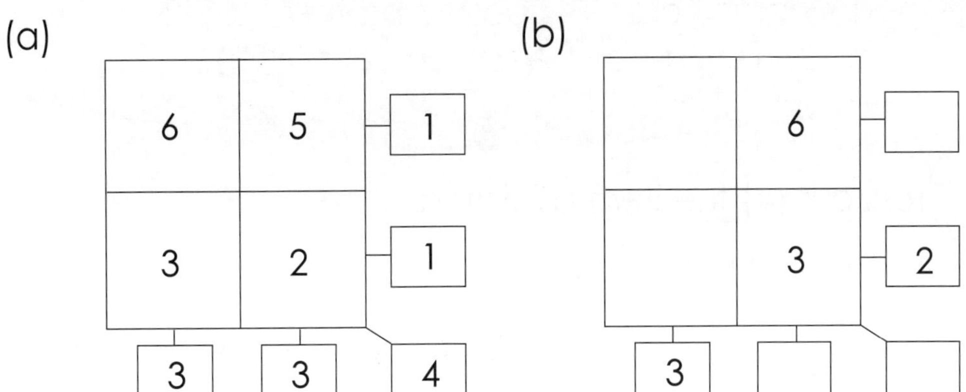

(c)

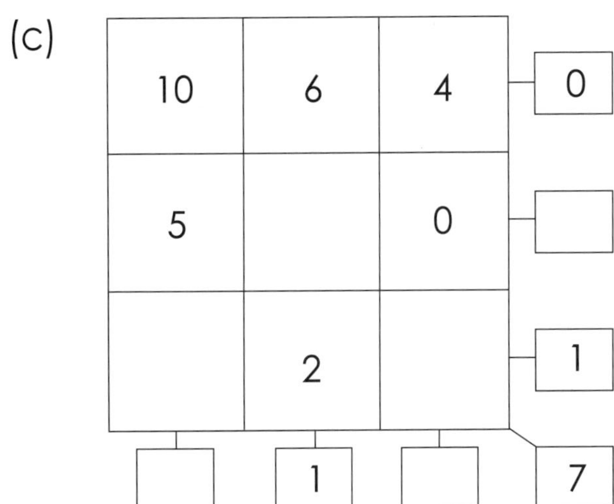

(d)

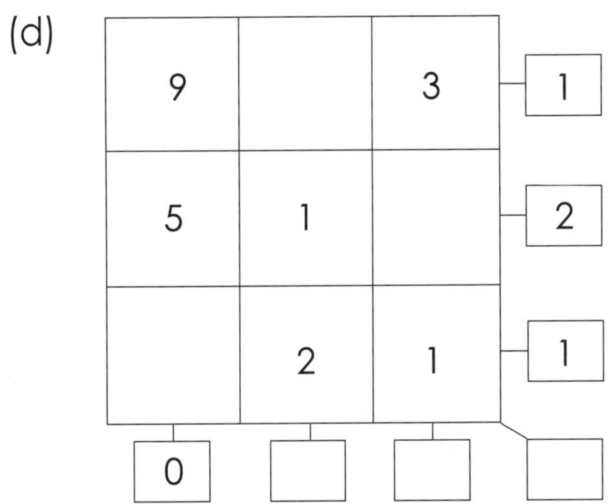

Topic 5: Ordinal Numbers

1. Cross out (×) the item as stated.

   (a) The 2nd last towel.

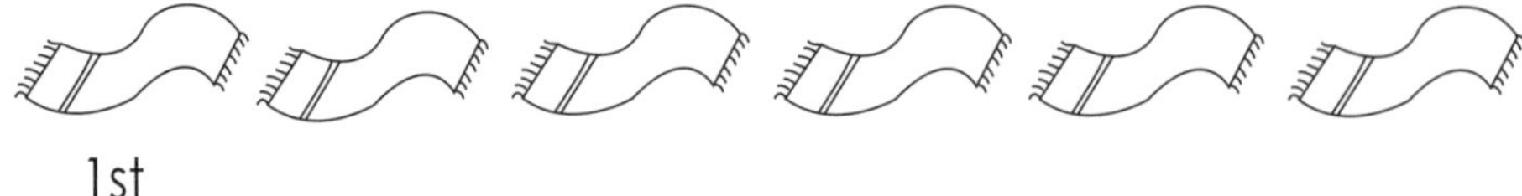

   (b) The 3rd rabbit from the left.

   (c) The 5th pen from the right.

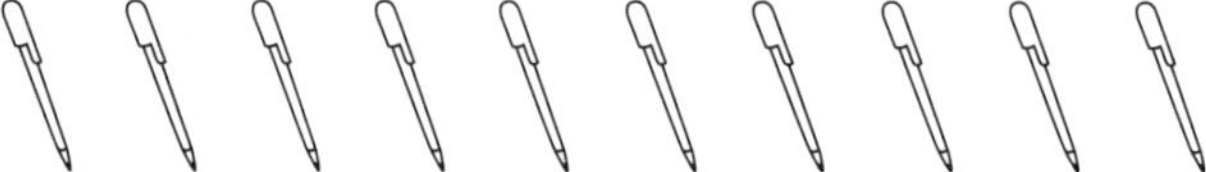

   (d) The 4th leaf.

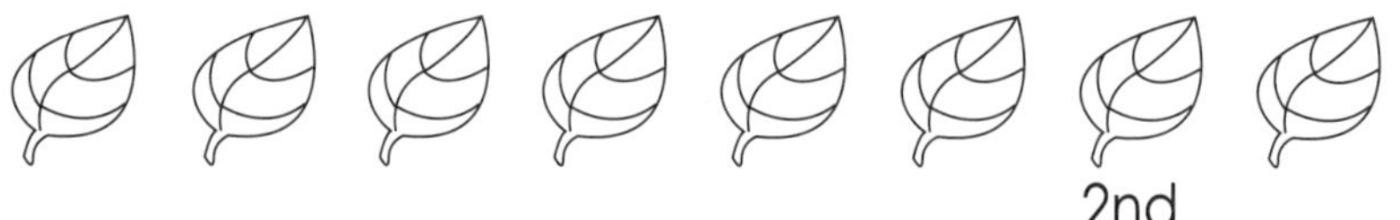

   (e) The 6th stool from the right.

   (f) The horse in the 3rd place.

2. Write out the position of the shaded animal in words.

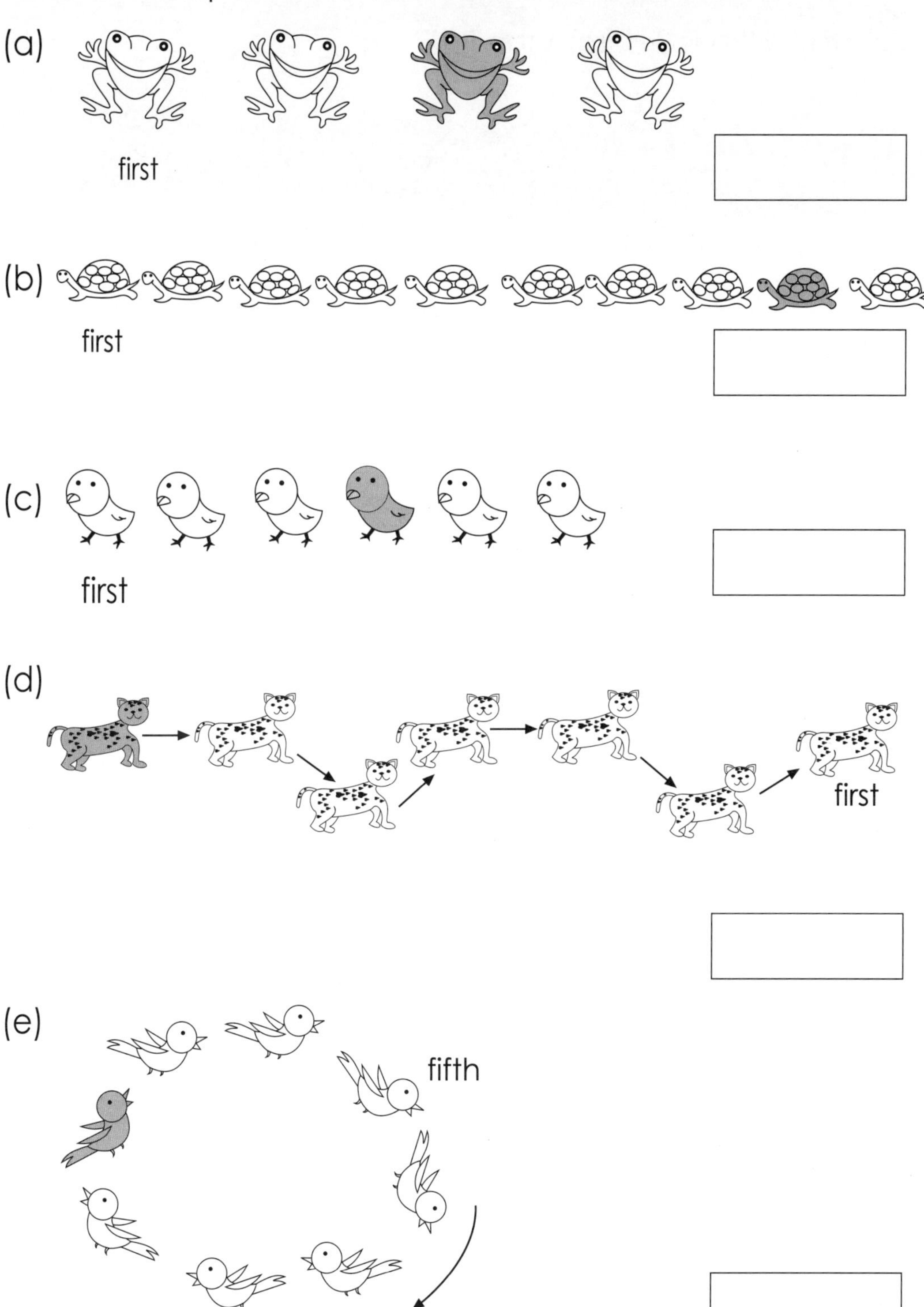

3. Do the following.

(a) Who is 3rd from the left?

__________ is 3rd from the left.

(b) Who is 4th from the right?

__________ is 4th from the right.

(c)

Paul is __________ from the __________.

(d) 

Nicholas is ________ in the race.

4. Write the ordinal positions in words.
   (a) 1st ____________ (b) 5th ____________
   (c) 8th ____________ (d) 2nd ____________
   (e) 10th ____________ (f) 6th ____________

WORD PROBLEMS

1. This is a line.

(a) Who is 4th in line?

____________ is 4th in line.

(b) Who is between the 2nd person and Andrea?

____________ is between the 2nd person and Andrea.

(c) Who is the 5th person counting from the back?

____________ is the 5th person counting from the back.

2. In a sports competition, the Red Team won 7 gold awards. The Green Team won 5 gold awards. The Blue Team won eight gold awards. The Yellow Team won 4 gold awards. Arrange the teams, beginning with the 1st position in the sports competition.

The	The	The	The
[ ]	[ ]	[ ]	[ ]
Team	Team	Team	Team
1st	2nd	3rd	4th

3. Sara is 5th in line. Shirley, who is the last in line, is just behind Sara. How many people are there in line?

There are ________ people in line.

4. Michelle is standing behind 4 people in a line. There are two people behind her. How many people are there in line?

There are ________ people in line.

5. Tom is standing in a row. He is 5th from the right and 4th from the left. How many children are there in the row?

There are ________ children in the row.

Take the Challenge!

1. In a race, Sally is running immediately behind James. James is in the 5th position. How many people are running ahead of Sally?

_______ people are running ahead of Sally.

2. Mark and Simon are lining up for food at a food stall. There are 3 people in front of Mark. There is one person between Mark and Simon. Which position is Simon in the line?

Simon is the _______ person in line.

3. Luis always stands immediately in front of Mason when they line up for school assembly. Shawn is behind Mason and there are two students in line between them. Shawn is the 10th student in line. How many students are in front of Luis in the line?

There are ________ students in front of Luis in line.

4. Look at the photograph of Class 1C.

(a) Where is Kelly in the photograph?

Kelly is in Row ________ , and ________ from the right.

(b) Where is John in the photograph?

John is in Row ________ , and ________ from the left.

5. In a taxi line, everyone needed a taxi for himself or herself. Maria exchanged her 3rd position with an old lady who was in the 8th position. After the old lady had got on a taxi, how many more taxis would have to leave before Maria got on hers?

________ more taxis would have to leave before Maria got on hers.

Topic 6: Numbers to 20

1. Count and color the rocks from 1 to 20 so that Kimmy can get across the pond.

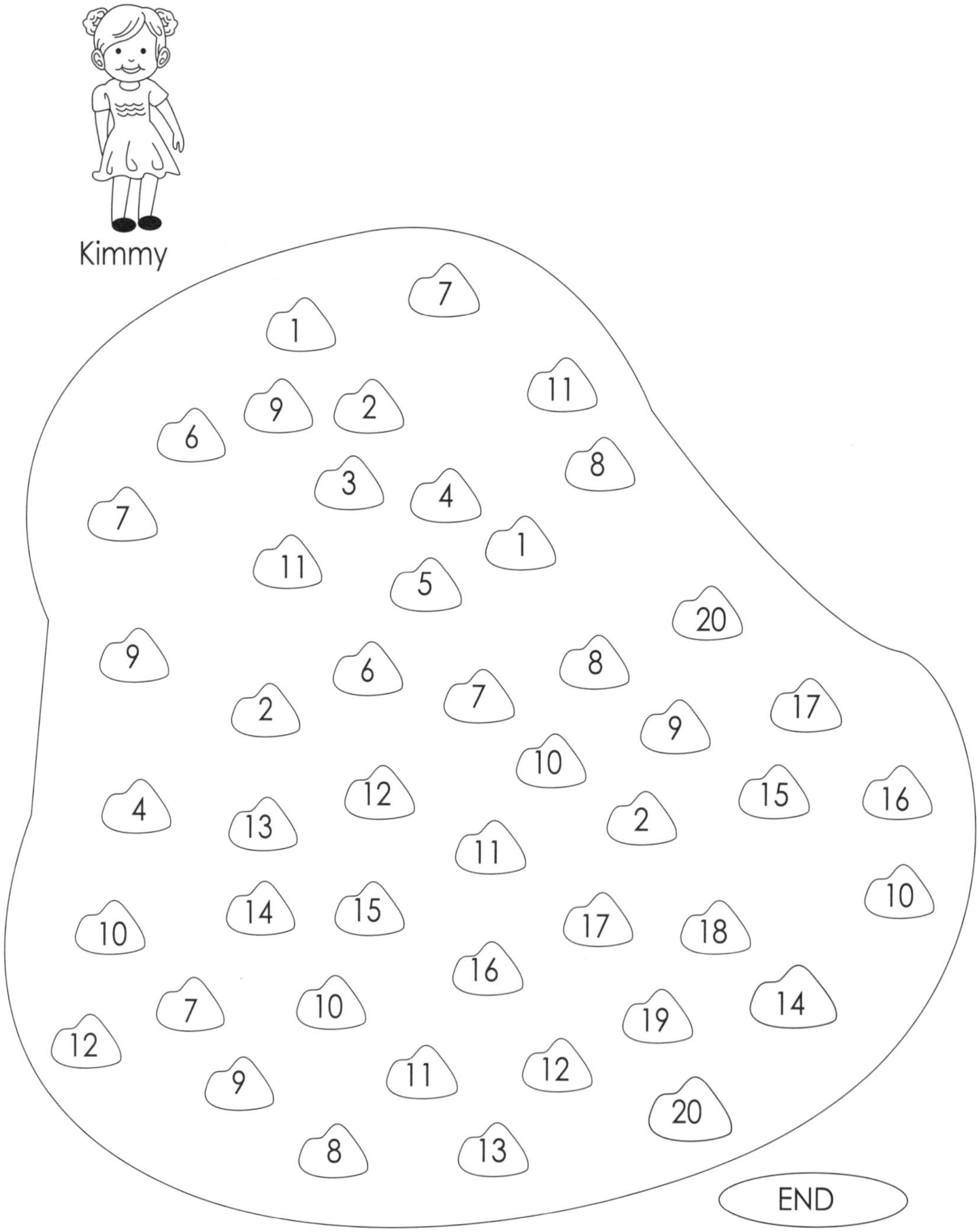

Kimmy

END

2. Count the number of items and write it in words.

(a) 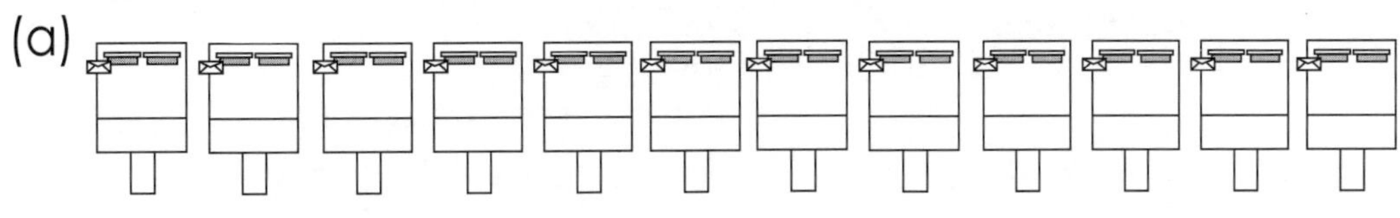

(b) 

(c) 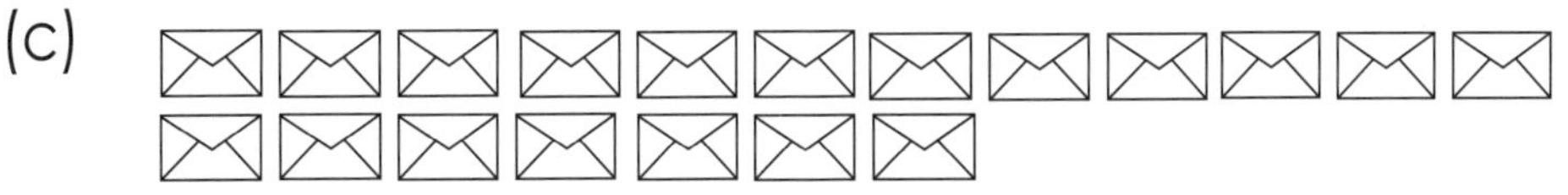

(d) 

(e) 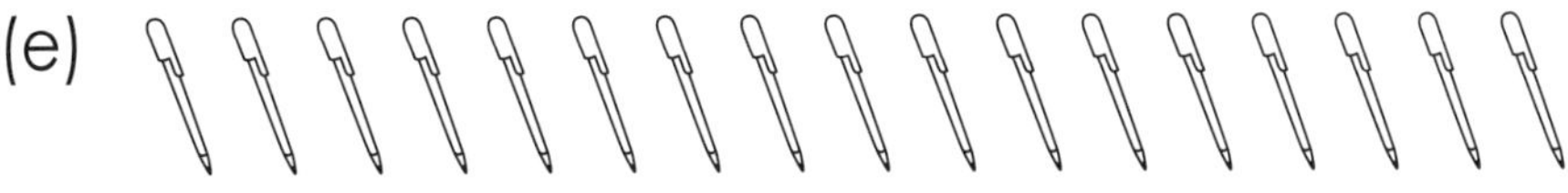

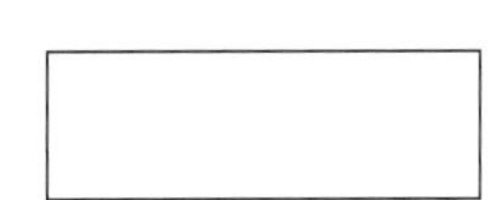

3. Complete the number bonds.

(a)

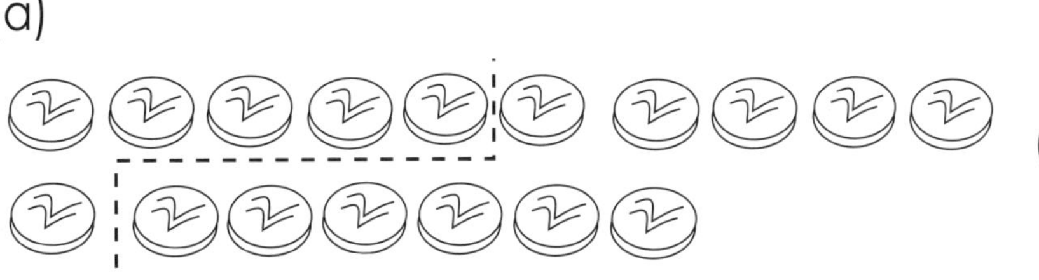

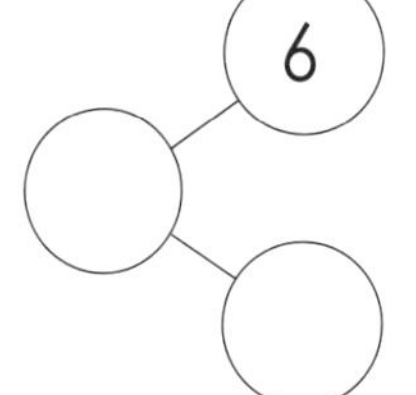

(b)

(c)

(d)

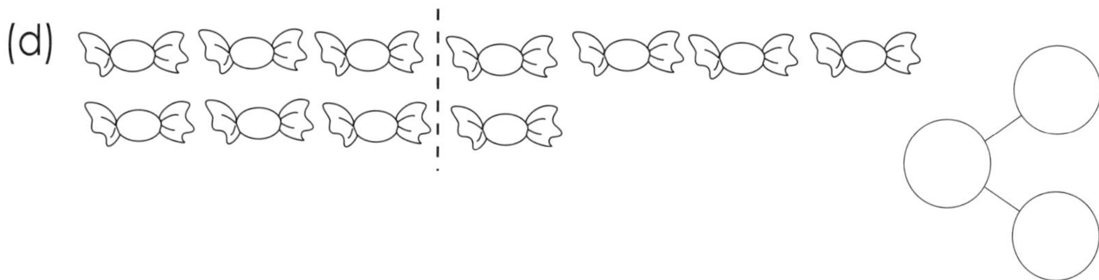

(e)

4. Color the elephant with the largest number.

5. Color the giraffe with the smallest number.

6. Arrange the numbers from the smallest to the largest.

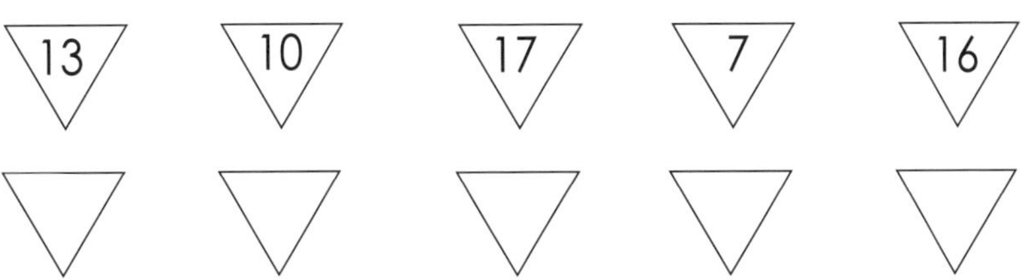

7. Arrange the numbers from the largest to the smallest.

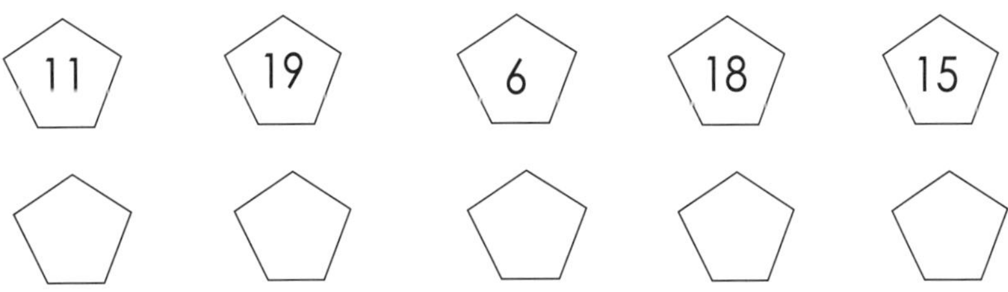

8. Write in numerals.

(a) twelve ________ (b) seventeen ________

(c) fifteen ________ (d) nineteen ________

9. Write in words.

(a) 13 ____________ (b) 11 ____________

(c) 20 ____________ (d) 16 ____________

10. Fill in the blanks.

(a) 10 ones and 9 ones make ________.

(b) 1 ten 7 ones = ________.

(c) 13 = ________ ten and ________ ones.

(d) ________ ones and 11 ones make 14.

(e) ________ tens ________ ones = 20.

(f) 8 ones and 5 ones make ________.

11. Check (✓) the correct statements and cross out (×) the wrong statements.

(a) 16 comes just after 15. ( )

(b) 15 is more than 17. ( )

(c) 14, 15, 16 is a correct number order. ( )

(d) 2 tens and 2 ones make 20. ( )

(e) 7 ones and 1 ten make 71. ( )

(f) 1 one and 1 one make 11. ( )

(g) 12 ones is equal to 12. ( )

(h) 18 is less than 9 ones and 1 ten. ( )

(i) 20 is more than 2 ones and 1 ten but less than 2 tens and 0 ones. ( )

(j) 1 ten and 3 ones is less than 15 ones but more than 11 ones. ( )

12. Complete the crossword puzzle with the clues.

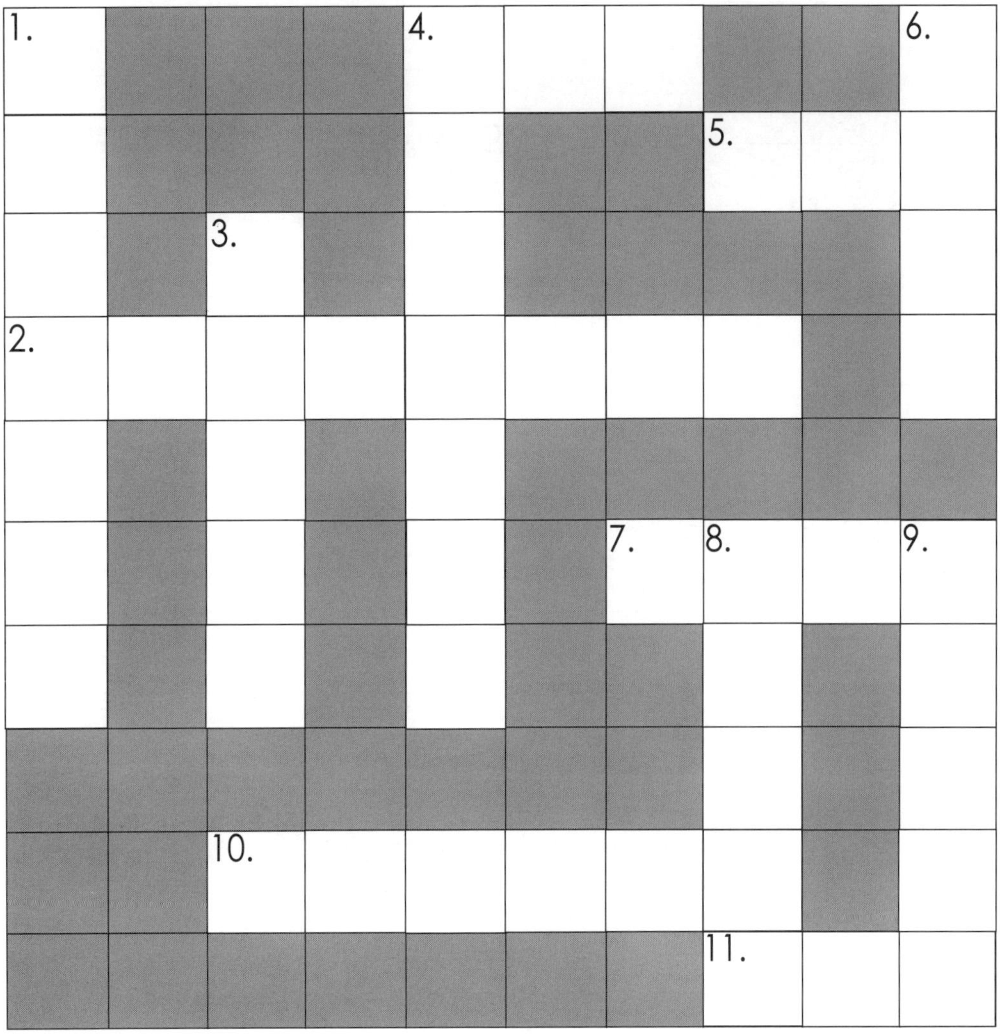
1.
4.
6.
5.
3.
2.
7.
8.
9.
10.
11.

Down:

1. ________ is between fourteen and sixteen.

3.
1st
Jeannie

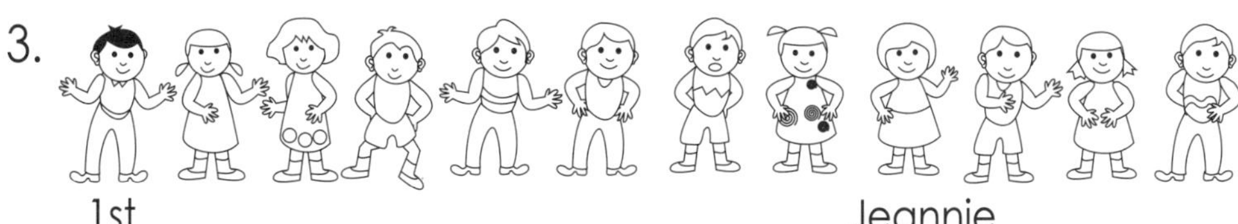

Jeannie is ________ in position.

4. ________ comes before 17.

6.

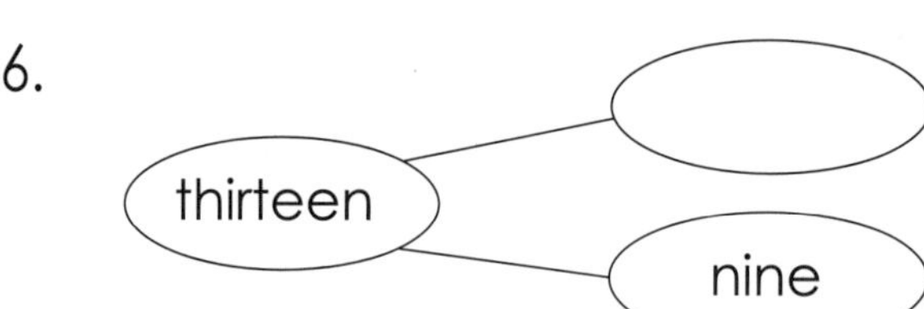

________ is the missing number in the number bond.

8. ________ ones and 9 ones make 17.

9. 4 ones, 3 ones and 0 tens make ________.

Across:

2.

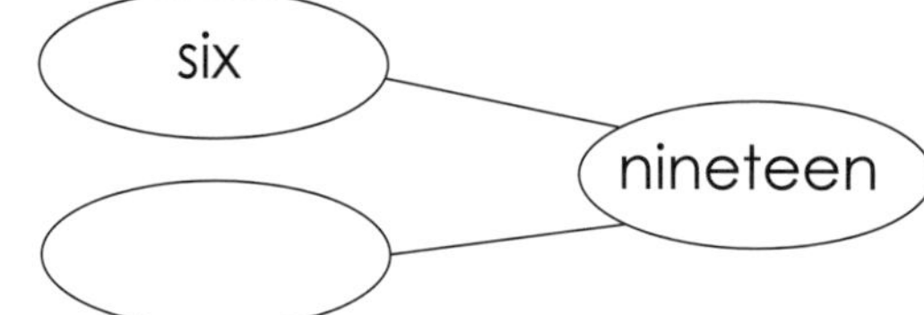

________ is the missing number in the number bond.

4. ________ comes just before 7.

5. ________ tens and 0 ones make 20.

7. 1 ten and 2 ones is ________ than 14 ones.

10. Magdeline is 7th in line. Sharon, who is just after Magdeline, is ________ in line.

11. 10 ones make 1 ________.

13. Fill in the missing numbers in each pattern.

(a)

WORD PROBLEMS

1. There are 10 apples on a tray. Another 4 apples are placed on the tray. How many apples are there on the tray altogether?

☐ and ☐ make ☐

There are ________ apples on the tray altogether.

2. Ten children are at a beach. Seven more children join them. How many children are there at the beach altogether?

☐ and ☐ make ☐

There are ________ children at the beach altogether.

3. Two letters of the alphabet are written on the board. The teacher writes another 10 more letters on the board. How many letters are there on the board altogether?

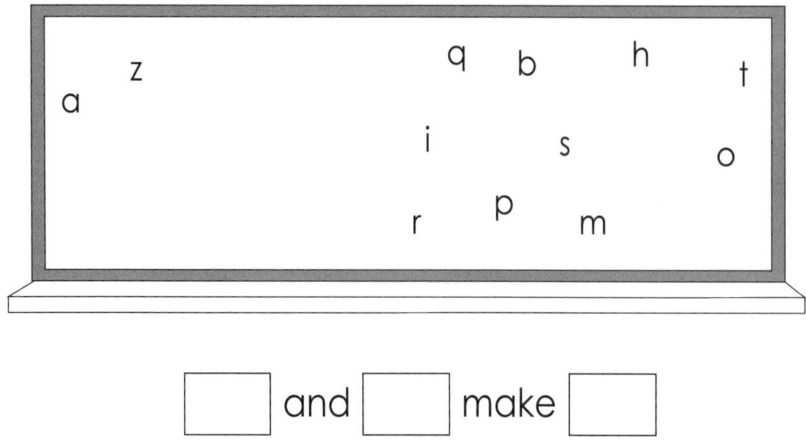

☐ and ☐ make ☐

There are ________ letters on the board altogether.

4. There are 6 fish in the tank. Daddy put 10 more fish into the tank. How many fish are there in the tank altogether?

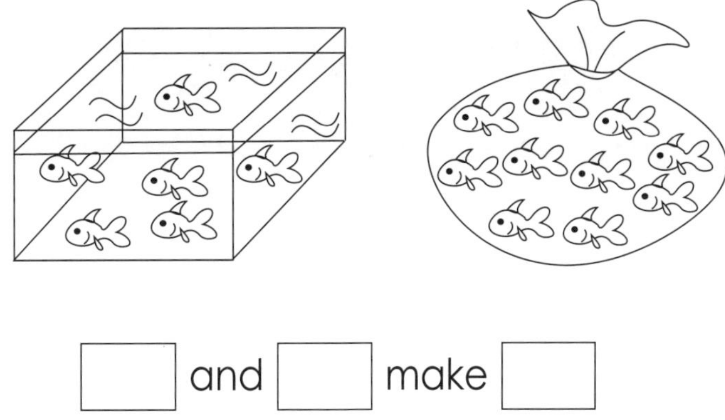

☐ and ☐ make ☐

There are ________ fish in the tank altogether.

5. Look at the picture. Which pond has more frogs?

Pond ________ has more frogs.

6. Look at the picture. Which table has fewer ants?

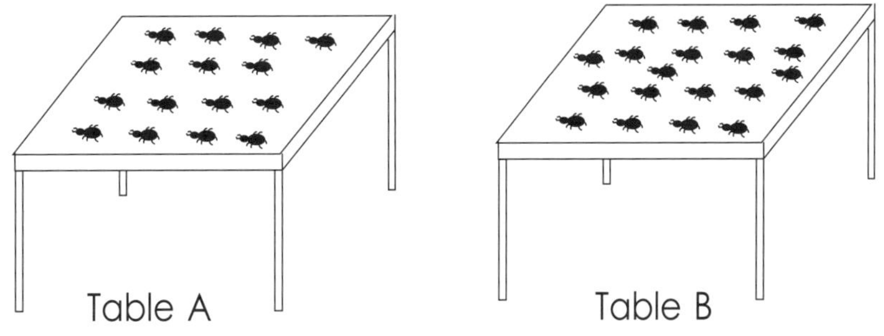

Table ________ has fewer ants.

7. Look at the picture. Who has more stamps?

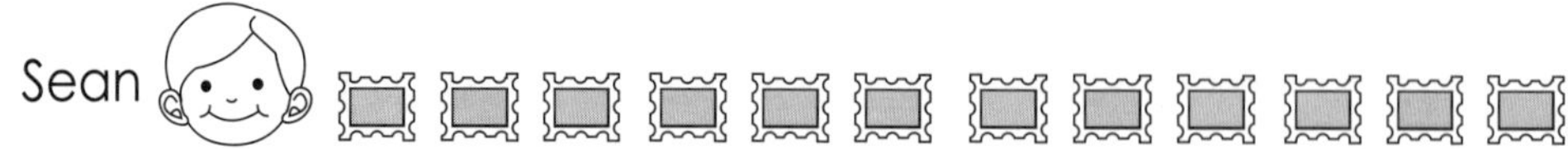

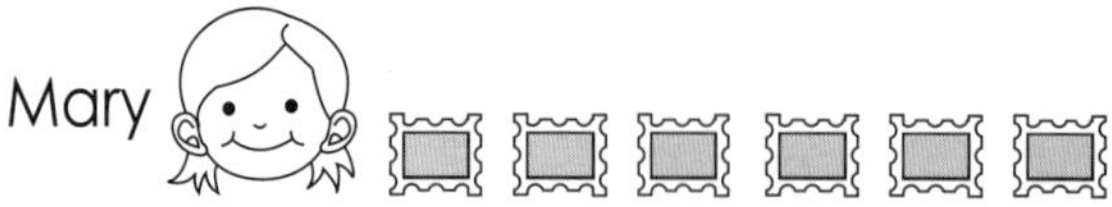

________ has more stamps.

How many more? ________ more

8. Look at the picture. Which pole has fewer cloths?

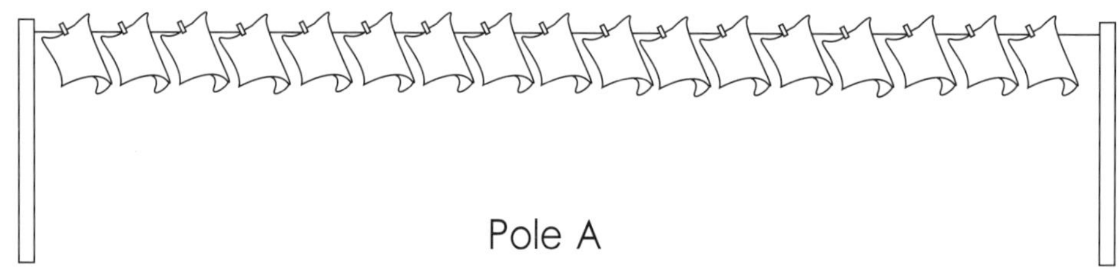

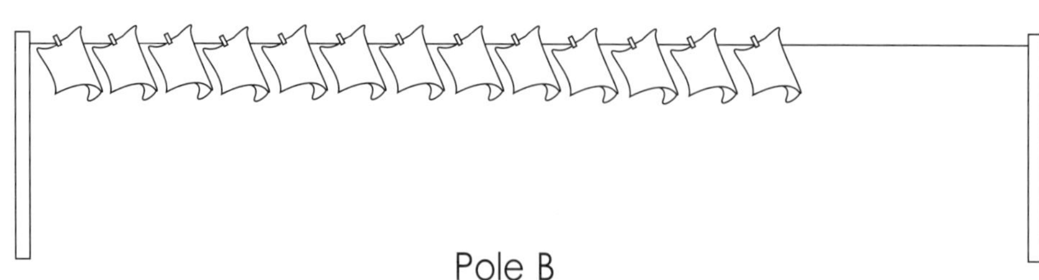

Pole ________ has fewer cloths.

How many fewer? ________ fewer

Take the Challenge!

1. Fill in the missing numbers in each pattern.

(a)

(b)

(c)

2. Fill in the missing number to complete the pattern.

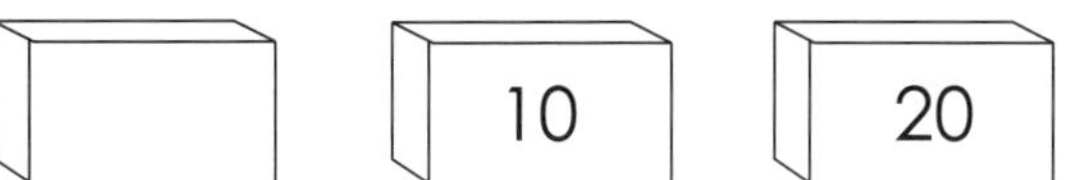

Topic 7: Addition and Subtraction Within 20

1. Add by 'counting on'.

   Example: 12 + 4 = 16
   Count 4 ones from 12: 13, 14, 15, <u>16</u>

   (a) 13 + 5 = ________ (b) 9 + 3 = ________

   (c) 8 + 4 = ________ (d) 15 + 3 = ________

   (e) 17 + 2 = ________ (f) 18 + 1 = ________

   (g) 6 + 6 = ________ (h) 7 + 4 = ________

2. Add by "making 10". Circle pictures to make 10 first. Then, fill in the missing numbers.

   (a)

   7 + 6 = 10 + 3

   (3) (3) = ________

   (b)

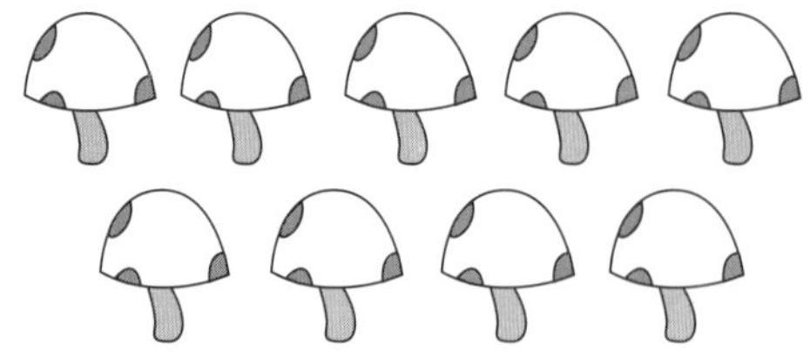

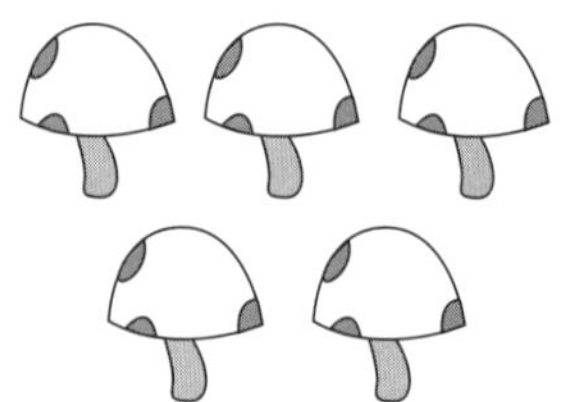

   9 + 5 = 10 + ________

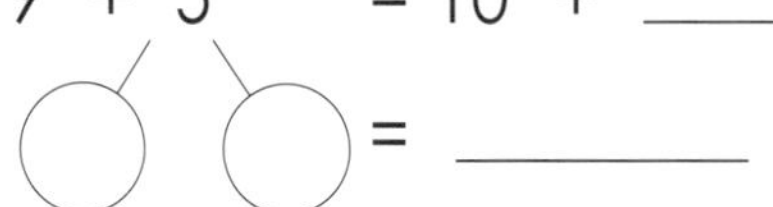

   ( ) ( ) = ________

(c) 

6 + 8 = 10 + ________

◯ ◯ = ________

(d) 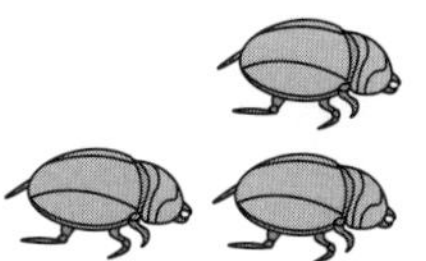

8 + 3 = 10 + ________

◯ ◯ = ________

(e) 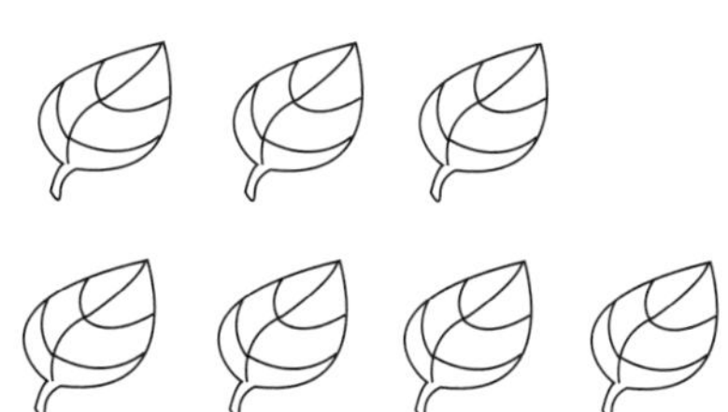

5 + 7 = 10 + ________

◯ ◯ = ________

(f) 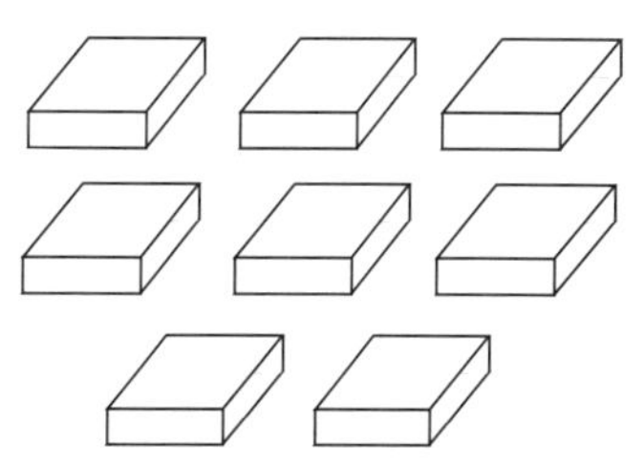

9 + 8 = 10 + ________

◯ ◯ = ________

3. Add using number bonds.

Example: 13 + 6 = <u>19</u>

Step 1: 13 + 6

(10) (3)

Step 2: Add 6 to 3.
3 + 6 = 9

Step 3: 10 + 9 = 19

Step 4: 13 + 6 = 19

(a) 14 + 3 = ________

(b) 12 + 4 = ________

(c) 15 + 4 = ________

(d) 8 + 11 = ________

(e) 11 + 8 = ________

(f) 13 + 3 = ________

(g) 2 + 16 = ________

(h) 17 + 2 = ________

(i) 13 + 5 = ________

(j) 3 + 11 = ________

4. Cross out the correct number of pictures. Fill in the missing numbers.

(a)

13 – 6 = ________

(b)

17 – 7 = ________

(c)

11 – 5 = ________

(d)

16 – 3 = ________

(e)

14 – 8 = ________

5. Subtract by 'counting backwards'.

Example: 11 – 3 = <u>8</u>
Count 3 ones backwards from 11: 10, 9, <u>8</u>

(a) 15 – 6 = ________ (b) 19 – 5 = ________

(c) 12 – 7 = ________ (d) 16 – 1 = ________

(e) 13 – 5 = ________ (f) 20 – 4 = ________

(g) 14 - 3 = ________ (h) 18 – 2 = ________

6. Subtract using number bonds.

Example: 16 – 4 = <u>12</u>

Step 1: 16 – 4

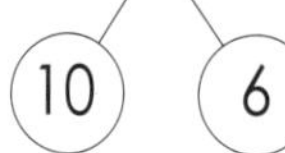

Step 2: Subtract 4 from 6.
6 – 4 = 2

Step 3: 10 + 2 = 12

Step 4: 16 – 4 = <u>12</u>

(a) 17 – 5 = ________ (b) 15 – 1 = ________

(c) 18 – 7 = ________ (d) 19 – 8 = ________

(e) 15 – 5 = ________

7. Subtract using number bonds.

Example: 13 – 7 = <u>6</u>

Step 1: 13 – 7

(3) (10)

Step 2: Subtract 7 from 10.
10 – 7 = 3

Step 3: 3 + 3 = 6

Step 4: 13 – 7 = <u>6</u>

(a) 12 – 6 = ________

(b) 16 – 9 = ________

(c) 12 – 3 = ________

(d) 11 – 4 = ________

(e) 14 – 6 = ________

8. Put "+" or "–" in the circle to make the number sentences correct.

(a) 5 ◯ 7 = 12

(b) 20 ◯ 5 = 15

(c) 8 ◯ 8 = 16

(d) 14 = 9 ◯ 5

(e) 19 ◯ 9 = 10

(f) 18 ◯ 18 = 0

9. Write 2 addition and 2 subtraction sentences for this picture. Complete the number bond.

(a) 

(b) ☐ + ☐ = ☐

(c) ☐ – ☐ = ☐

(d) ☐ – ☐ = ☐

(e) 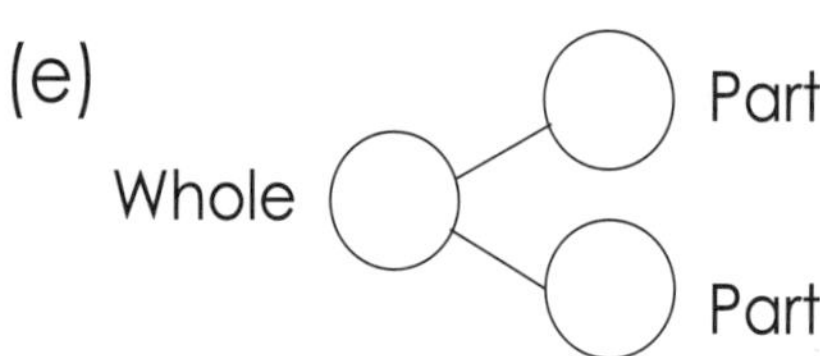

10. Look at the picture. Count, then add or subtract correctly.

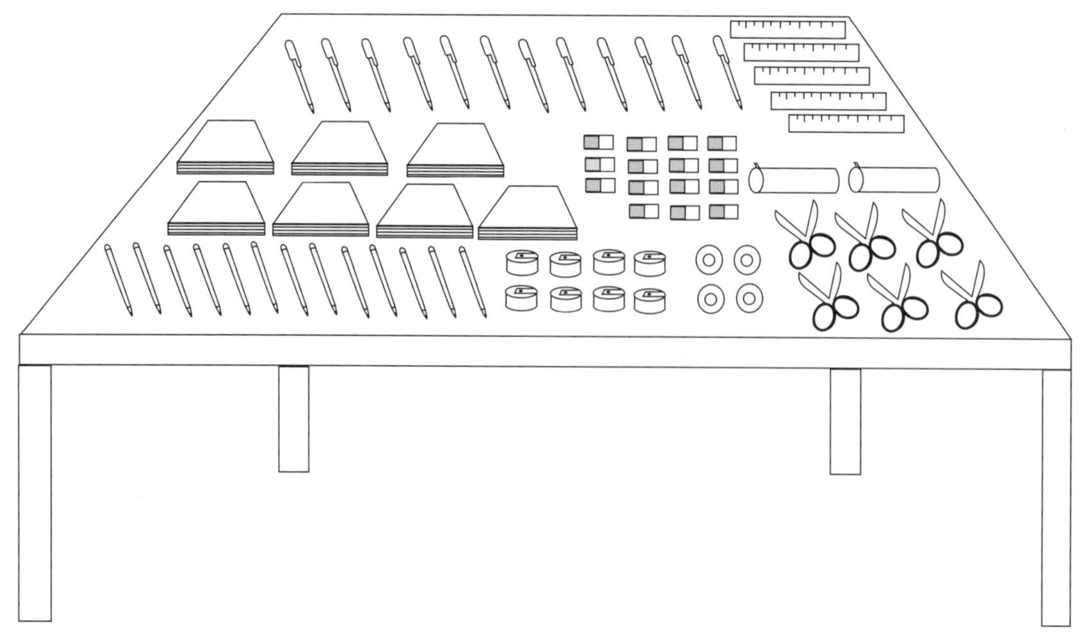

(a) ☐  + ☐ = ________

(b) ☐  + ☐ 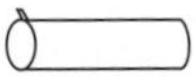 = ________

(c) ☐ 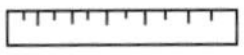 + ☐ = ________

(d) ☐ + ☐ 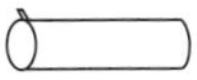 = ________

(e) ☐  – ☐ = ________

(f) ☐  – ☐ 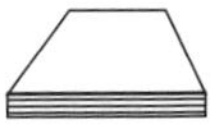 = ________

(g) ☐ – ☐  = ________

(h) ☐ – ☐  = ________

11. Fill in the blanks.

(a) 10 + 8 = ________

(b) 5 + ________ = 14

(c) ________ – 6 = 13

(d) 7 is ________ less than 12.

(e) 19 is ________ more than 11.

(f) 14 is 2 more than ________.

(g) 10 is 5 less than ________.

(h) 7 + 9 = ________

(i) 17 – 8 = ________

(j) 16 – ________ = 9

(k) 12 – 2 = 7 + ________.

(l) 18 – 5 = 6 + ________.

(m)

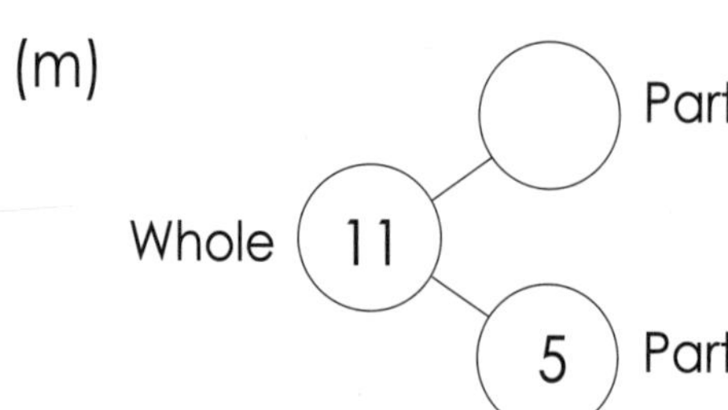

(n)

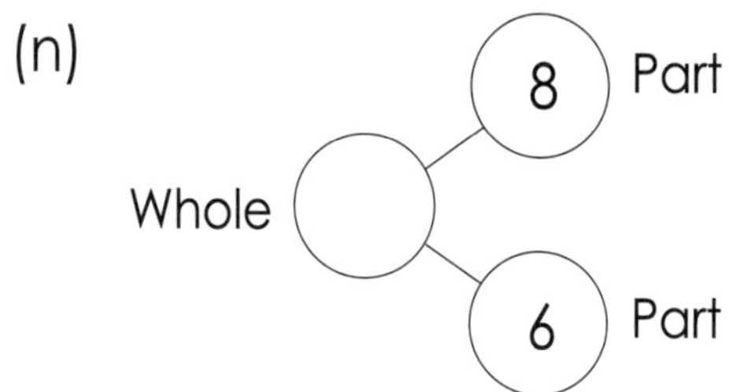

12. Guess the correct number.

(a)

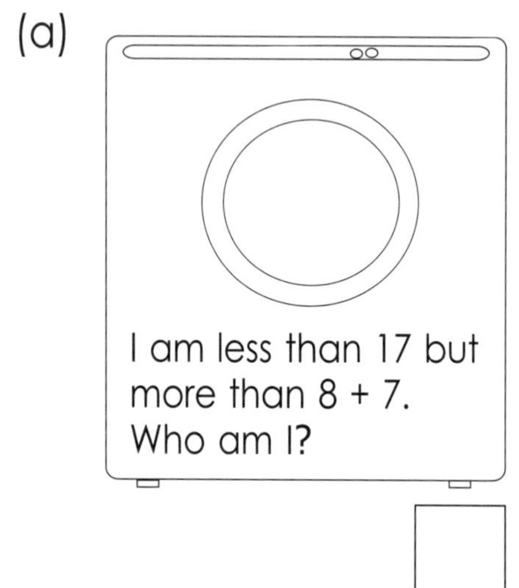

(b)

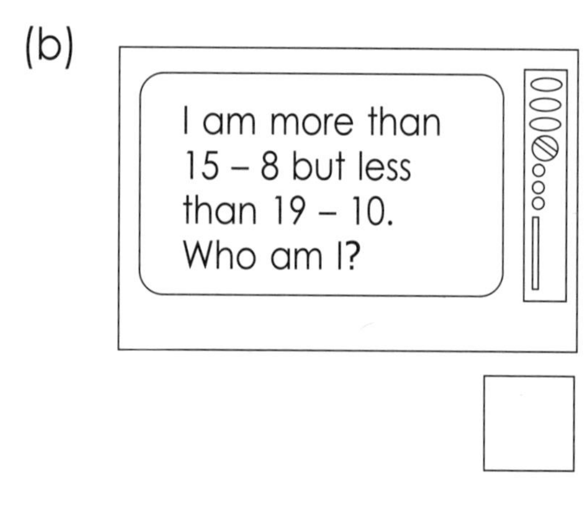

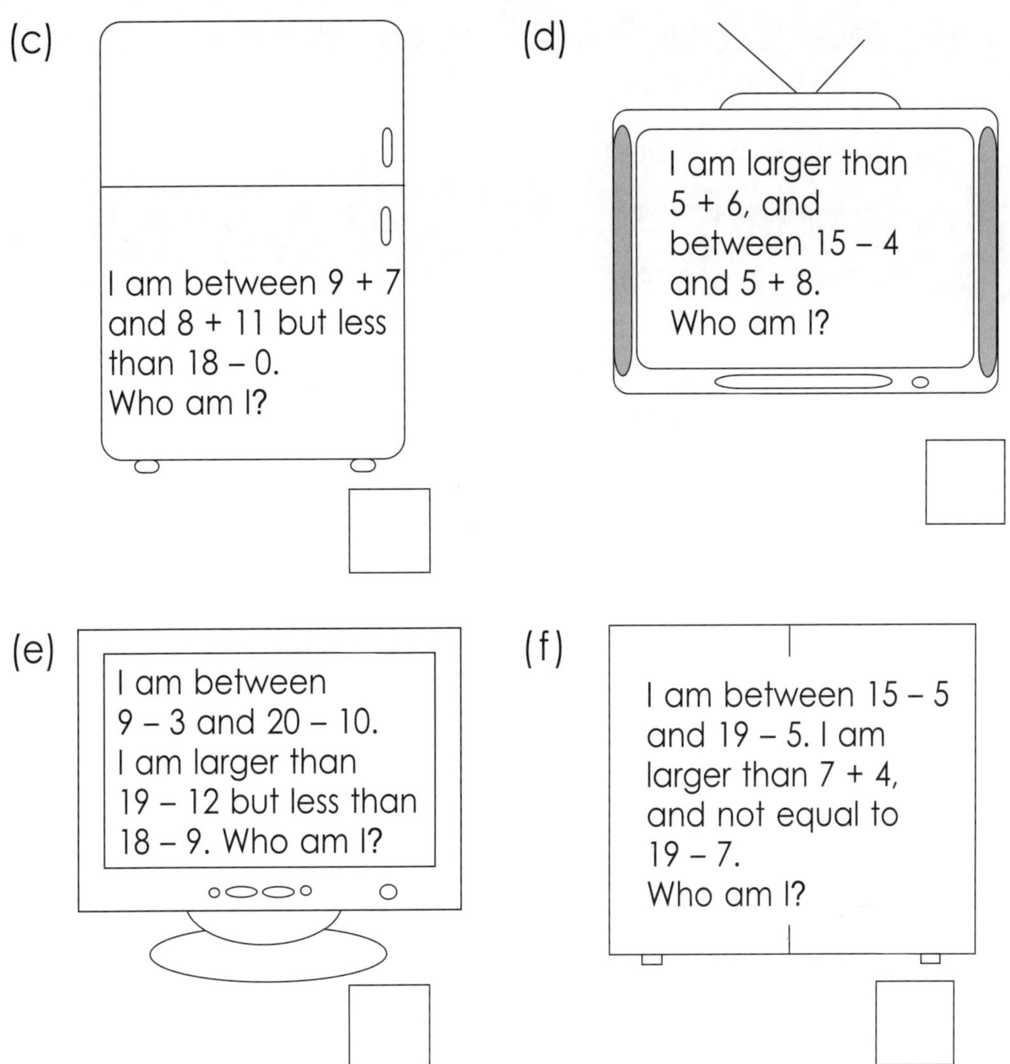

13. Check (✓) the correct statements and cross out (✗) the wrong statements.

(a) 15 + 4 is equal to 19. ( )

(b) Take 7 away from 15, the answer is 7. ( )

(c) 8 and 3 is less than 4 and 6. ( )

(d) 17 – 11 is larger than 14 – 6. ( )

(e) The numbers 17, 18 and 19 are all larger than 14 + 3. ( )

(f) Take 11 away from 16, the answer is the same as 19 – 14. ( )

(g) 4 + 8 is not equal to 17. ( )

(h) Adding 13 – 7 to 5, the answer is larger than 10. ( )

WORD PROBLEMS

1. Sophia has 8 bags. Mandy has 7 bags. How many bags do they have altogether?

☐ + ☐ = ☐

They have ______ bags altogether.

2. Ginny and Laura share 17 pieces of candy. Laura gets 9 pieces of candy. How many pieces of candy does Ginny have?

☐ – ☐ = ☐

Ginny has ______ pieces of candy.

3. After giving 7 hair clips to her friend, Lydia had 11 hair clips left. How many hair clips did Lydia have at first?

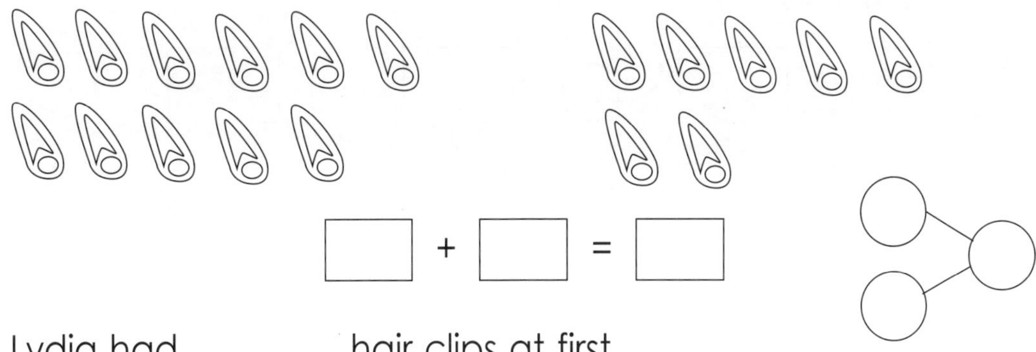

☐ + ☐ = ☐

Lydia had ________ hair clips at first.

4. Barbara bought 19 eggs from the market. On the way home, she broke 6 of them. How many eggs were not broken?

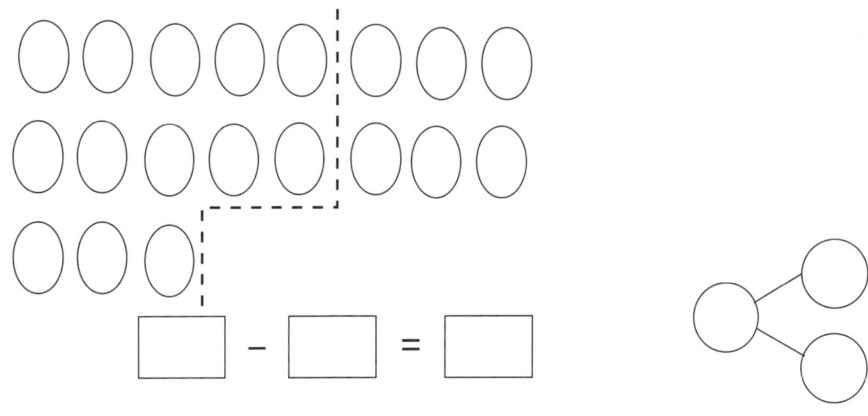

☐ – ☐ = ☐

________ eggs were not broken.

5. Greg has 16 shells. Joseph has 9 shells fewer than Greg. How many shells does Joseph have?

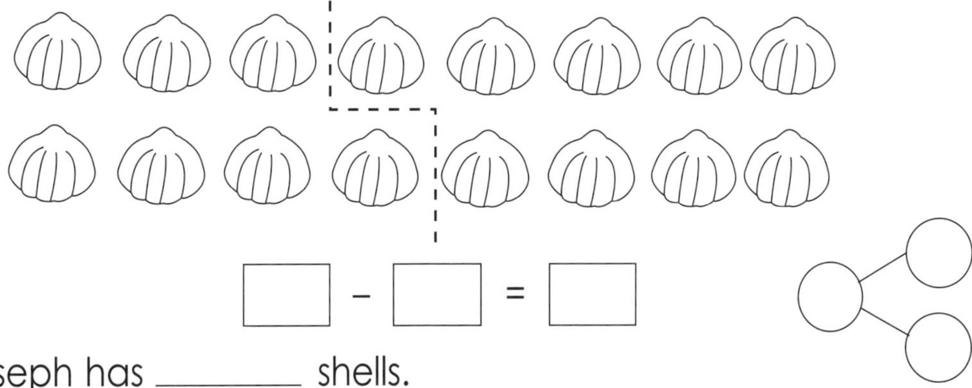

☐ – ☐ = ☐

Joseph has ________ shells.

6. There were 9 bees and 5 dragon flies in the garden. Six bees flew away. How many insects are there in the garden now?

☐ ○ ☐ = ☐

☐ ○ ☐ = ☐

There are ________ insects in the garden now.

7. Daniel is 12 years old. His brother, Joshua, is 3 years older than him. His sister, Ann, is 4 years younger than Joshua.

(a) How old is Joshua?

☐ ○ ☐ = ☐

Joshua is ________ years old.

(b) How old is Ann?

☐ ○ ☐ = ☐

Ann is ________ years old.

8. In a basket, there are 11 cherries and 6 guavas.

(a) How many more cherries than guavas are there?

☐ ○ ☐ = ☐

There are ________ more cherries than guavas.

(b) How many fruits are there altogether?

☐ ○ ☐ = ☐

There are ________ fruits altogether.

Take the **Challenge!**

1. Fill in the correct numbers at the ends such that the sum of any two end numbers gives the number in the middle of the line joining these two end numbers.

   [Clue: Use 'guess and check' method.]

   Example:

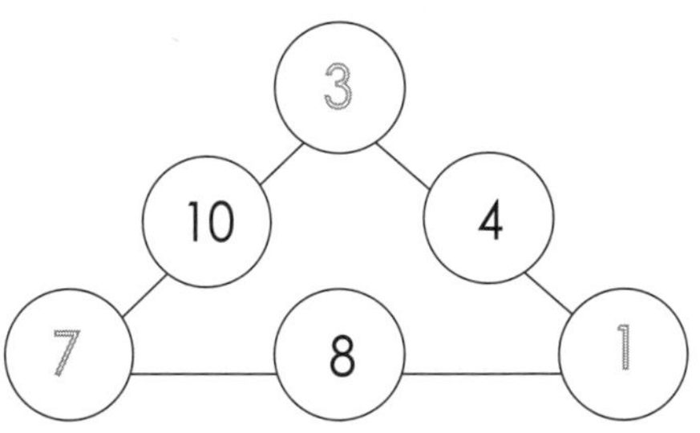

Check:
3 + 7 = 10
7 + 1 = 8
1 + 3 = 4

(a) [Hint: Check: 3, 4, 5 or 6]

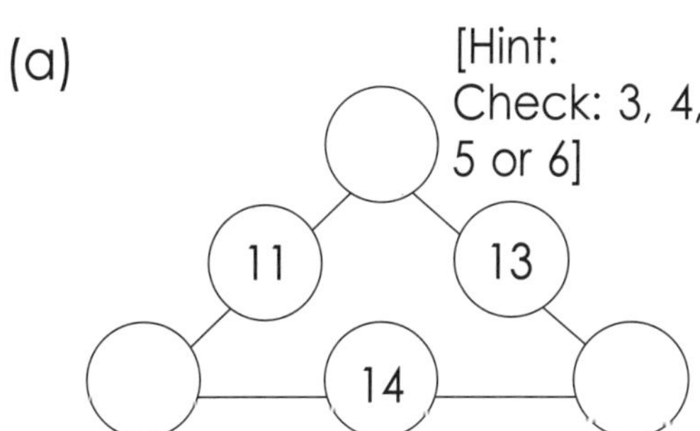

(b) [Hint: Check: 6, 7, 8 or 9]

14
12
8

(c) [Hint: Check: 10, 11, 12 or 13]

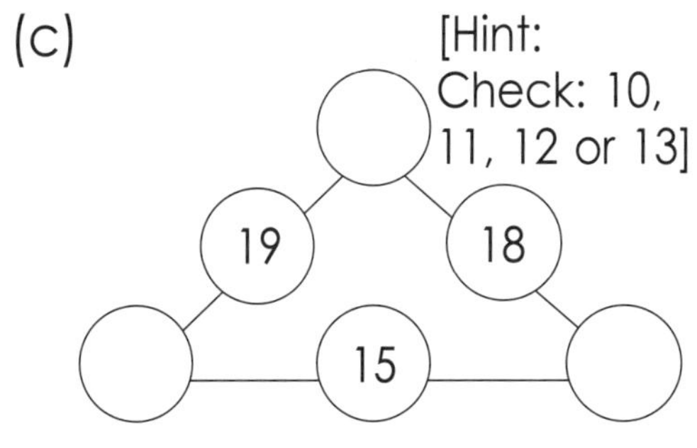

(d) [Hint: Check: 7, 8, 9 or 10]

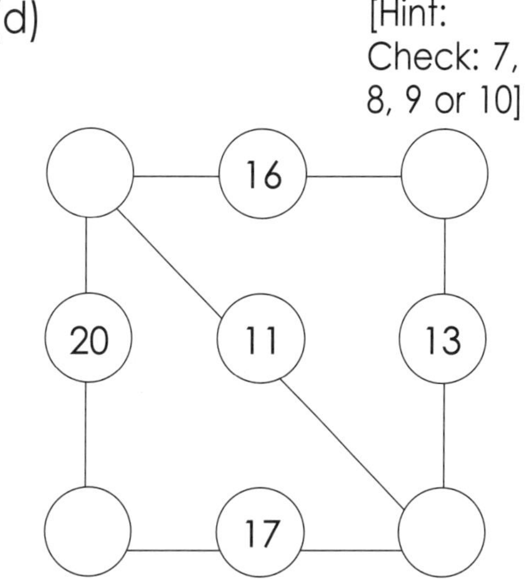

2. Fill in the correct numbers at the ends such that the difference of any two end numbers gives the number in the middle of the line joining these two end numbers. Use numbers within 20 to fill in the missing end numbers.

   [Note: The difference of two numbers means subtracting the smaller number from the larger number.]

   [Clue: There are many possible ways. You may start by filling in any number within 20 at any one end and then check if the answers at the other two ends can both be within 20. If not, start with another number within 20.]

   Example:

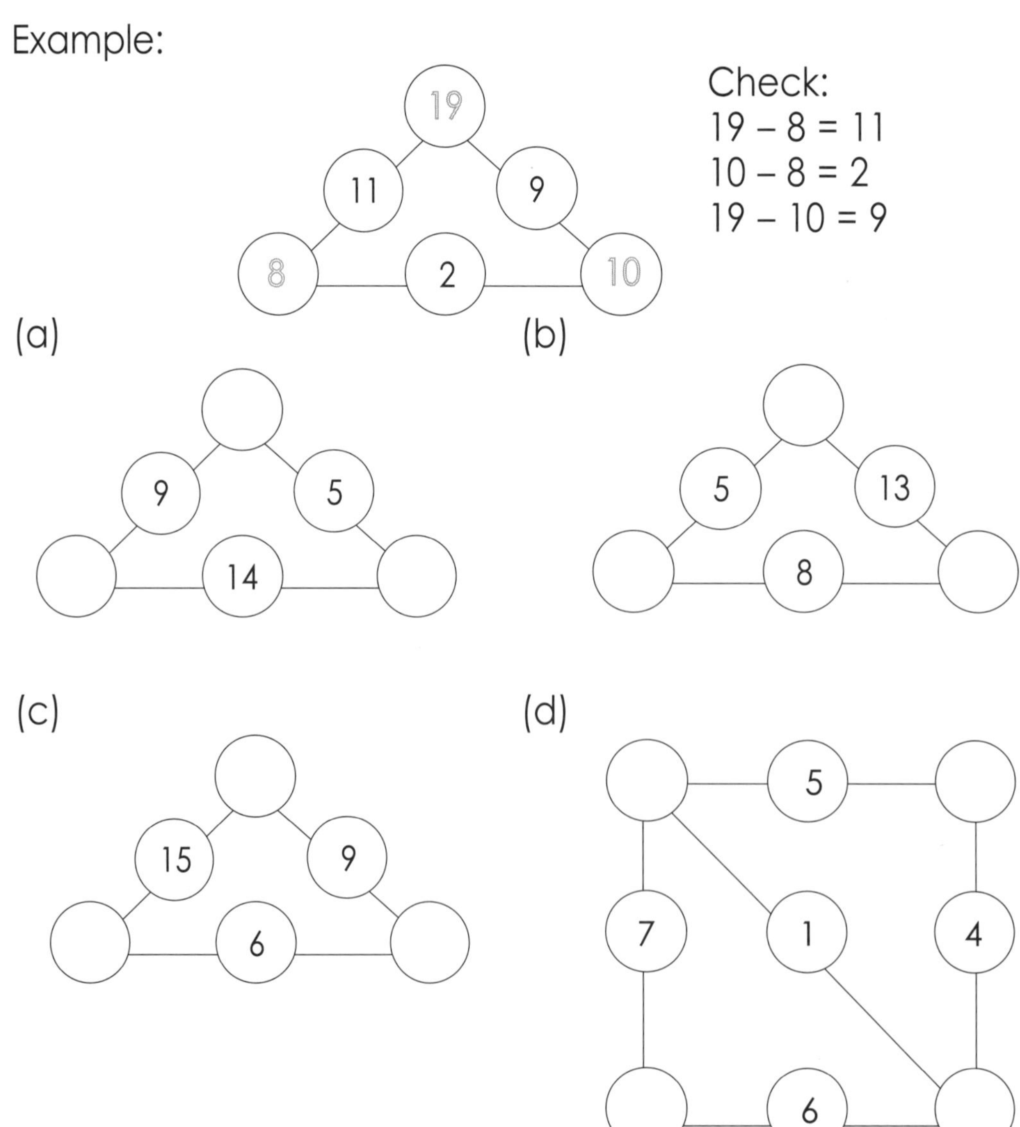

Topic 8: Shapes and Patterns

1. Color the picture by using the given color code.

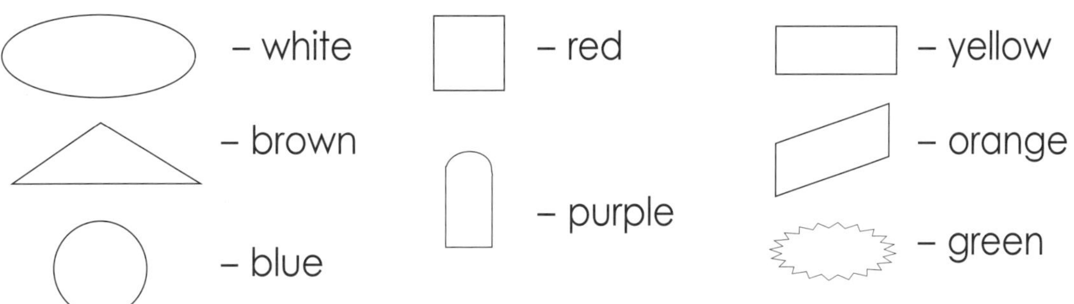

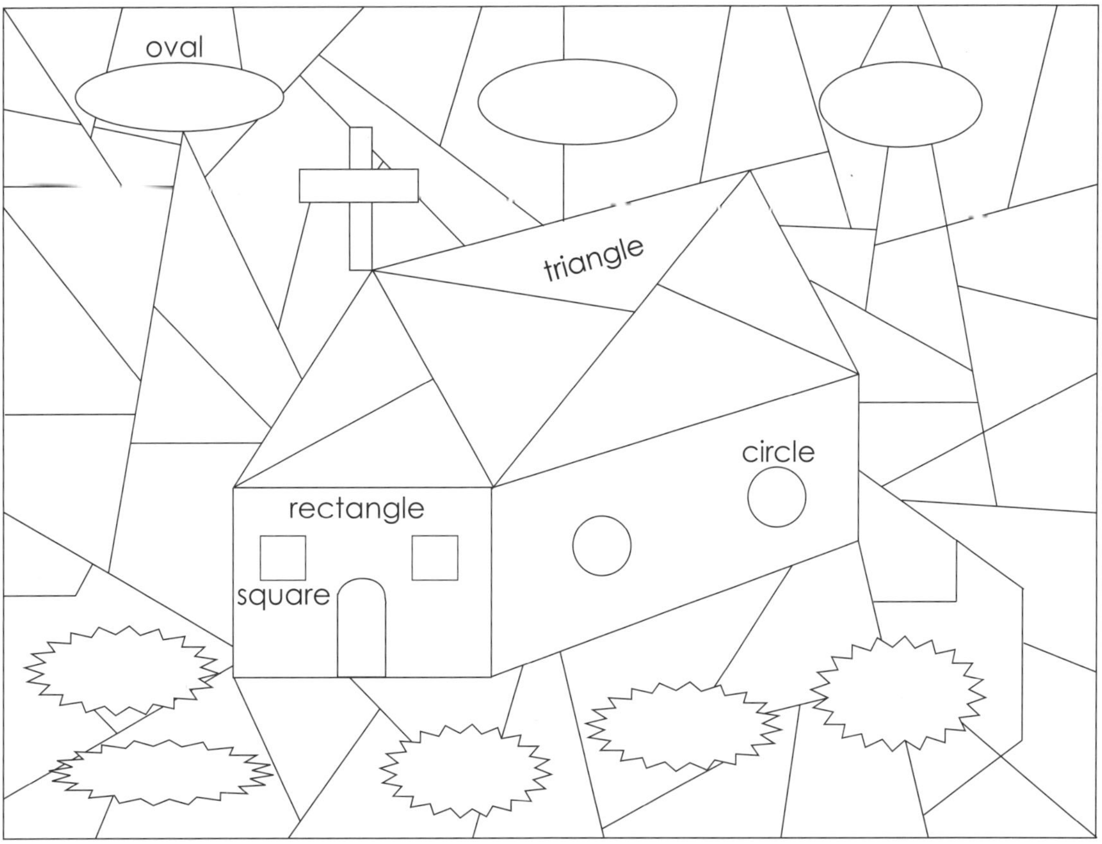

oval

triangle

circle

rectangle

square

2. Color two items of the same shape in each set of figures.

(a)

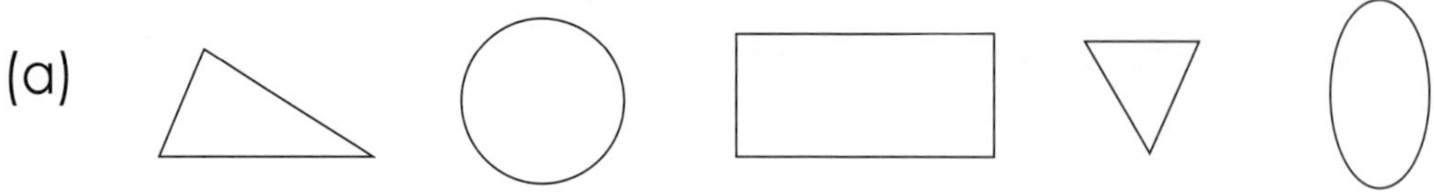

(b)

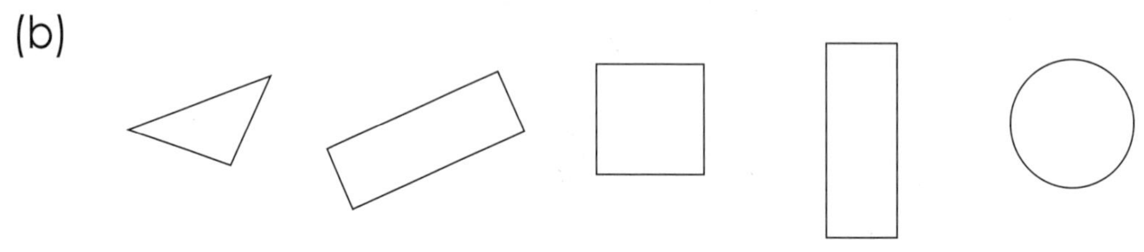

(c)

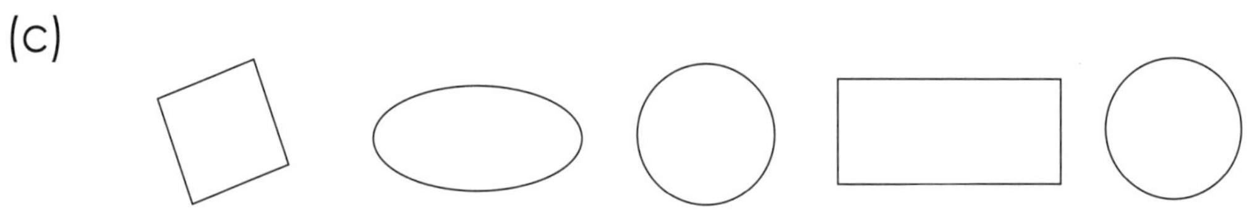

(d)

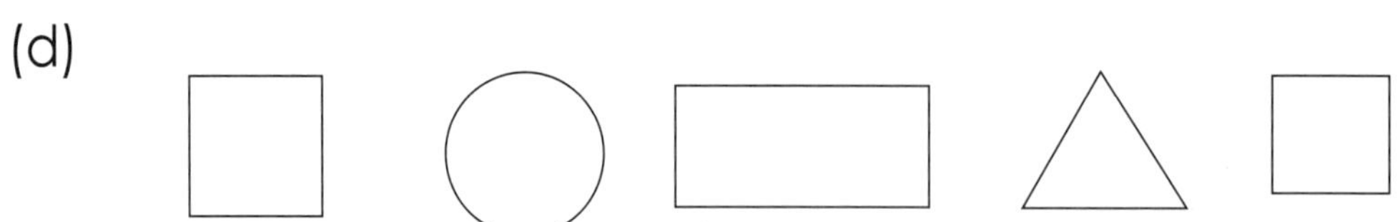

(e)

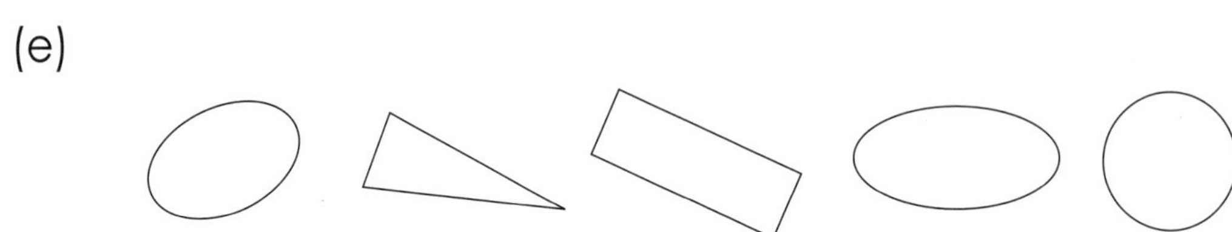

3. Cross out (×) the diagram that does not belong to the set.

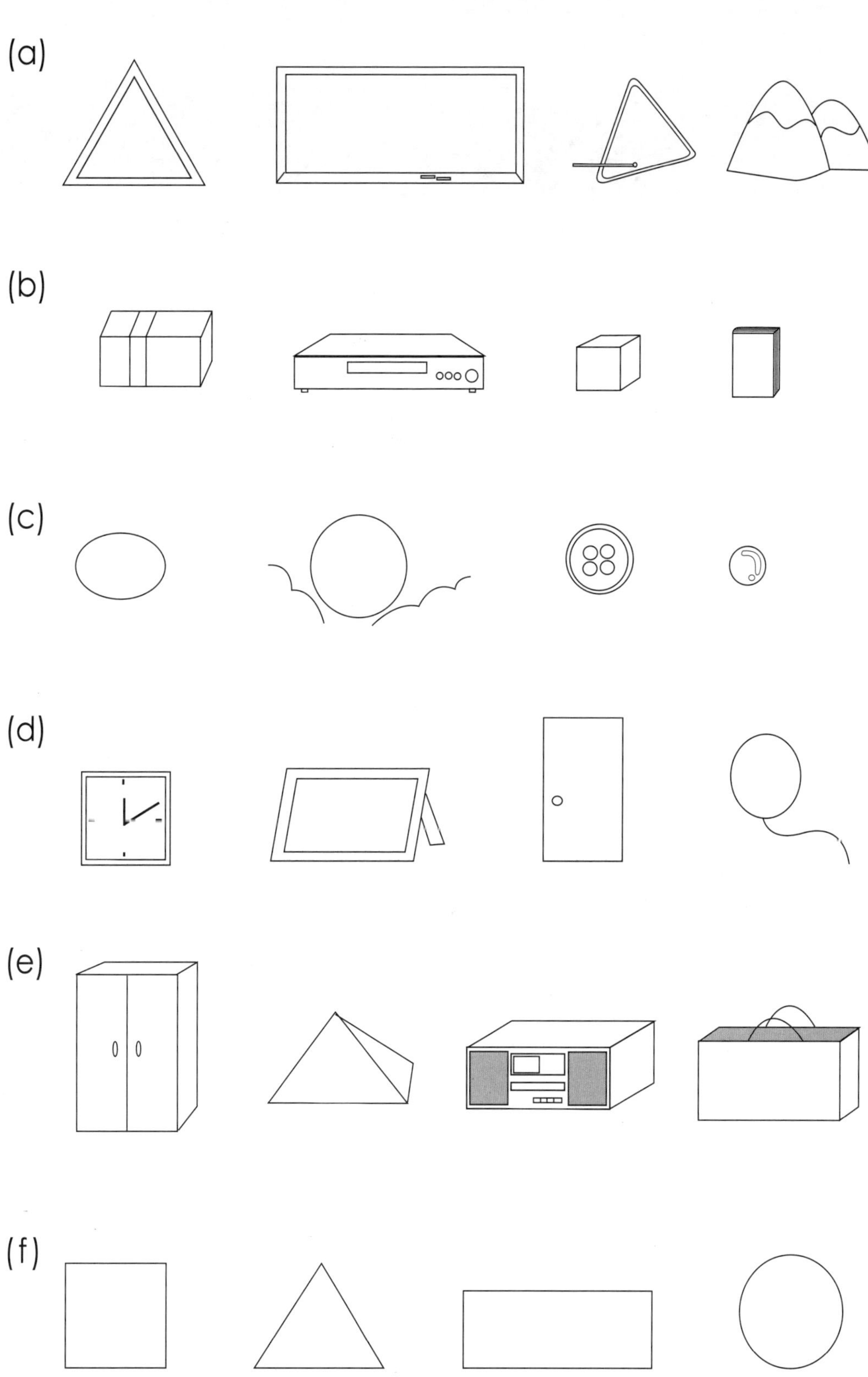

4. Color the two figures that will form a square.

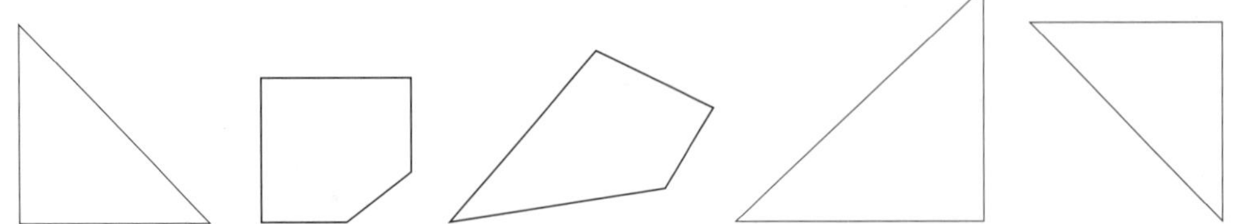

5. Color the two figures that will form a rectangle.

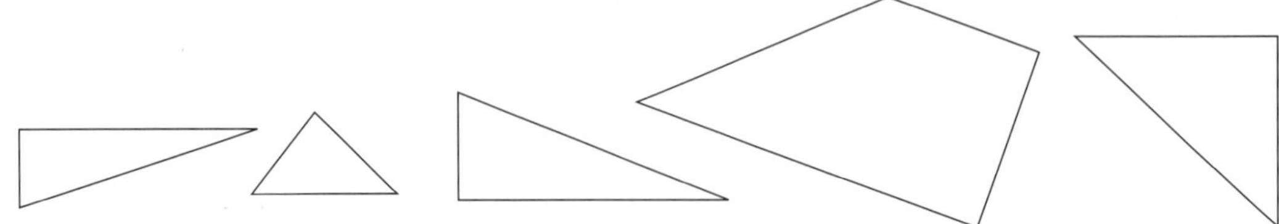

6. Color the two figures that will form a circle.

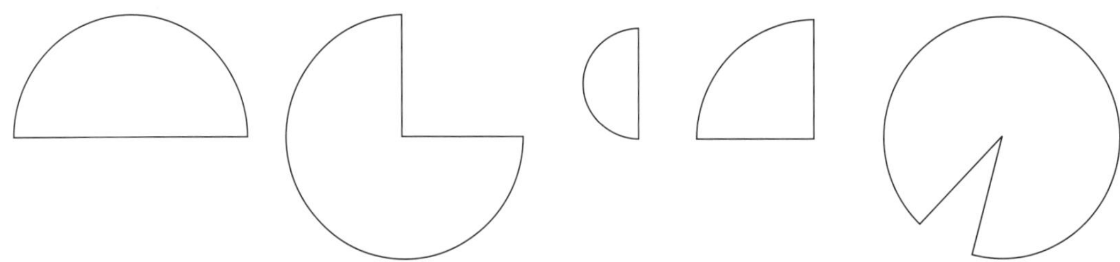

7. Count the number of triangles and squares in each figure.

(a)

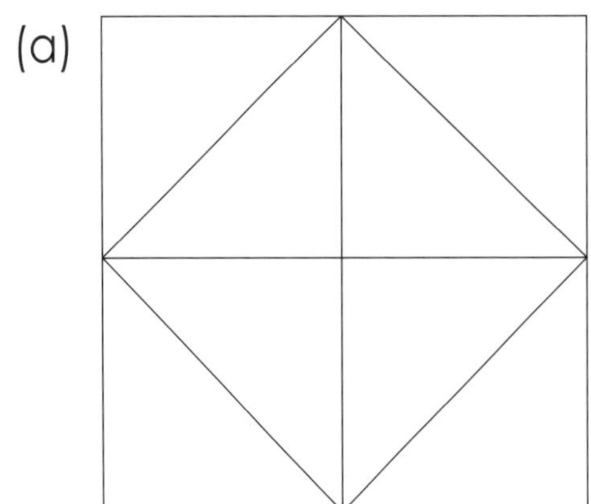

There are ________ triangles.

There are ________ squares.

There are more ______________ than ______________.

How many more? ________ more

(b)

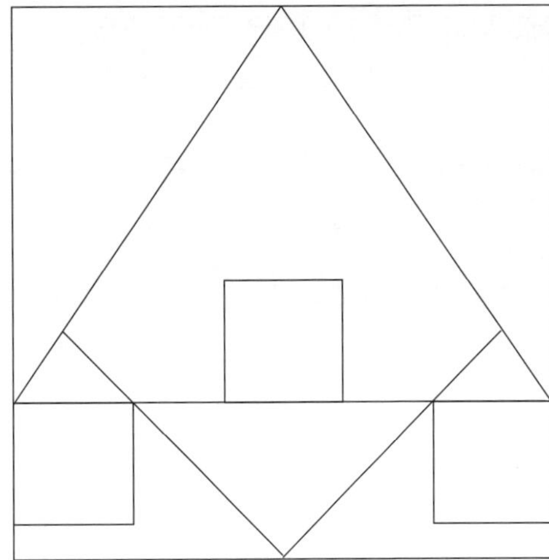

There are ________ triangles.

There are ________ squares.

There are ________ triangles and squares altogether.

There are ________ more ____________ than ____________.

8. (a) Color the smallest triangle in the picture.

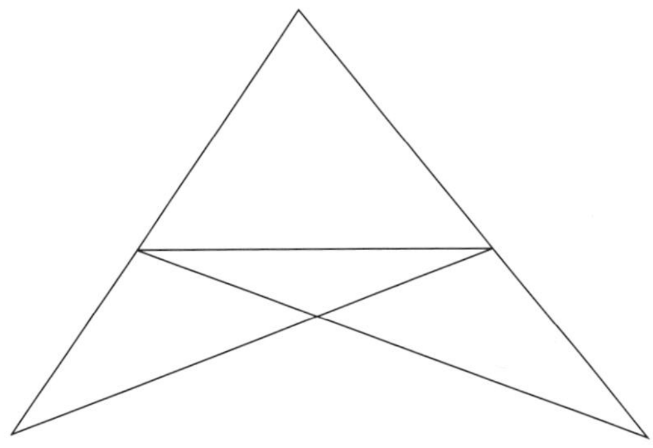

(b) How many triangles are there in the picture?

There are ________ triangles.

9. (a) Color the biggest circle in the picture.

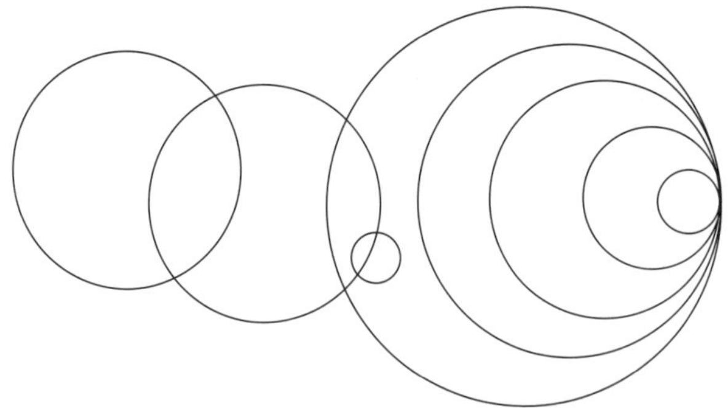

(b) How many circles are there in the picture?

There are ________ circles.

10. (a) Color the smallest rectangle in the picture.

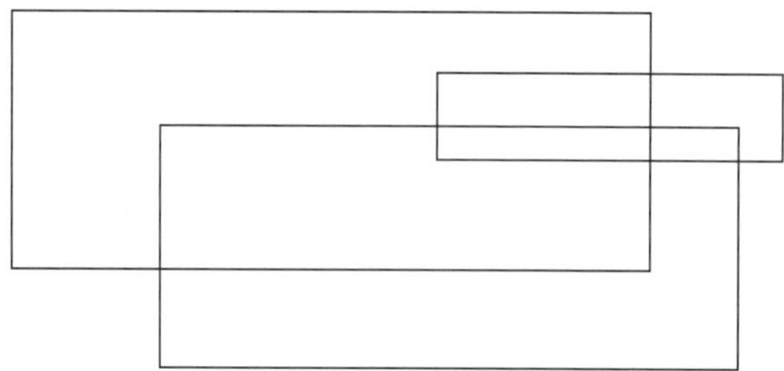

(b) How many rectangles are there in the picture?

There are ________ rectangles.

11. Draw the figure that comes next.

(a) 

____

(b) 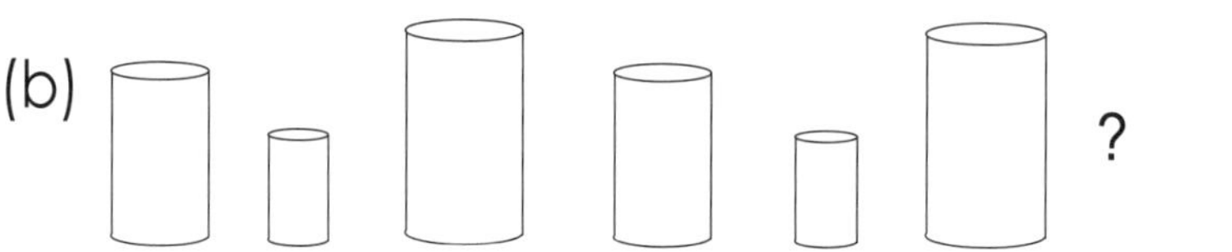

?

____

(c)

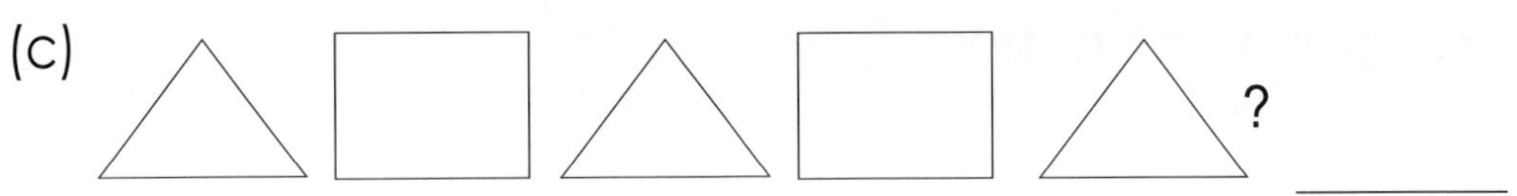

(d)

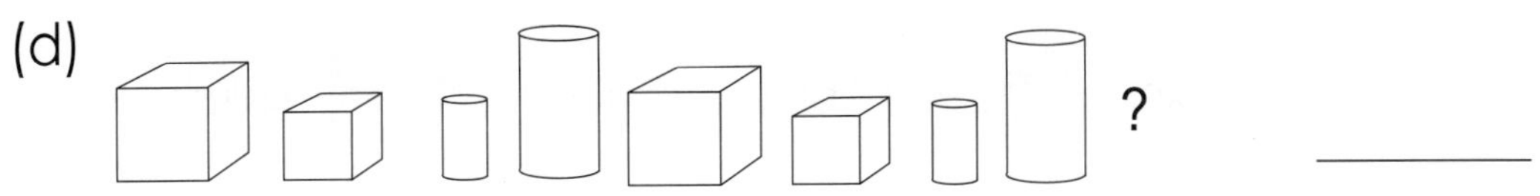

(e)

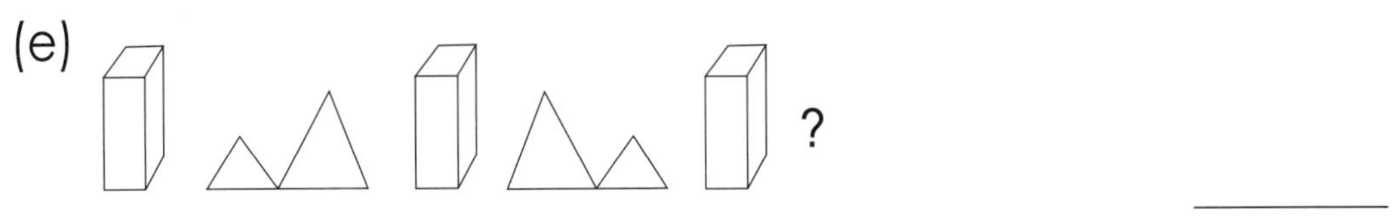

(f)

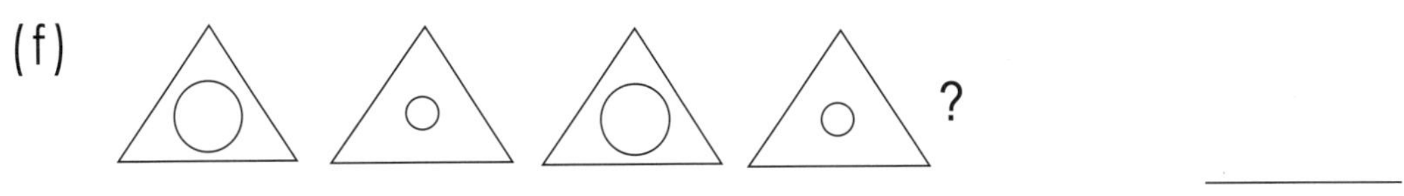

(g)

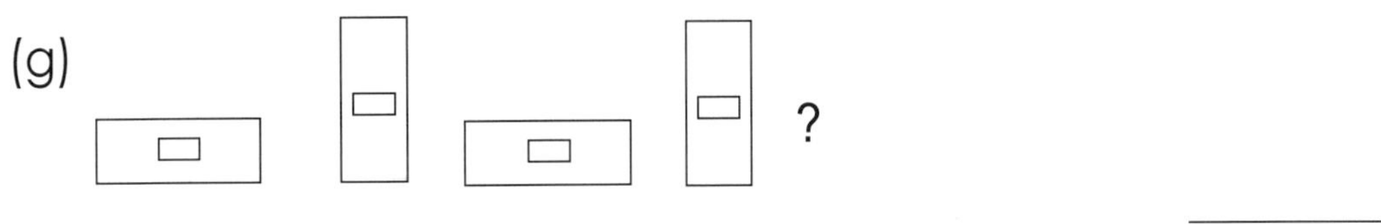

12. Look at the pattern.

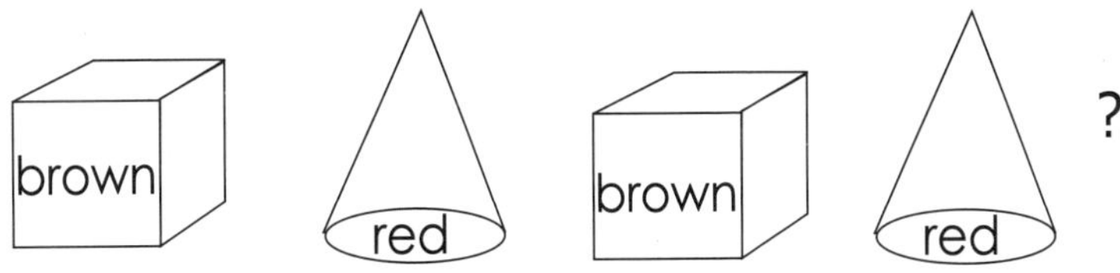

(a) Draw the next figure. ______________

(b) What is its color? ______________

13. Look at the pattern.

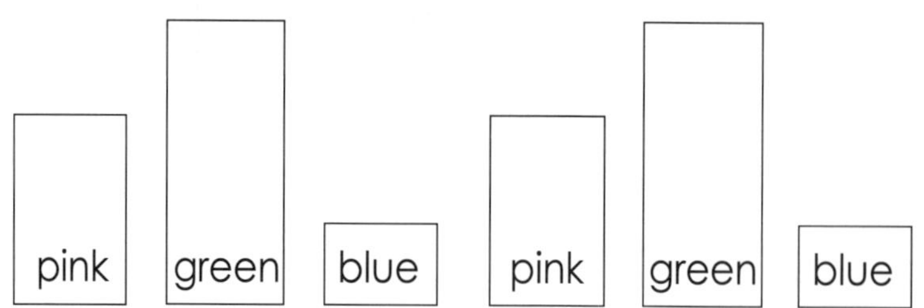

(a) Draw the next figure. ________________

(b) What is its color? ________________

14. Look at the pattern.

(a) Draw the next figure. ________________

(b) What is its color? ____________

15. Look at the pattern.

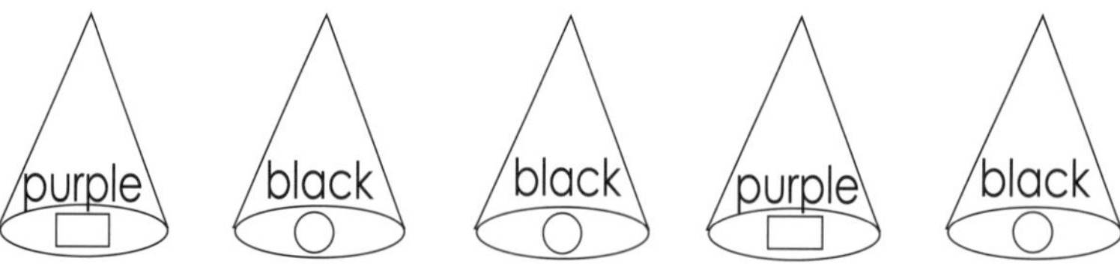

(a) Draw the next figure. ____________

(b) What is its color? ____________

Take the Challenge!

1. Draw the figure that comes next.

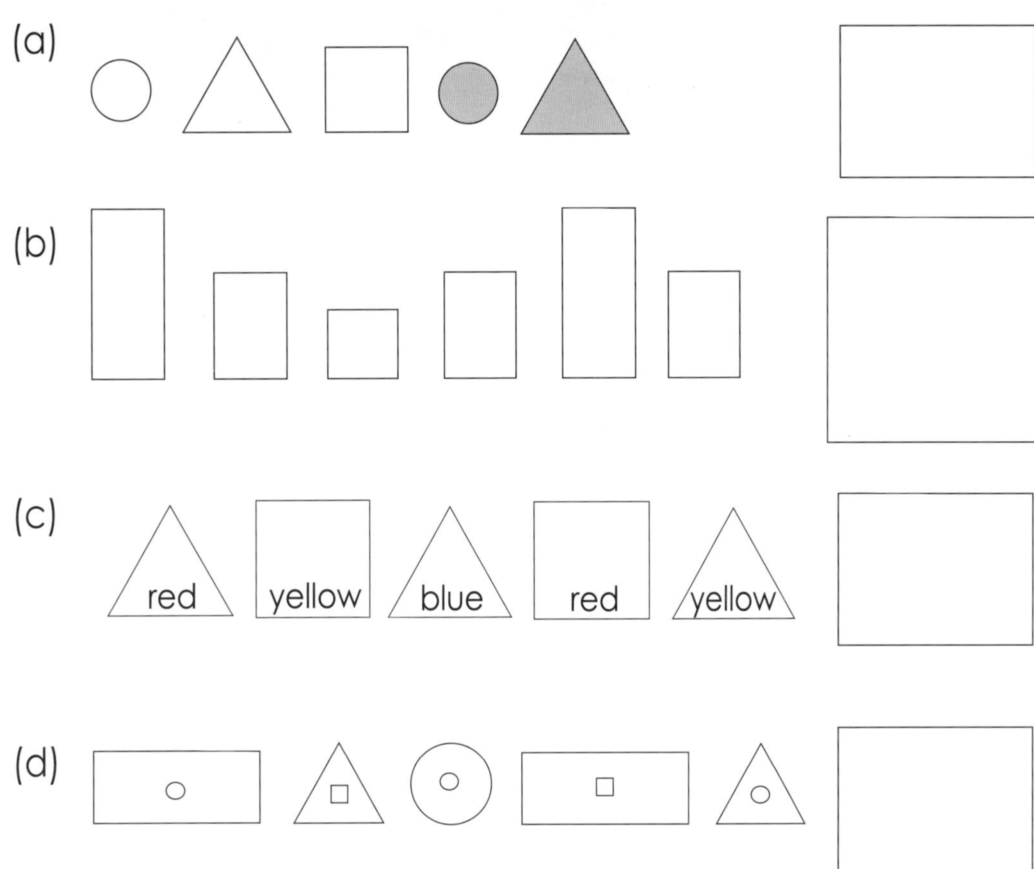

2. Look at the pattern.

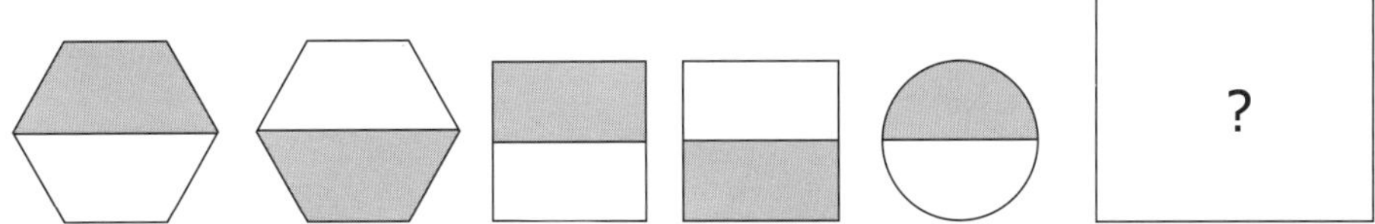

Circle the correct figure that comes next.

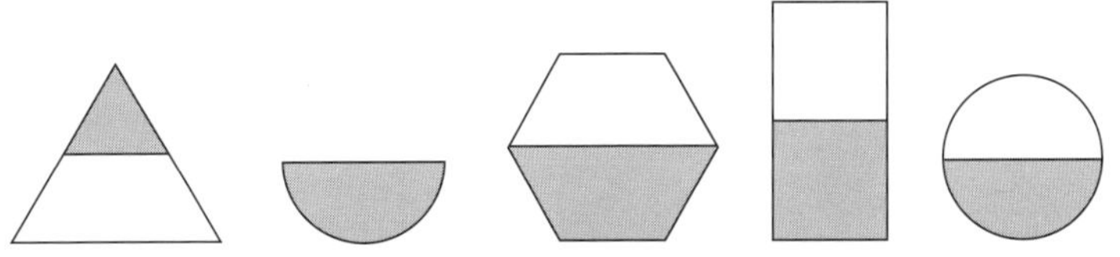

3. Look at the pattern.

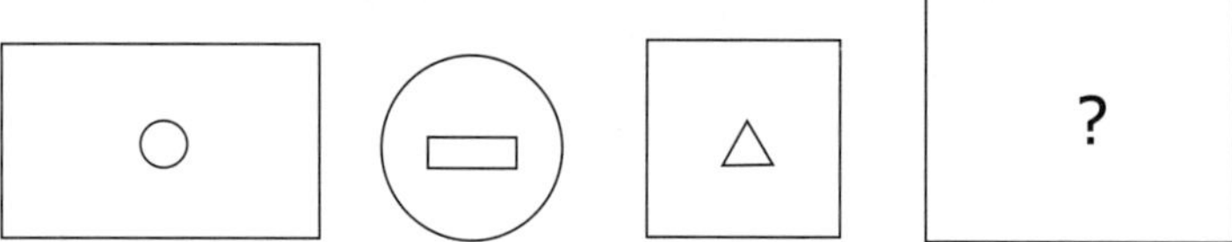

Circle the correct figure that comes next.

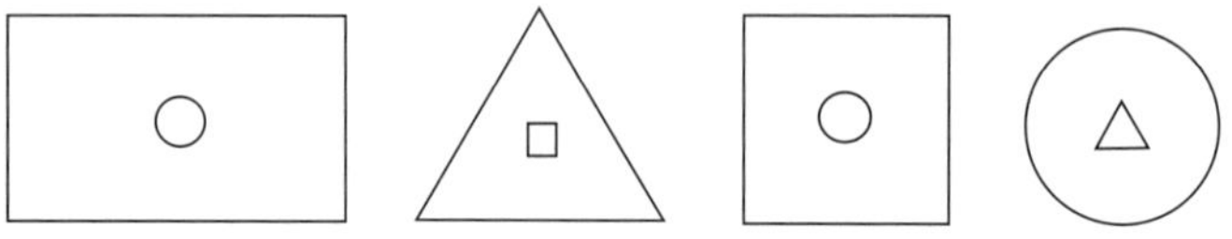

Topic 9: Length

1. Fill in the blanks.

(a)

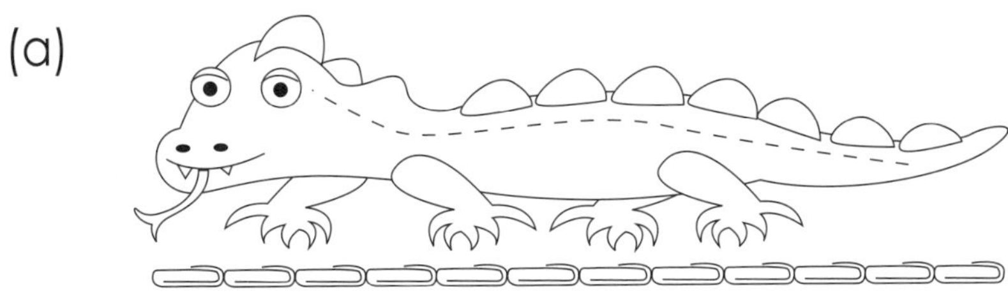

The iguana is about ________ paper clips long.

(b)

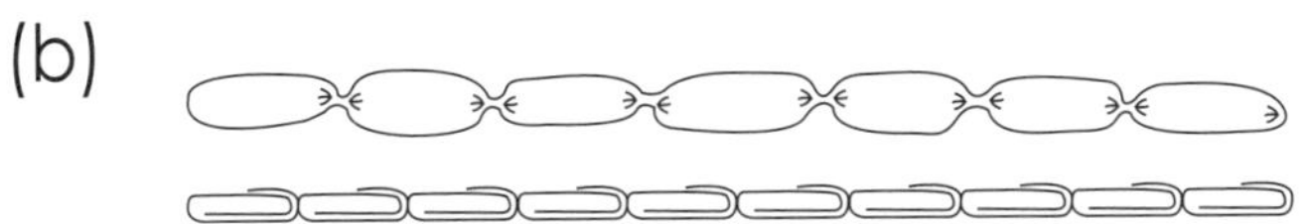

The string of sausages is about ________ paper clips long.

(c)

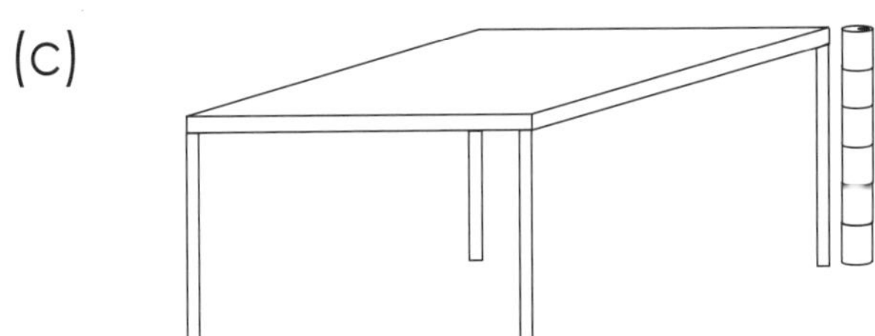

The dining table is about ________ cans tall.

(d)

Timothy is as tall as ________ bricks.

(e)

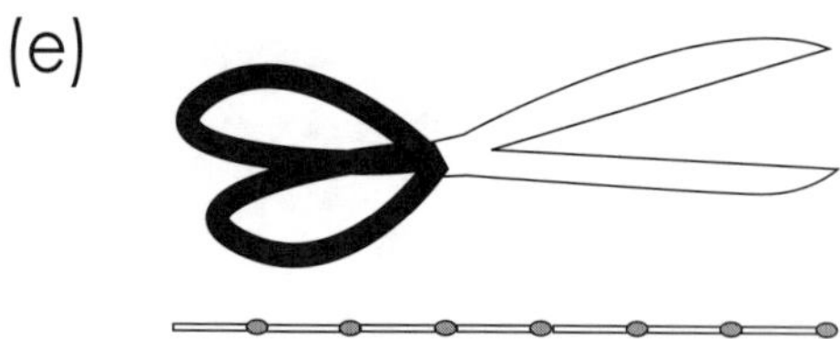

The pair of scissors is as long as ________ matchsticks.

2. Draw a shorter pencil.

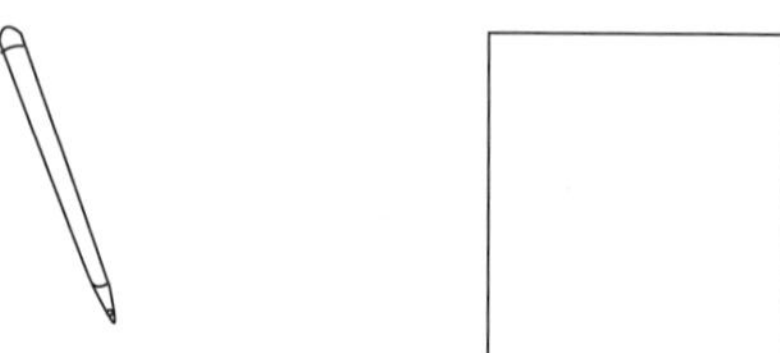

3. Draw a longer pair of pants.

4. Draw a taller mug.

5. Draw a higher hill.

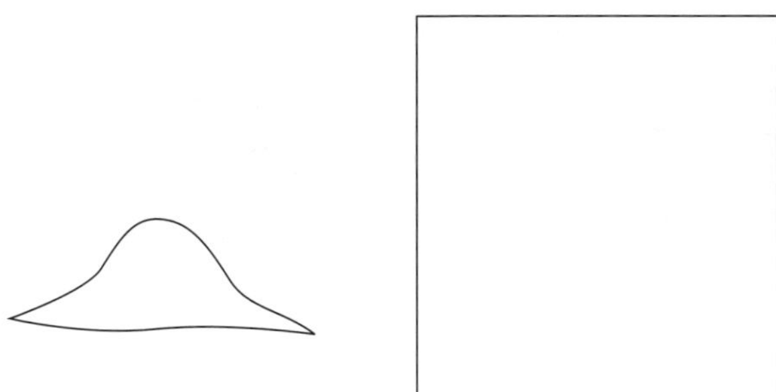

6. Draw a shorter stool.

7. Color the shortest girl.

8. Color the longest worm.

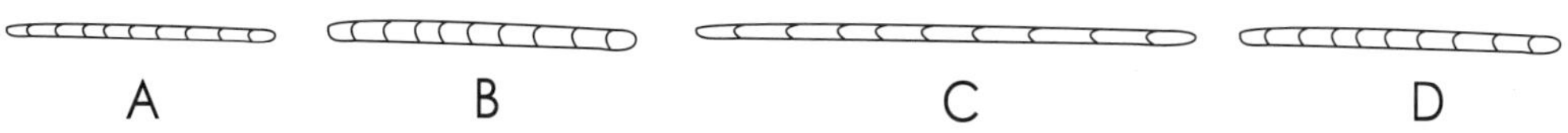

9. Color the tallest object.

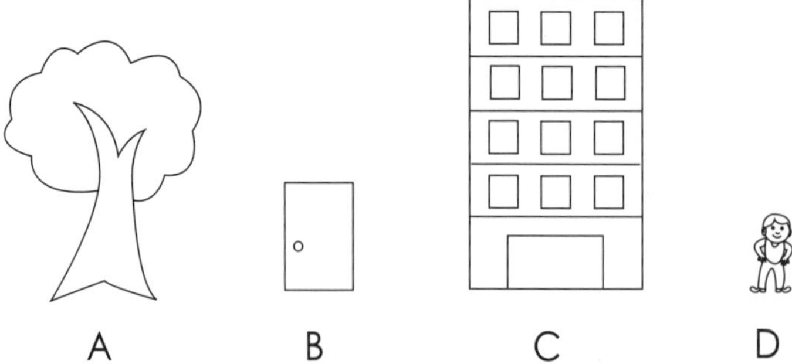

10. Color the highest ball.

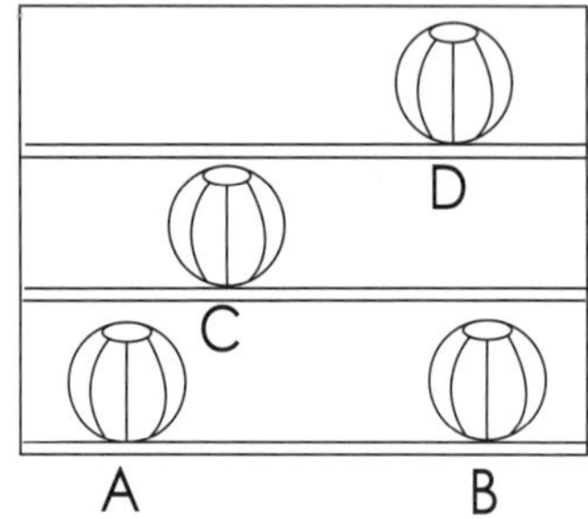

11. Color the shortest leaf.

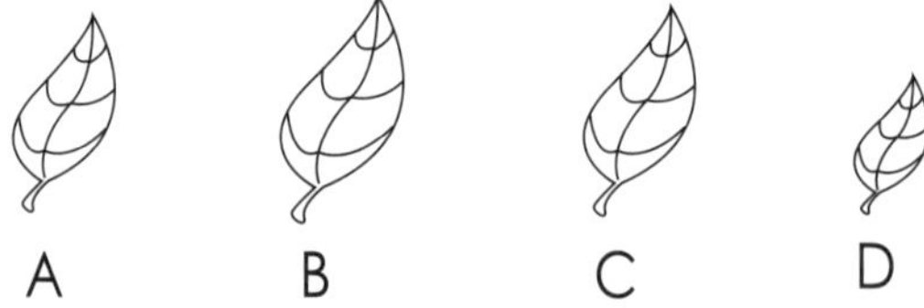

12. Circle the longest word.

love family children parents

13. Circle the shortest letter.

14. Cross out (×) the tallest hat.

15. Circle the longest string.

16. Cross out (×) the highest picture frame on the wall.

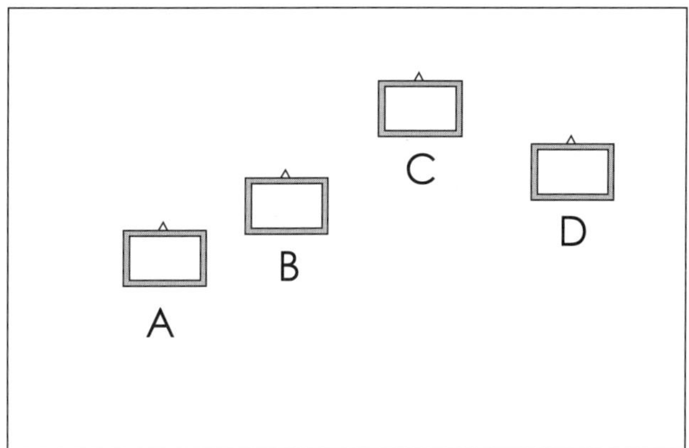

17. Fill in the blanks.

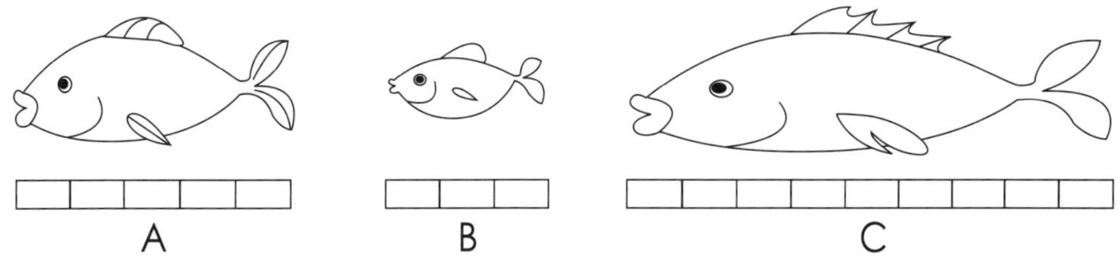

(a) There are ________ types of fish.

(b) Fish A is about ________ ☐ long.

(c) Fish B is about ________ long.

(d) Fish C is about ________ long.

(e) Fish B is ____________________ than Fish A.

(f) Fish C is ____________________ than Fish B.

(g) Fish A is ____________________ than Fish C.

(h) Fish ________ is the shortest.

(i) Fish ________ is the longest.

18. Fill in the blanks.

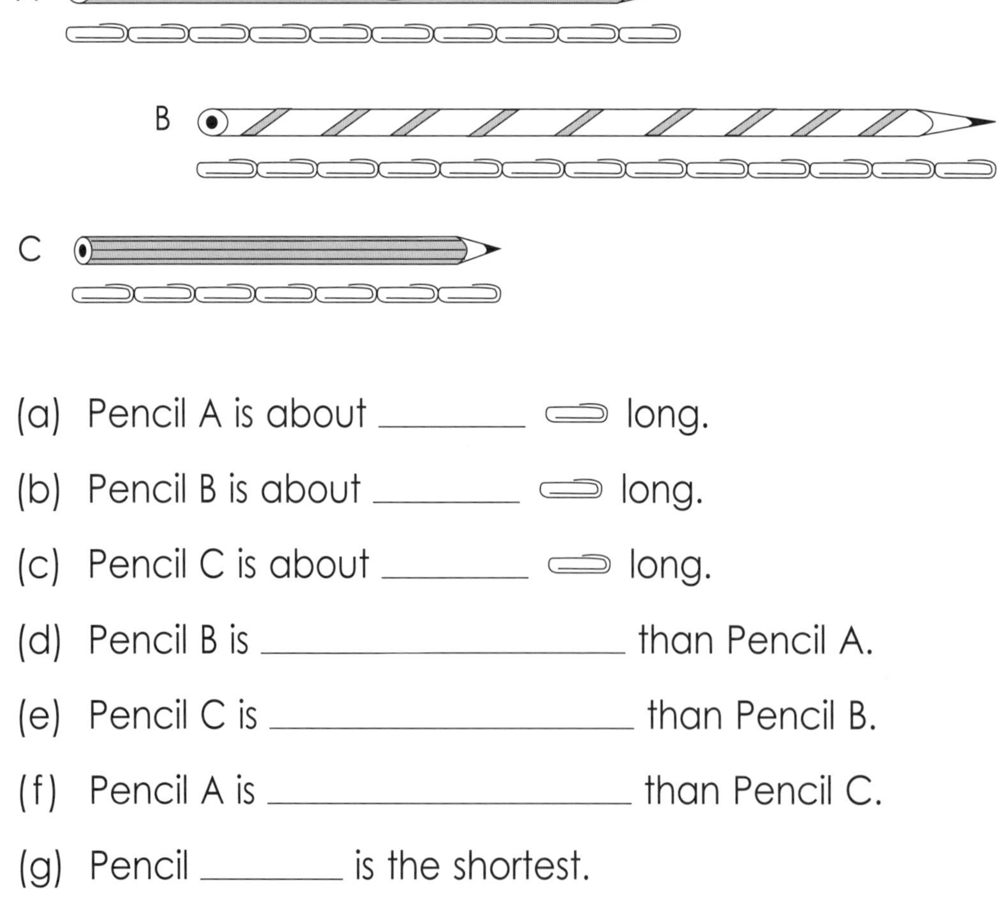

(a) Pencil A is about ________ long.

(b) Pencil B is about ________ long.

(c) Pencil C is about ________ long.

(d) Pencil B is ____________________ than Pencil A.

(e) Pencil C is ____________________ than Pencil B.

(f) Pencil A is ____________________ than Pencil C.

(g) Pencil ________ is the shortest.

(h) Pencil ________ is the longest.

19. Fill in the blanks with any of the words given.

shorter than, longer than, longest, shortest, as long as

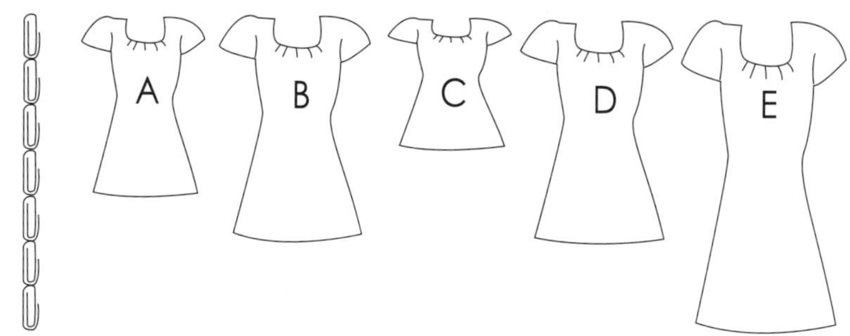

(a) Dress C is the ____________________________.

(b) Dress E is the ____________________________.

(c) Dress A is ____________________________ Dress C.

(d) Dress B is ____________________________ Dress D.

(e) Dress E is ____________________________ Dress D.

(f) Dress A is ____________________________ Dress B.

20. Fill in the blanks.

(a) Sean's height is about ________ [bottle] tall.

(b) Melanie's height is about ________ [bottle] tall.

(c) Kristine is ____________________ than Sam.

(d) Melanie is ____________________ than Sean.

(e) Vance is as tall as ____________________.

(f) Sam is ____________________ than Sean.

WORD PROBLEMS

1. Stick A is about 7 ⊂⊃ long. Stick B is about 8 ⊂⊃ long. What is the total length of the two sticks?

   □ ○ □ = □

   The total length of the two sticks is about ________ ⊂⊃.

2. One ribbon is about 6 ▭ long. Another ribbon is about 5 ▭ long. What is the total length of the two ribbons?

   □ ○ □ = □

   The total length of the two ribbons is about ________ ▭.

3. Umbrella A is about 9 ⊖— long. Umbrella B is about 4 ⊖— long. What is the total length of the two umbrellas?

   □ ○ □ = □

   The two umbrellas are about ________ ⊖— long.

4. Ruler A is about 11☐ long. Ruler B is about 7 ☐ longer than Ruler A. What is the length of Ruler B?

☐ ○ ☐ = ☐

The length of Ruler B is about ________ ☐.

5. A rail car is about 5 🚗 long. What is the length of 2 rail cars?

☐ ○ ☐ = ☐

The length of 2 rail cars is about ________ 🚗.

6. Bob is about 7 ▯ tall. He is about 9 ▯ shorter than Sam. How tall is Sam?

☐ ○ ☐ = ☐

Sam is about ________ ▯ tall.

7. One chair is about 5 ▯ tall. How tall are three chairs?

☐ ○ ☐ ○ ☐ = ☐

Three chairs are about ________ ▯ tall.

8. Dress A is about 4 long. Dress B is about 5 long. Dress C is about 7 long. What is the total length of the 3 dresses?

☐ ○ ☐ ○ ☐ = ☐

The total length of the 3 dresses is about ________ .

Take the Challenge!

1. Draw the figure that comes next in each box.

(a)

(b)

(c)

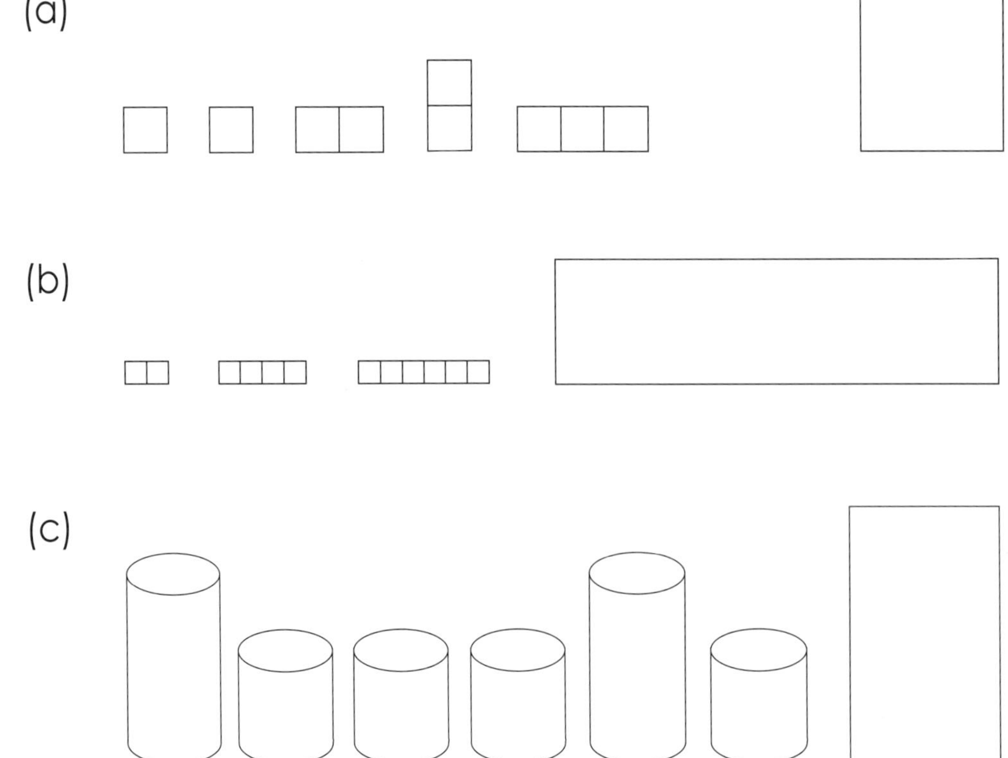

(d)

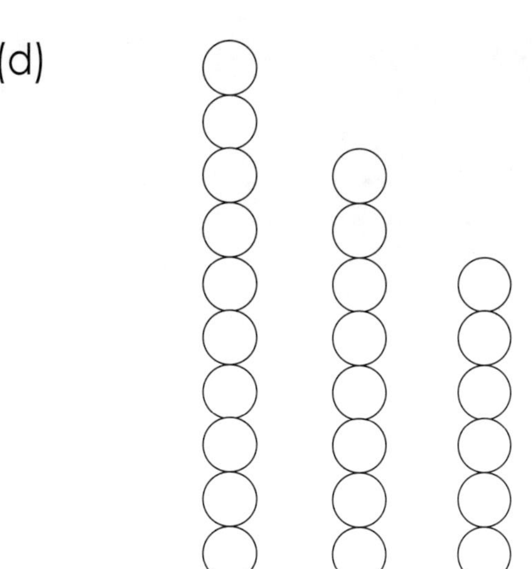

(e)

2. This is a toy train. Fill in the blanks.

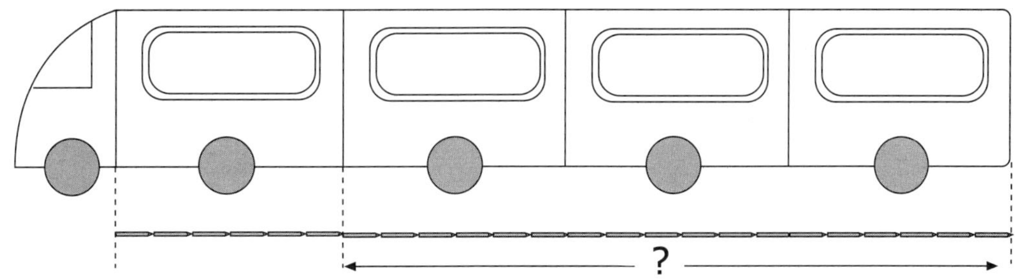

(a) The train has ________ rail cars.

(b) Each rail car is about ________ ▭ long.

(c) The length from the beginning of the 2nd car to the end of the train is about ________ ▭ long.

Topic 10: Weight

1. Fill in the blanks.

(a)

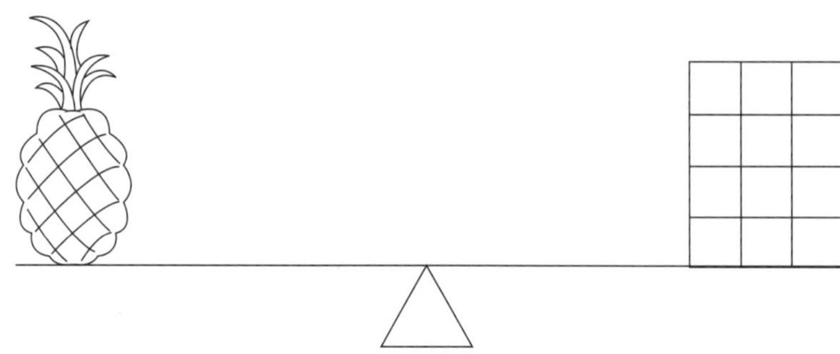

The weight of the pineapple is about ________ □.

(b)

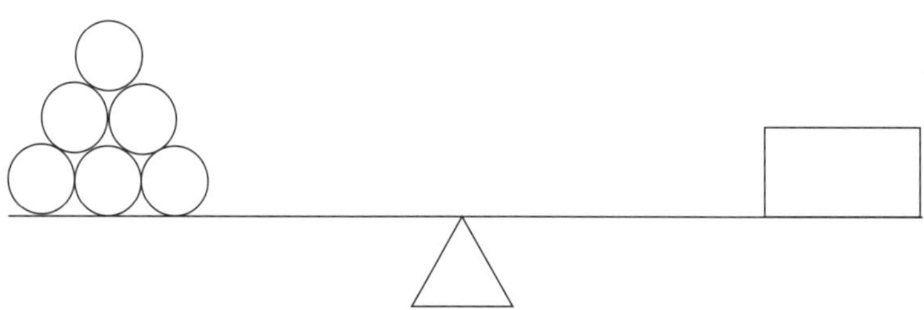

The box weighs about ________ ○.

(c)

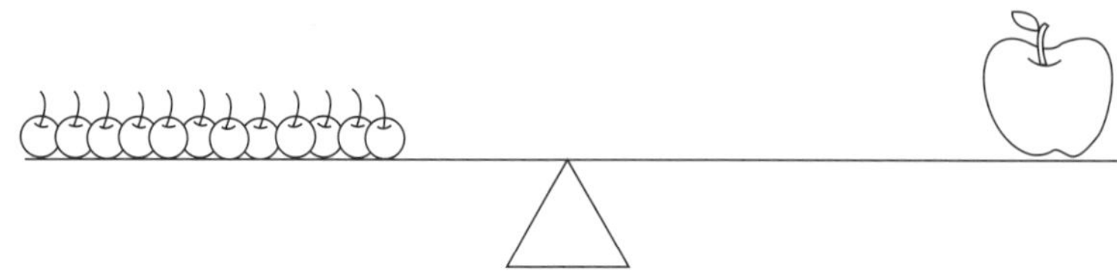

The weight of ________ apple(s) is equal to the weight of ________ cherries.

(d)

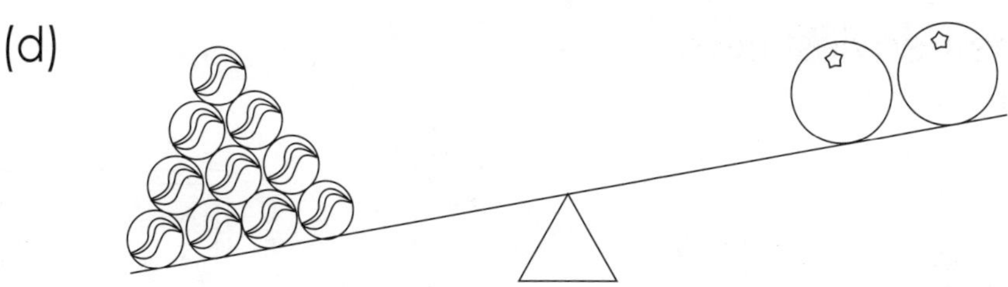

The weight of ________ oranges is less than the weight of ________ marbles.

(e)

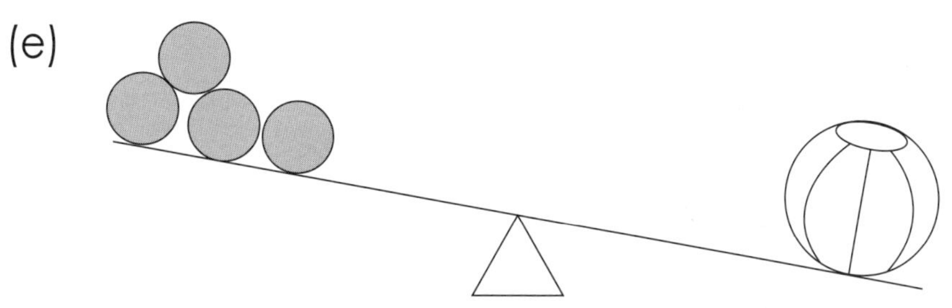

The weight of a ball is ________________ than the weight of 4 balls.

2. Color the heavier item.

3. Color the lighter item.

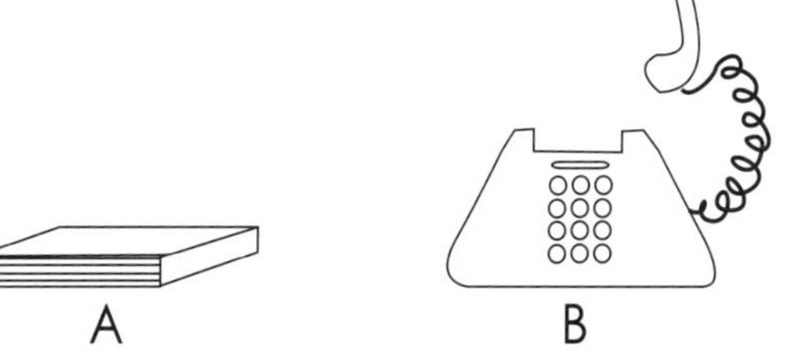

4. Color the heaviest item.

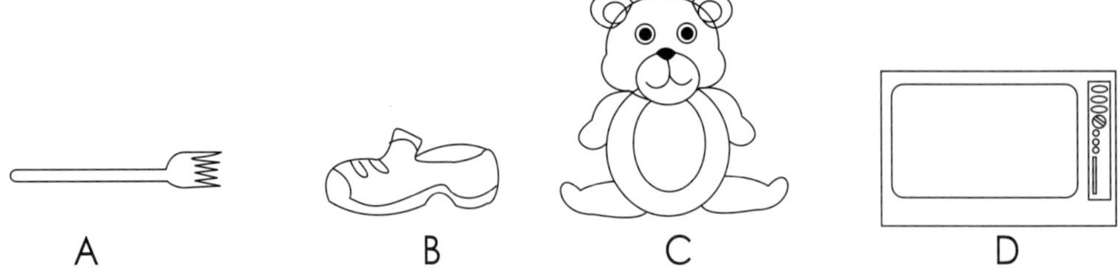

5. Color the lightest item.

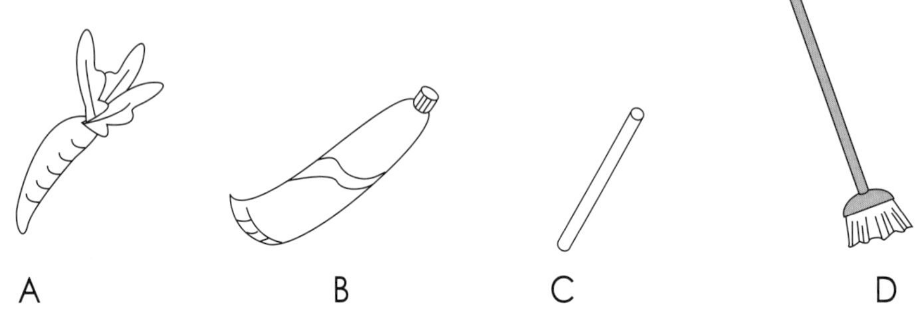

6. Color the heavier animal.

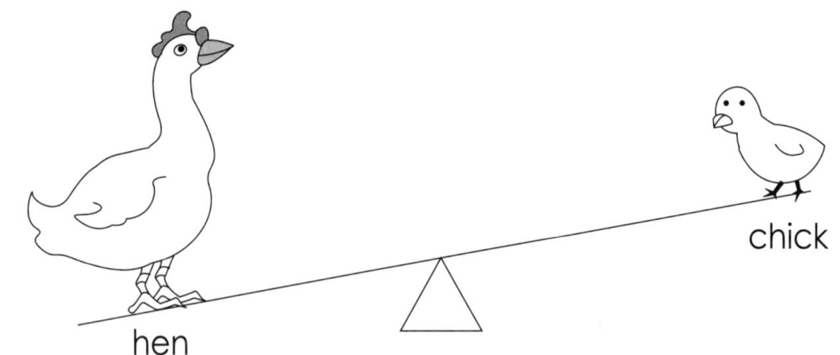

7. Arrange the items from the lightest to the heaviest.

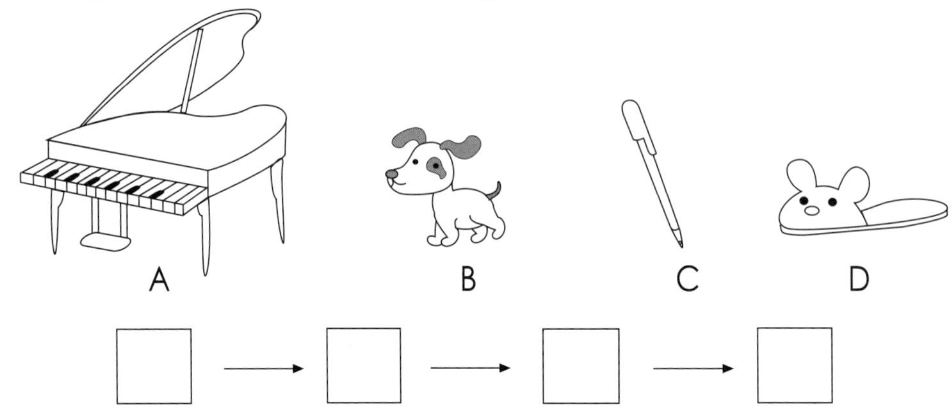

8. Arrange the items from the heaviest to the lightest.

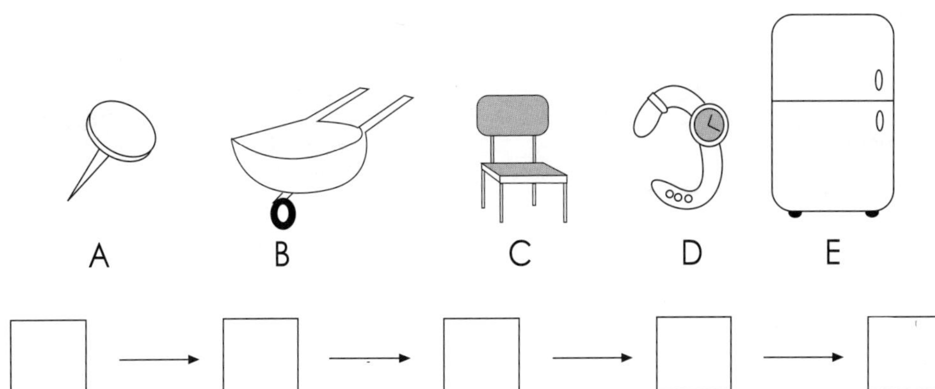

9. Color the lightest item and cross out (✖) the heaviest item.

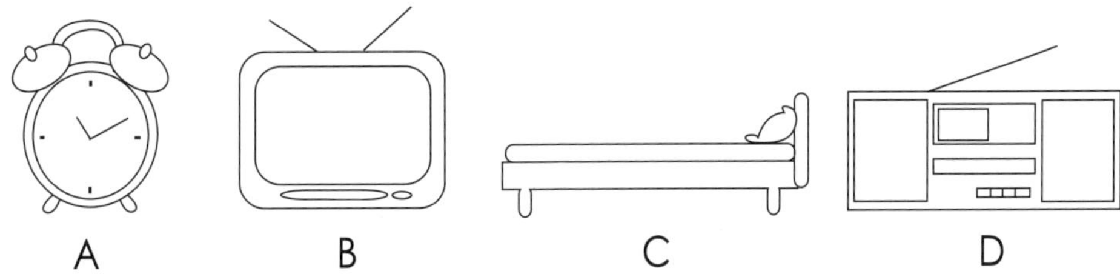

10. Fill in the blanks.

(a) The cat weighs about ________ ▪.

(b) The rat weighs about ________ ▪.

(c) The ________ is heavier.

(d) The ________ is lighter.

(e) Fill in the correct boxes with the words "cat" and "rat".

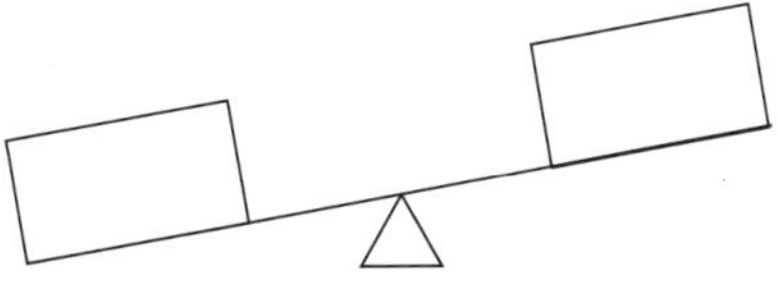

11. Fill in the blanks.

(a) Baby A weighs about ________ ○.

(b) Baby B weighs about ________ ○.

(c) Baby ________ is heavier.

(d) Baby ________ is lighter.

(e) Fill in the correct boxes with the words "Baby A" and "Baby B".

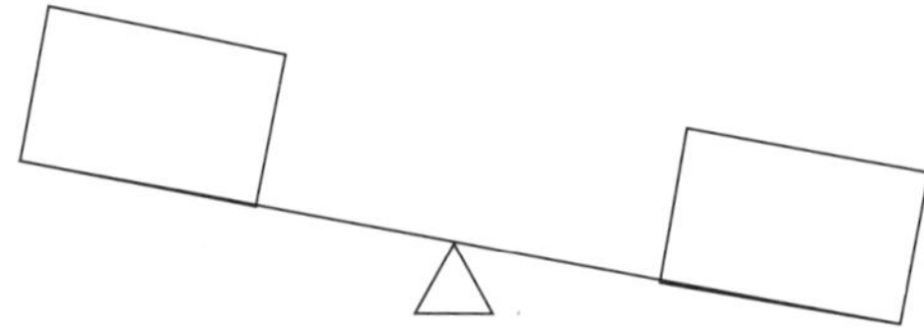

12. Fill in the blanks. Use ▩ as 1 unit.

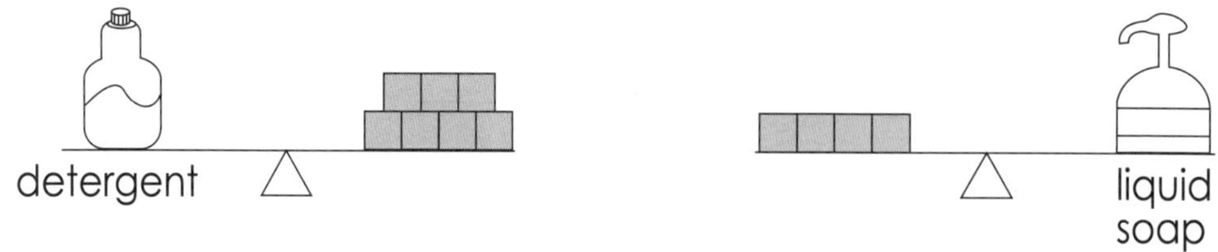

(a) The bottle of detergent weighs about ________ units.

(b) The bottle of liquid soap weighs about ________ units.

(c) The bottle of ____________________ is heavier.

(d) The bottle of ____________________ is lighter.

13. Fill in the blanks. Use ⊚ as 1 unit.

(a) The weight of the can of milk is about ________ units.

(b) The clock weighs about ________ units.

(c) The ______________________________ is heavier.

(d) The ______________________________ is lighter.

14. Fill in the blanks. Use ▭ as 1 unit.

(a) The weight of the jar of candy is about ________ units.

(b) The jar of jam weighs about ________ units.

(c) The jar of _____________ is heavier.

(d) The jar of _____________ is lighter.

WORD PROBLEMS

1. A bowl weighs about 5▪. The weight of a plate is about 3▪ more than the weight of the bowl. What is the weight of the plate?

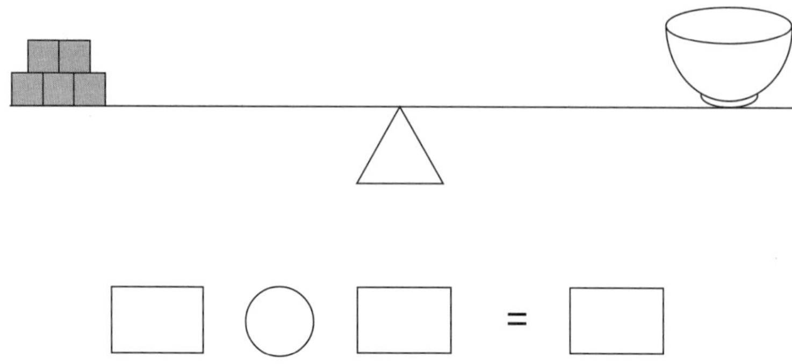

☐ ○ ☐ = ☐

The plate weighs about ________ ▪.

2. A papaya weighs about 8 marbles less than a watermelon. The watermelon weighs about 15 marbles. What is the weight of the papaya?

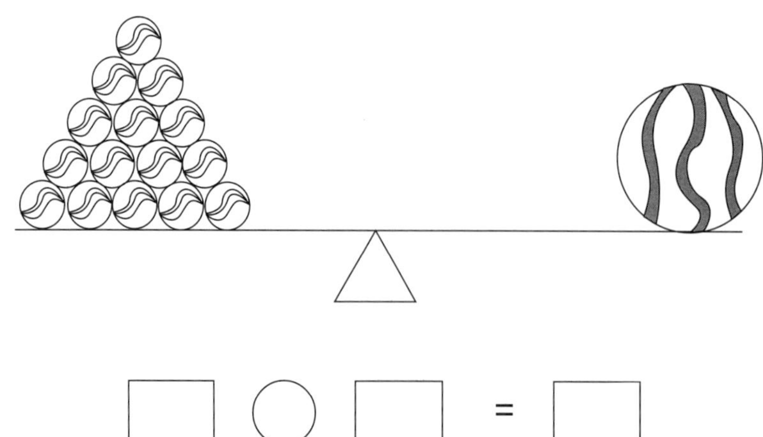

☐ ○ ☐ = ☐

The weight of the papaya is about ________ marbles.

3. A knife weighs about 9● more than a spoon. What is the weight of the knife if the spoon weighs about 2●?

☐ ◯ ☐ = ☐

The knife weighs about ________ ●.

4. A banana and an apple together weigh about 12 ■. The banana weighs about 6 ■. What does the apple weigh?

☐ ◯ ☐ = ☐

The apple weighs about ________ ■.

5. A book weighs about 7 ▢. Another book weighs about 4 ▢. What is the total weight of the two books?

☐ ◯ ☐ = ☐

The total weight of the two books is about ________ ▢.

6. A watch weighs about 4◯. A wallet weighs about 9◯. What is the total weight of the two objects?

□ ◯ □ = □

The total weight of the two objects is about __________ ◯.

7. The weight of Chair A is about 8▭. The weight of Chair B is about 7▭. What is the total weight of the two chairs?

□ ◯ □ = □

The total weight of the two chairs is about __________ ▭.

8. Pen A weighs about 5⬭. The weight of Pen B is about 7⬭ more than the weight of Pen A. How much does Pen B weigh?

□ ◯ □ = □

Pen B weighs about __________ ⬭.

9. Each ◇ stands for 1 unit.

Casey weighs about 11◇. Casey is about 7◇ lighter than Kim. How much does Kim weigh?

□ ◯ □ = □

Kim weighs about __________ units.

10. Each □ stands for 1 unit.
The weight of a papaya is about 8□. A watermelon is about 5□ heavier than a papaya. How much does a watermelon weigh?

□ ○ □ = □

A watermelon weighs about ________ units.

11. Each ▢ stands for 1 unit.
Fish A weighs about 6▢. Fish A weighs about 8▢ less than Fish B. What is the weight of Fish B?

□ ○ □ = □

The weight of Fish B is about ________ units.

12. Each ○ stands for 1 unit.
A bag of candy weighs about 3○. A bag of marbles weighs about 9○ more than the bag of candy. What is the total weight of the two bags?

□ ○ □ ○ □ = □

The total weight of the two bags is about ________ units.

Take the Challenge!

1. Fill in the blanks with any of the given words or letters of the alphabet.

heavier than, lighter than, as heavy as, heaviest, lightest, A, B, C, D, E

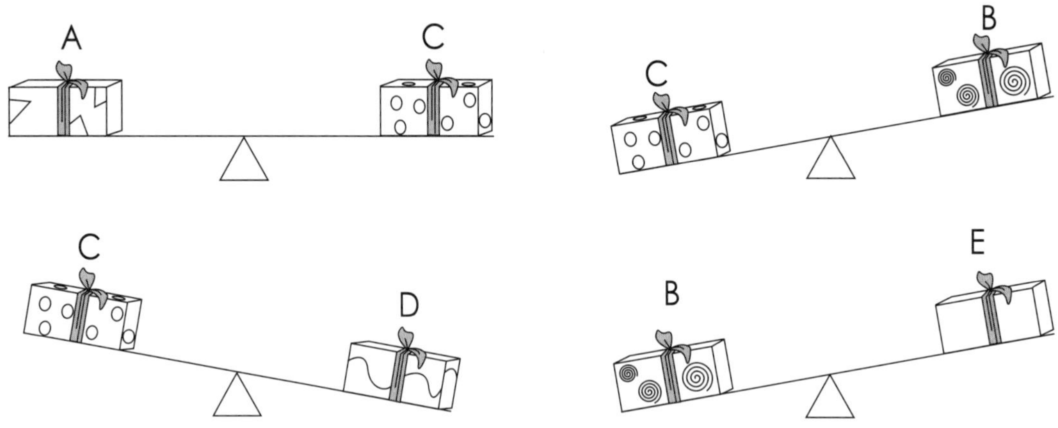

(a) Present C is ____________________ Present A.

(b) Present B is ____________________ Present C.

(c) Present A is ____________________ Present B.

(d) Present D is ____________________ Present C.

(e) Present B is ____________________ Present D.

(f) Present E is ____________________ Present B.

(g) Present C is ____________________ Present E.

(h) Present E is ____________________ Present D.

(i) Present A is ______________________ Present E.

(j) Present ______________________ is the heaviest.

(k) Present ______________________ is the lightest.

(l) Present A and Present C together are ______________________ Present C and Present D together.

2. Fill in the blanks. Each ▭ stands for 1 unit.

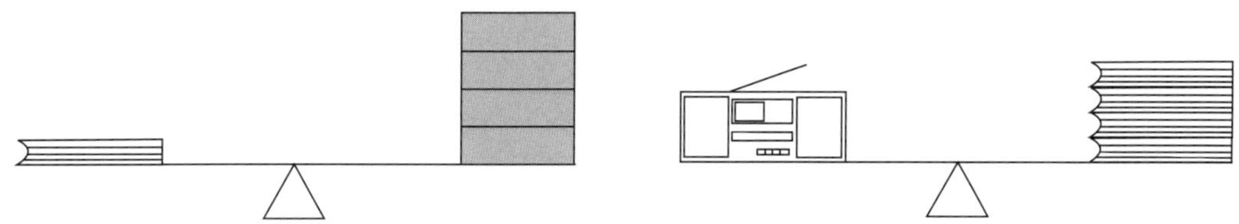

(a) The book weighs about ________ units.

(b) The radio weighs about ________ books.

(c) The radio weighs about ________ units.

Mid-Year Review

PART 1

1. Check (✓) the set with the most number of items.

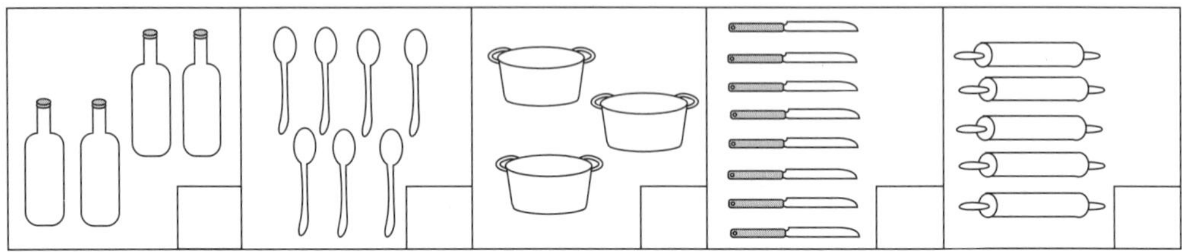

2. Write an addition sentence for this picture.

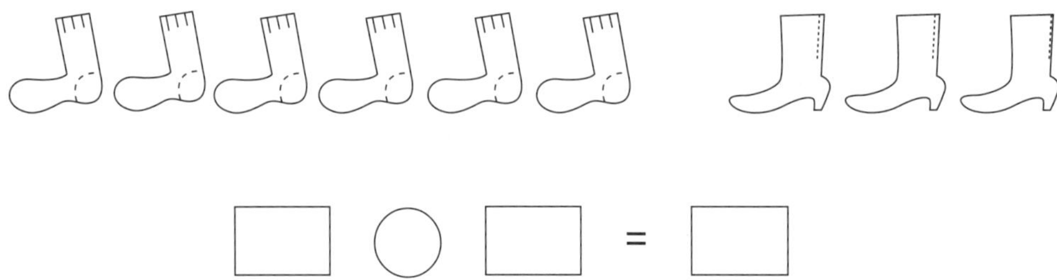

3. How many more dolls are there than toy bears?

There are ________ more dolls than toy bears.

4. Look at the diagram and answer the questions.

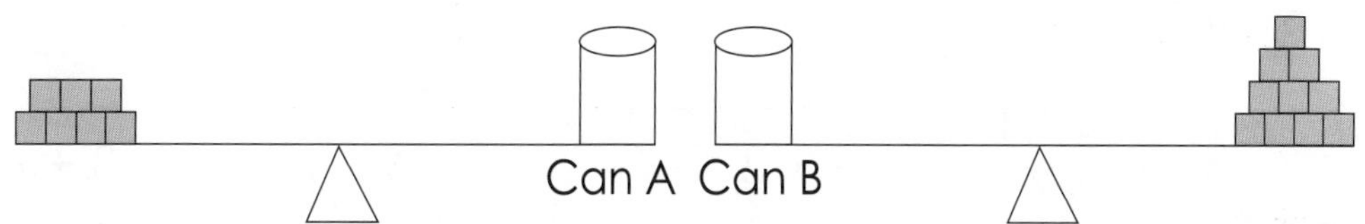

(a) Can A weighs about ________ ■.

(b) Can B weighs about ________ ■.

(c) Can ________ is heavier than Can ________.

5. △ is 2 more than 7. Check (✓) the sets with the same answer as △.

3 + 5	7 – 2	1 less than 10.	10 – 3	4 more than 5.
☐	☐	☐	☐	☐

6. Look at the picture. Complete the number bond.

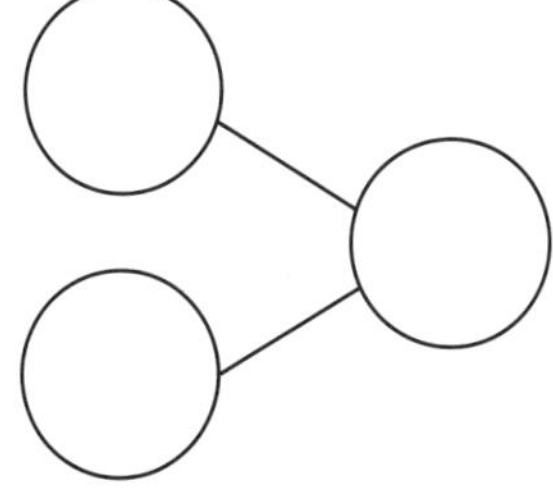

7. The number of matches in each matchbox is shown on top of the box. Color the matchbox that has the least number of matches.

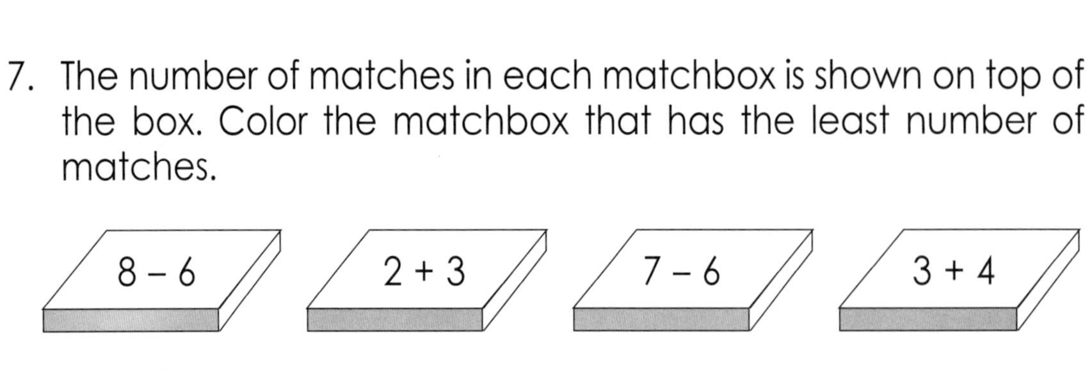

8. Color the pieces that make up the picture on the right.

9. Cross out (×) the flower in the 3rd position.

10. Count and write the number in words.

11. Arrange the numbers, starting from the smallest.

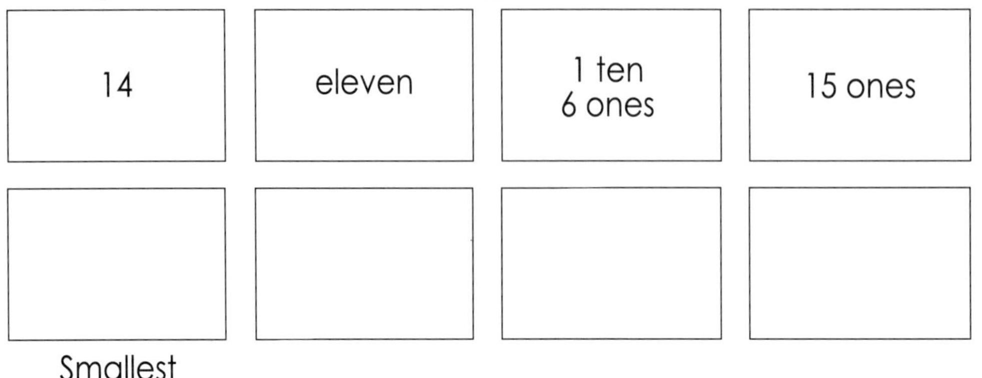

12. Work out each of the following.
Check (✓) the one that gives the largest answer.

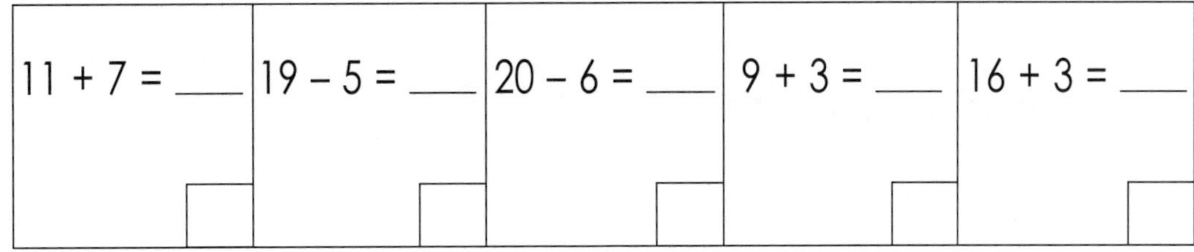

13. Complete the number bond.

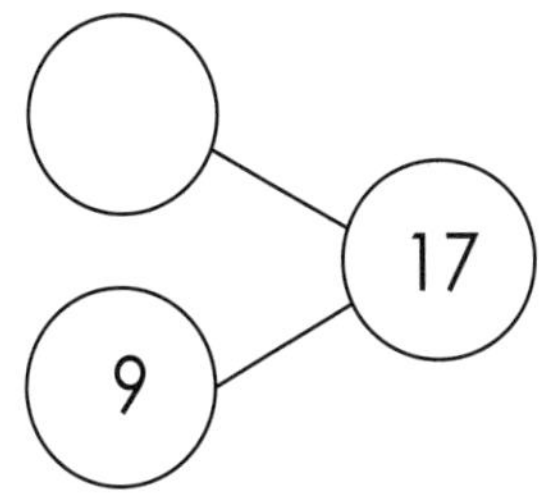

14. 3 less than 14 ones is ________.

15. Work out each of the following.
Check (✓) the one that does not give an answer of 19.

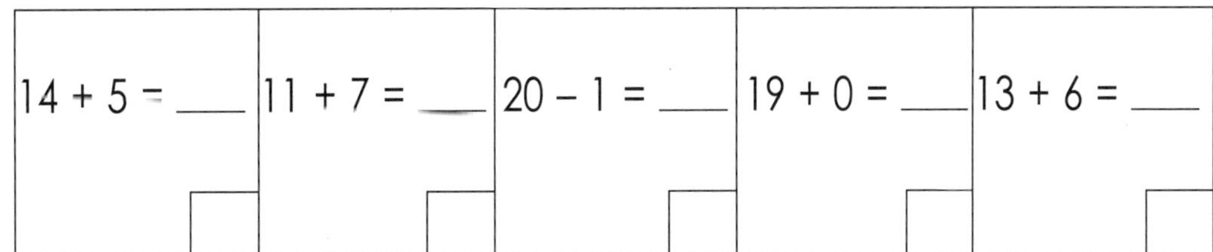

16. How many more circles are there than triangles?

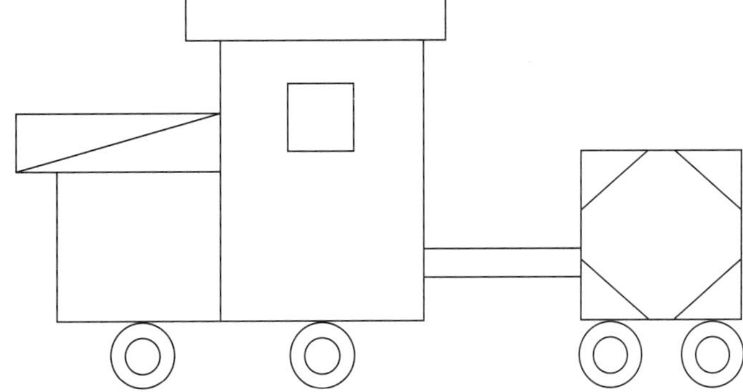

There are ________ more circles than triangles.

17. Fill in the missing number in the box.

☐ + 4 = 17 − 3

18. Draw a shorter ruler.

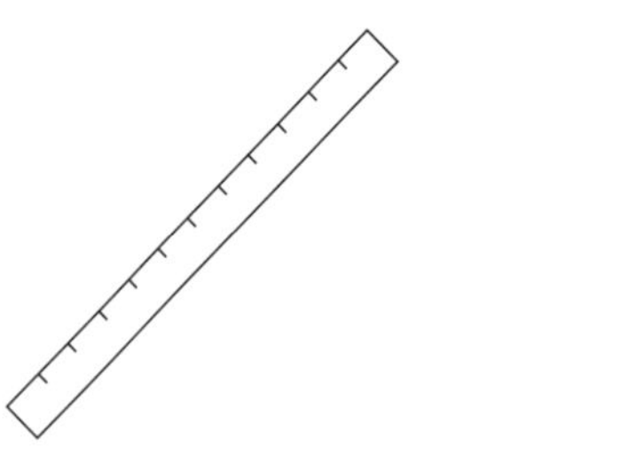

19. Put in "+" or "–" to complete the each number sentence.

(a) 14 ☐ 9 = 5 (b) 9 ☐ 6 = 15

20. ________ ten(s) and ________ ones = 16 ones

21. 13 comes before ________ and after 12.

22. Write the correct number sentence with the given numbers and sign.

12,	–,	5,	17

☐ ○ ☐ = ☐

23. Fill in the missing number.

24. Color two items of the same shape.

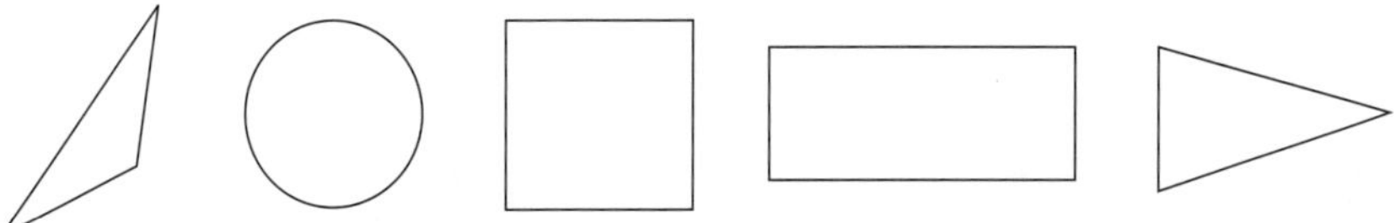

25. Look at the picture. Fill in the missing numbers.

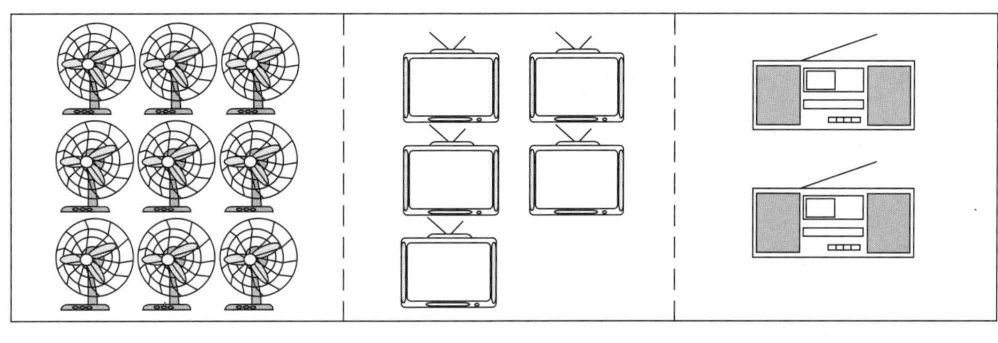

$\square + \square + \square = \square$

26. Fill in the missing number in the box.

$\square - 7 = 5 + 3$

27. Color the two numbers to make 11.

28. Complete the pattern by drawing the next shape in the box on the right.

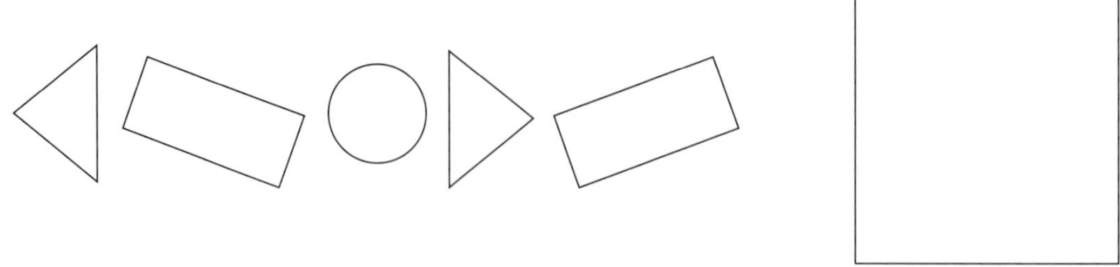

29. Fill in the missing number in the box.

18 – [ ] = 19 – 10

30. Circle the shortest item and cross out (×) the tallest item.

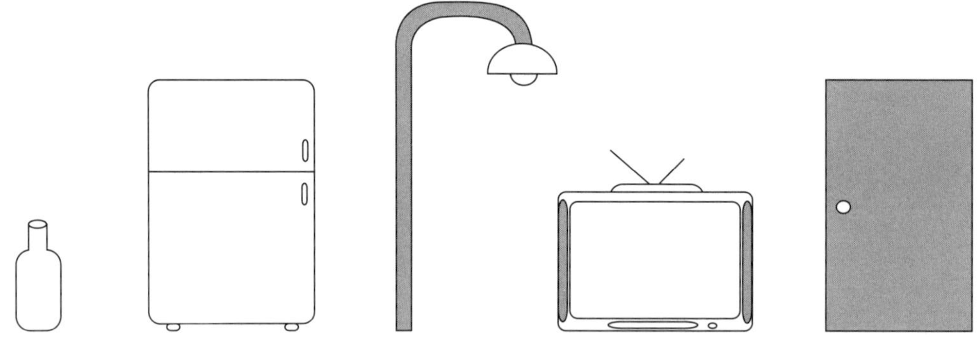

31. Fill in the missing numbers.

32. Write a correct number sentence with the given numbers and signs.

7, =, +, 16, 9

____

33. This is a line at the taxi-stand.

(a) Who is in the 3rd position? ____________

(b) Who is between the 4th and 6th person in line?

____

34. How many triangles are there in this figure? ________

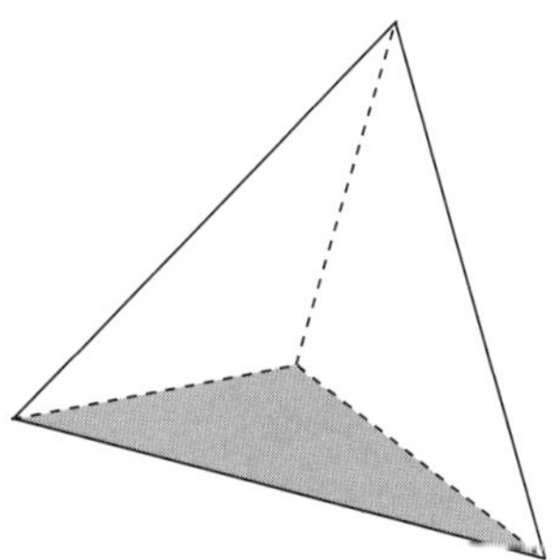

35. Study these diagrams. Fill in the correct answers.

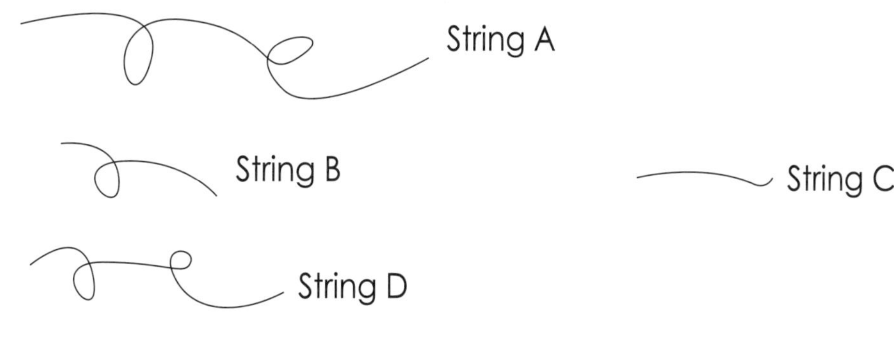

(a) String ________ is longer than String D.

(b) String ________ is the shortest.

(c) String ________ is the longest.

36. Fill in the missing numbers.

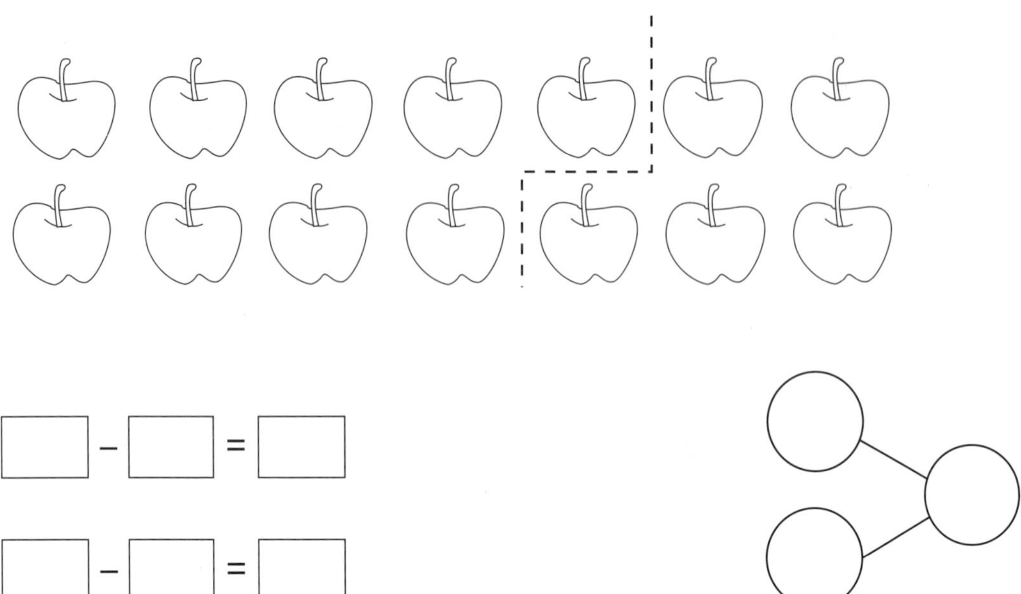

37. ________ tens – 6 = 14 ones

38. Color all the squares in the figure.

39. Color some more to make 18. Complete the number bond.

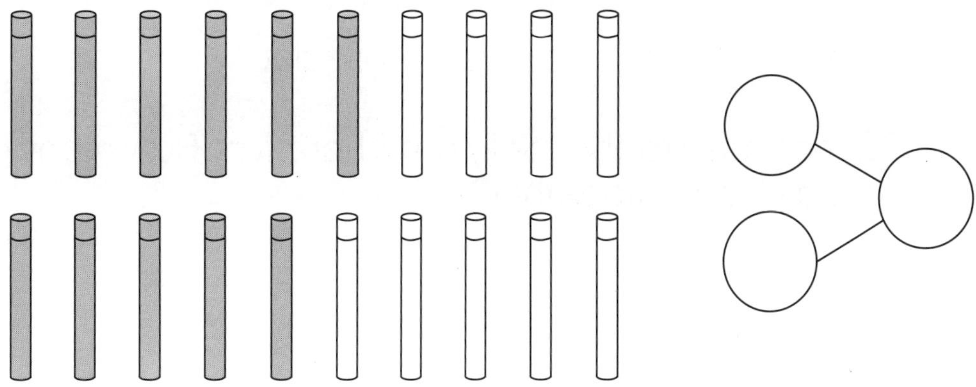

40. Study the picture. Fill in the correct answers.

(a) Sally is as tall as ____________.

(b) Derick is taller than ____________.

(c) ____________ is the tallest.

(d) ____________ is the shortest.

PART 2

Solve these problems. Show your work clearly.

41. Carmen has 4 rabbits. Sally has 3 hamsters. How many animals do they have altogether?

☐ ○ ☐ = ☐

They have ________ animals altogether.

42. Mom baked 8 cakes. Terry ate 5 of them. How many cakes were left?

☐ ○ ☐ = ☐

________ cakes were left.

43. My brother has 2 pencils. I have 8 more pencils than my brother. How many pencils do I have?

☐ ○ ☐ = ☐

I have ________ pencils.

44. There are 7 fishes in a pond. There are 2 less frogs than fishes in the pond. How many frogs are there in the pond?

☐ ○ ☐ = ☐

There are ________ frogs in the pond.

45. A rope and a ruler together are about 17 screws long. The ruler is about 5 screws long. How long is the rope?

☐ ○ ☐ = ☐

The rope is about ________ screws long.

46. Dorothy has 11 chickens in her farm. She has 4 less chickens than Jansen. How many chickens does Jansen have?

☐ ○ ☐ = ☐

Jansen has ________ chickens.

47. In a line, Jacob is the 2nd last. He is standing behind Sean. Sean is in the 6th position. How many people are there in line?

There are ________ people in line.

48. Mrs. Chase buys 19 fun-size bags of potato chips. She gives 3 bags to Samuel and 8 bags to Nathaniel. How many bags of potato chips does she have left?

☐ ○ ☐ ○ ☐ = ☐

Mrs. Chase has ________ bags of potato chips left.

49. Uncle Sam bought 6 carrots, 7 potatoes and 4 tomatoes. How many vegetables did he buy altogether?

☐ ○ ☐ ○ ☐ = ☐

Uncle Sam bought ________ vegetables altogether.

50. The total of ☆ and # is 18. Take ☆ away from #, the answer is 4. What are the numbers, ☆ and #?

☆ = ________ ,   # = ________

More Challenging Problems

1. Fill in the circles with the numbers 1, 2, 3, 4, 5, 6, 7, 8 and 9 to make the three number sentences correct. Each number can only be used once. The number 2 has been filled in for you.

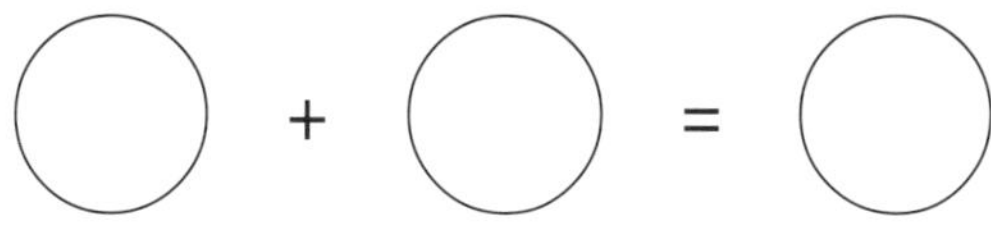

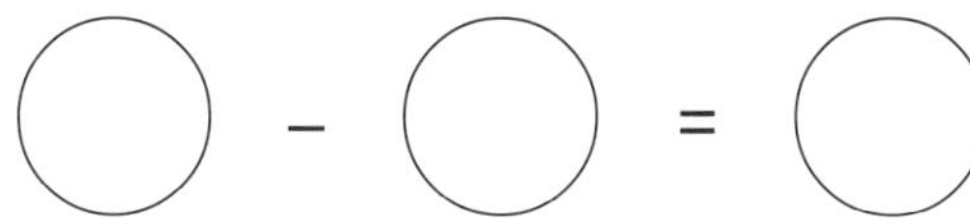

2. Miss June arranges 19 students in a row from the shortest to the tallest. If Maria stands right in the middle of the row, which position does she stand from the tallest student?

3. Complete the following number patterns.

(a) 4, 12, 20, 28, 36, ________, ________, ________.

(b) 85, 80, 75, 70, ________, ________, ________.

(c) 10, 9, 20, 8, 30, 7, 40, 6, ________, ________, ________.

(d) 66, 60, 54, 48, ________, ________, ________.

(e) 3, 4, 5, 4, 5, 6, 5, 6, 7, ________, ________, ________.

4. In the following number pattern, which number does not follow the pattern? Circle it.

2, 3, 5, 8, 12, 17, 29.

5. If △△ = ○○○

and □□□□ = ○○,

how many □ are there in △△?

6. If 1 ♡ = 2 □
   and 1 □ = 4 ●,
   how many ● are there in 1 ♡?

7. Fill in the circles with the numbers 1, 2, 3, 4 and 5 such that the numbers in any straight line add up to 10.

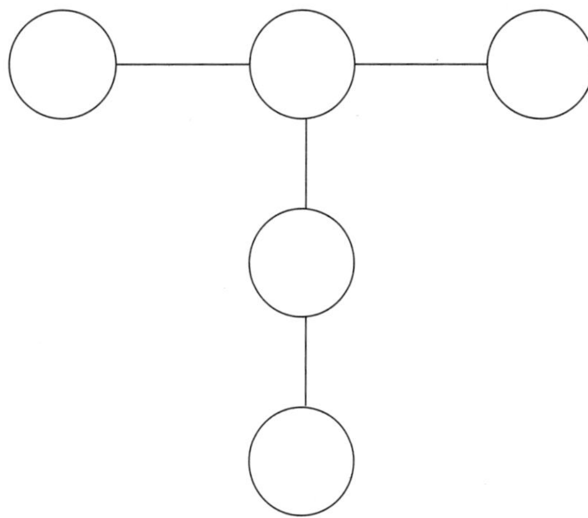

8. Fill in the circles with the numbers 1, 2, 3, 4 and 5 such that the numbers in any straight line add up to 7.

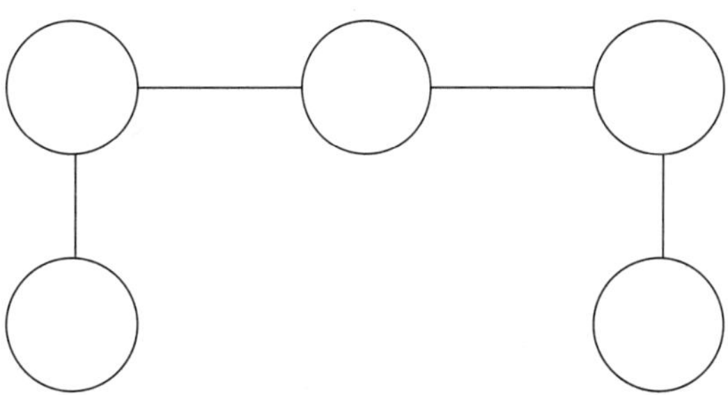

9. Kyle is third in line. He is ahead of Samantha. There are three people between Kyle and Samantha. If Samantha is the second last in line, how many people are there in line?

10. Anne, Sue, Pat and Kim took part in a swimming competition. With the clues given below, can you find out the positions of the 4 girls?

    Clues:
    a. Anne came in 3rd.
    b. Pat was not the 1st and Kim was not the 4th.
    c. Sue was not the winner.
    d. Pat was slower than Sue.

	Position
Anne	______
Sue	______
Pat	______
Kim	______

11. If △ + △ + △ = ☆ + ☆,

△ + ☆ = 5,

and ○ – ☆ = 9,

find the values of △, ☆ and ○.

△ = ________

☆ = ________

○ = ________

12. Find the values of □, ○ and △.

□ + ○ = 10

□ – ○ = 6

○ + ○ + ○ + ○ = □

△ + ○ + □ = 15

□ = ________

○ = ________

△ = ________

13. Find the values of X and Y.

X = ________

Y = ________

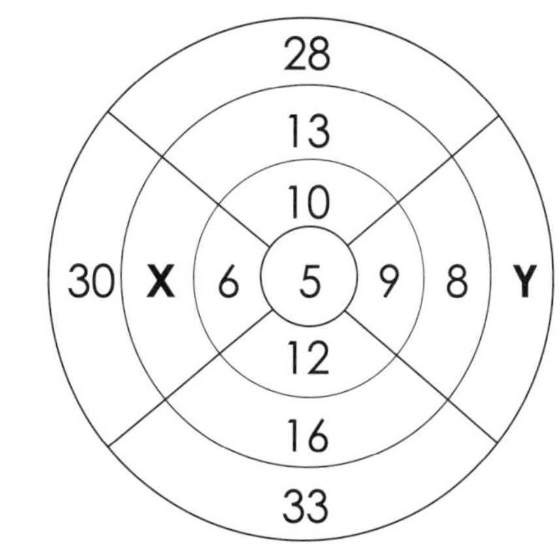

14. Can you make 5 triangles of equal size with 11 matches? Draw the diagram below.

15. Fill in the missing numbers in the circles.

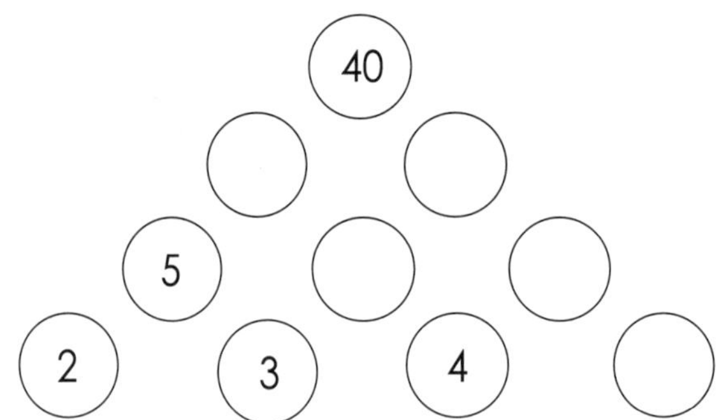

16. Crack the following secret code:

If ↑<↑↑ = 16

and <<↑↑< = 34,

then ↑↑<<<↑<<↑ stands for ________.

17. Study these diagrams. Which object is the heaviest and which is the lightest?

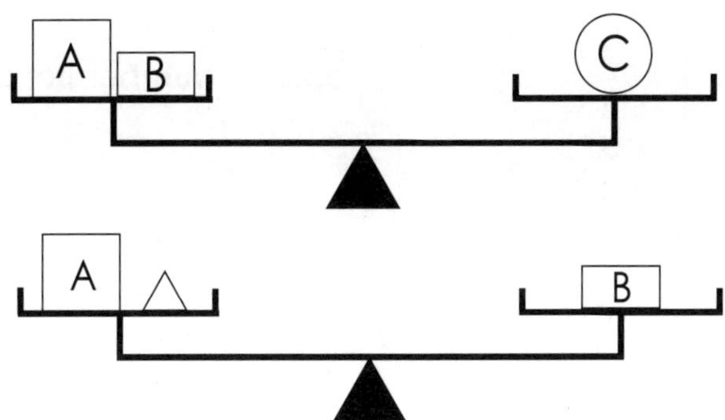

Object ________ is the heaviest.

Object ________ is the lightest.

18. Five animals are standing in a row. The dog is 4th from the left and 2nd from the right. The cat is 3rd from the left. The rabbit is between the mouse and the cat. There is also a duckling in the row.
Can you name the animals in their correct positions? Write the answers in the boxes below.

19. Each piece of cake has 3 layers – chocolate, vanilla and strawberry. Can you think of 6 different ways to combine the 3 flavors on a piece of cake? Mark '1' for chocolate, '2' for vanilla and '3' for strawberry on the cakes below. One has been done for you.

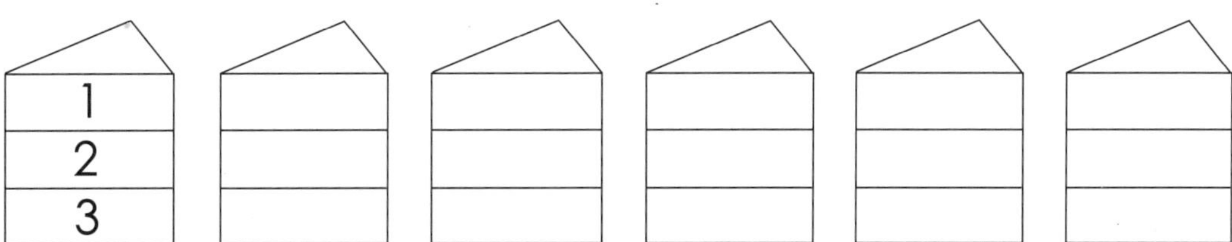

Answers

Topic 1: Numbers to 10

1. Match:
   - (a) and 5 (b) and 0
   - (c) and 10 (d) and 3
   - (e) and 6 (f) and 7
   - (g) and 9 (h) and 4
   - (i) and 2 (j) and 8
2. MATH IS FUN!
3. (a) 2 (b) 3 (c) 3
   (d) 2 (e) 5 (f) 4
5. (a) three (b) eight
   (c) nine (d) two
6. (a) 6 (b) 3
   (c) 2 (d) 1
7. (a) four (b) five
   (c) seven (d) ten
   (e) zero
8. (a) Six (b) Three
   (c) Seven (d) four
   (e) five (f) one
   (g) Nine (h) ten
   (i) Zero (j) eight
   (k) two

N	B	A	W	T	W	O	C
I	O	H	V	P	S	N	H
N	X	T	H	R	E	E	N
E	R	S	J	I	V	I	S
D	F	I	V	E	E	G	K
Y	G	X	T	E	N	H	B
Q	Z	E	R	O	M	T	Y
Z	U	N	I	F	O	U	R

9. Count from left to right:
   (a) Check 3rd box. (b) Check 2nd box.
   (c) Check 4th box. (d) Check 1st box.

Word Problems

1. 5 2. 9 3. 7
4. 3, 2 5. Tom 6. B
7. A 8. Rachel

Take the Challenge!

1. Ben, 4 2. Monday, 3

3. (a) 6, 5 (b) 6 (c) 7

Topic 2: Number Bonds

2. (a) 2 (b) 7 (c) 5
   (d) 4 (e) 7 (f) 4
   (g) 5 (h) 5 (i) 4
   (j) 4 and 4, or 1 and 7, or 2 and 6, or 3 and 5, or 0 and 8.
3.

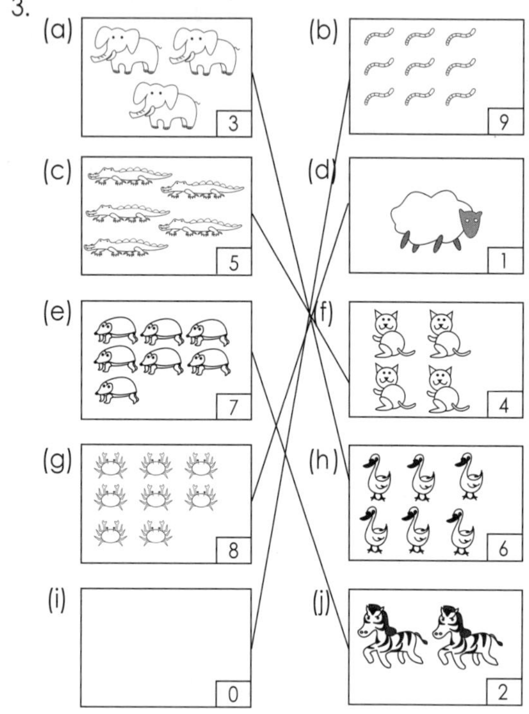

4. (a)

(b)

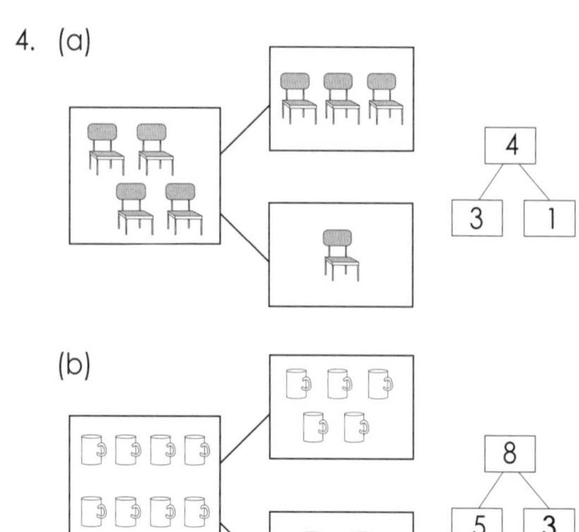

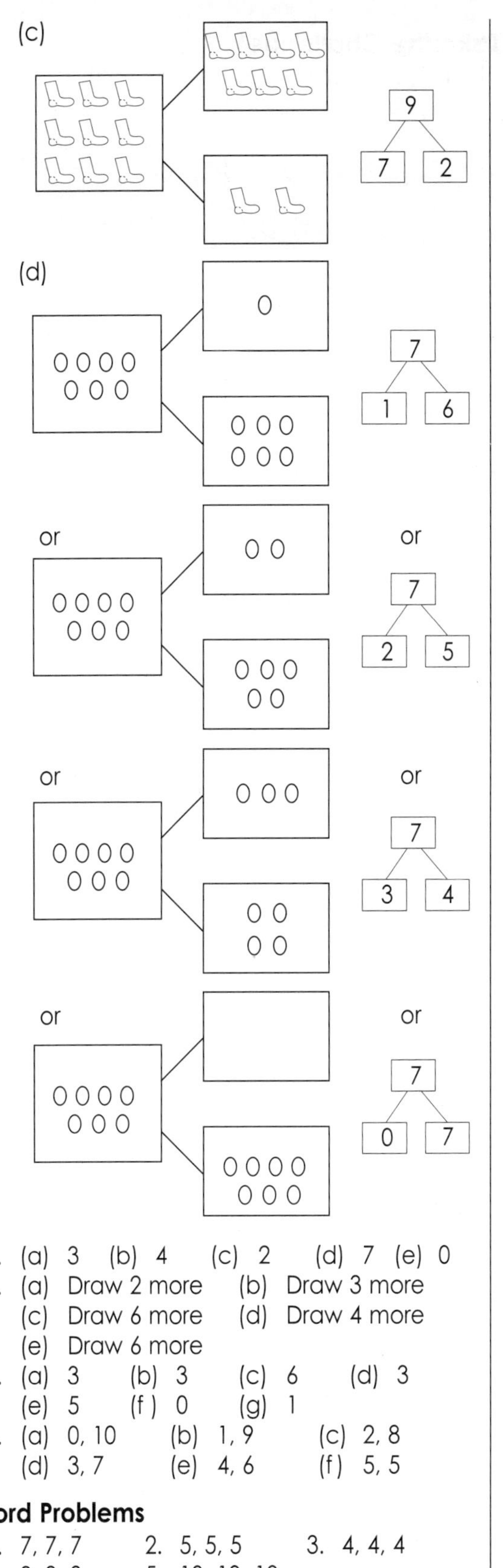

5. (a) 3 (b) 4 (c) 2 (d) 7 (e) 0
6. (a) Draw 2 more (b) Draw 3 more
   (c) Draw 6 more (d) Draw 4 more
   (e) Draw 6 more
7. (a) 3 (b) 3 (c) 6 (d) 3
   (e) 5 (f) 0 (g) 1
8. (a) 0, 10 (b) 1, 9 (c) 2, 8
   (d) 3, 7 (e) 4, 6 (f) 5, 5

Word Problems

1. 7, 7, 7
2. 5, 5, 5
3. 4, 4, 4
4. 8, 8, 8
5. 10, 10, 10

Take the Challenge!

1.

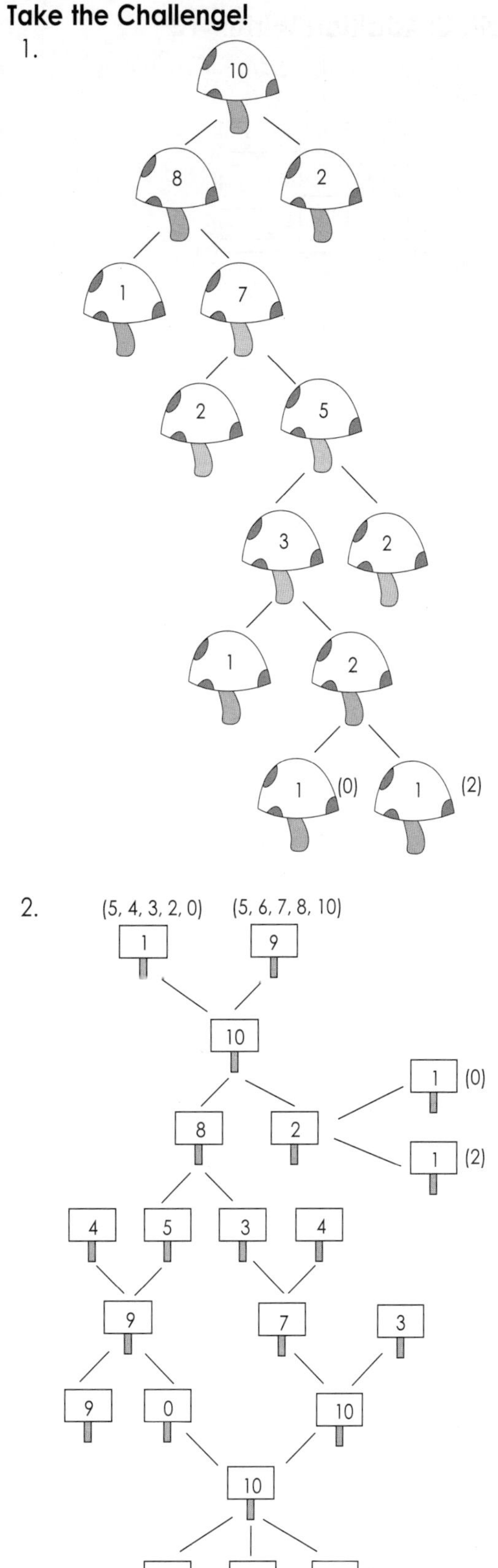

2.

Topic 3: Addition Within 10

1. (a) 2, 5 (b) 5, 6 (c) 4, 6
   (d) 4, 9 (e) 0, 8
2. (a) 2 + 3 = 5
   (b) 4 + 1 = 5
   (c) 1 + 7 = 8
   (d) 4 + 4 = 8
   (e) 5 + 2 = 7
   (f) 4 + 3 = 7
   (g) 0 + 6 = 6
   (h) 4 + 5 = 9
   (i) 3 + 6 = 9
   (j) 3 + 3 = 6
3. (a) 8 (b) 10
   (c) 6 (d) 9
   (e) 7 (f) 5
   (g) 8 (h) 10
4. (a) 8, 8, 8 (b) 7, 7, 7
   (c) 5, 5, 5 (d) 6, 6, 6
   (e) 10, 10, 10 (f) 9, 9, 9
   (g) 10, 10, 10
5. (a) 3, 4; 3 + 4 = 7; 7
   (b) 5, 2; 5 + 2 = 7; 7
   (c) 4, 2; 4 + 2 = 6; 6
6. (a) 1 + 4 = 5 (b) 2 + 5 = 7
   (c) 0 + 9 = 9 (d) 4 + 6 = 10
   (e) 3 + 5 = 8
7. (a) 5, 5 (b) 6, 6
   (c) 4, 4 (d) 4, 4
   (e) 3, 3 (f) 0, 0
   (g) 1, 1 (h) 1, 1
8. (a) 9 and 1, or 6 and 4
   (b) 3 (c) 4
   (d) 6 (e) 2, 6
   (f) 4 and 4, or 2 and 6
   (g) 3
9. (a) 6, 6 (b) 9, 9
   (c) 5, 5 (d) 10, 10
   (e) 8, 8 (f) 8, 8
   (g) 7 (h) 8
   (i) 10

Word Problems

1. 4 + 2 = 6
2. 6
3. 2 + 3 + 4 = 9
4. 3 + 2 = 5
5. 6
6. 3 + 2 + 4 = 9

Take the Challenge!

1. (a) 3 (b) 4 (c) 5 (d) 6
   (e) 2 (f) 2 (g) 1
2. (a)
   (b) ,
   (c) , or ,
   (d) , or ,
3. (a) Funland (b) 6

Topic 4: Subtraction Within 10

1. (a) 3 (b) 7, 2 (c) 6, 3
   (d) 9, 5 (e) 10, 7
2. (a) 3 (b) 4 (c) 4
   (d) 4 (e) 1 (f) 5
   (g) 7 (h) 0
3. (a) 2, 8 – 2 = 6, 6 (b) 2, 7 – 2 = 5, 5
   (c) 4, 6 – 4 = 2, 2 (d) 1, 6 – 1 = 5, 5
4. (a) 5, 5, 5 (b) 5, 5, 5
   (c) 4, 4, 4
5. (a) 7, 7 (b) 1, 1 (c) 2, 2
   (d) 6, 6 (e) 4, 4 (f) 10, 10
   (g) 3 (h) 5 (i) 8
   (j) 10
6. (a) 3 (b) 8 (c) 5
   (d) 3 (e) 6 (f) 4
   (g) 6 (h) 6 (i) 5
   (j) 2 (k) 6 (l) 2
   (m) 7 (n) 10
8. (a) 2 (b) 6 (c) 4
   (d) 1 (e) 3 (f) 7
9. (a) × (b) ✓ (c) ✓
   (d) × (e) × (f) ✓
   (g) × (h) ✓ (i) ×
   (j) ✓
10. (a) 5 (b) 10, 2 (c) 1, 7
    (d) 9, 2 (e) 10 (f) 6, 2
    (g) 5, 1

Word Problems

1. 7 – 3 = 4, 4

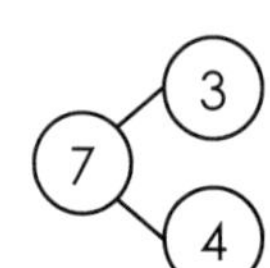

2. 10 – 4 = 6, 6

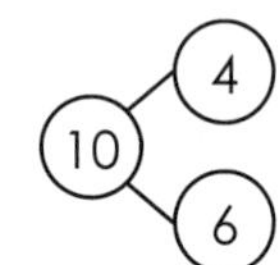

3. 6 – 2 – 2 = 2, 2

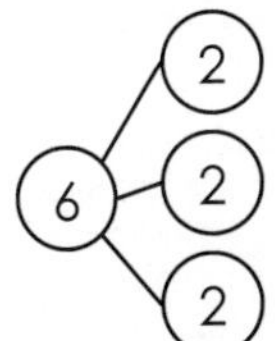

4. 8 – 5 = 3, 3

8 → 5, 3

5. 9 – 4 = 5, 5

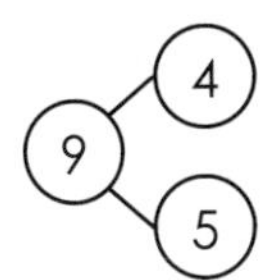

6. 8 – 6 = 2, 2

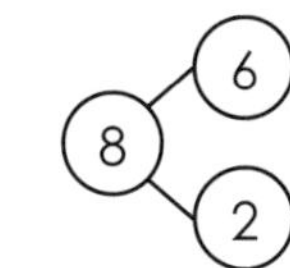

7. 10 – 3 = 7, 7

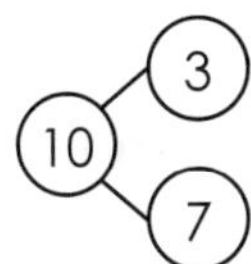

8. 9 – 3 = 6, 6

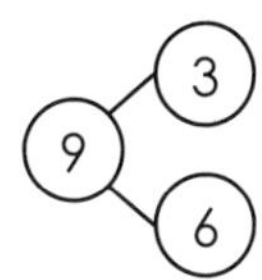

Take the Challenge!

1. 4, 6
2. (b)

8	6	2
5	3	2
3	3	5

(c)

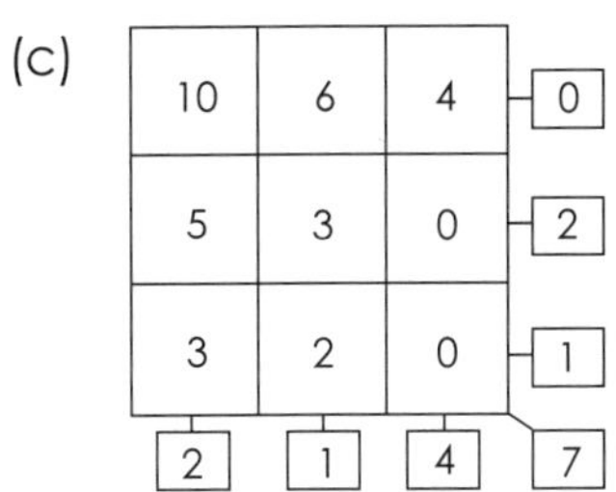

10	6	4	0
5	3	0	2
3	2	0	1
2	1	4	7

(d)

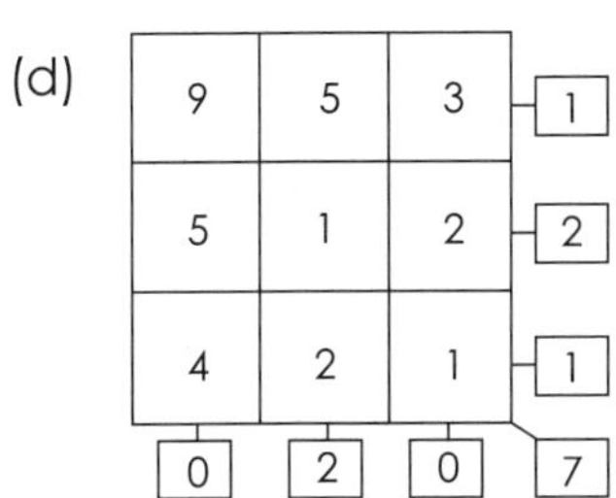

9	5	3	1
5	1	2	2
4	2	1	1
0	2	0	7

Topic 5: Ordinal Numbers

1. (a)

(b)

(c)

(d)

(e)

(f)

2. (a) third (b) ninth (c) fourth
   (d) seventh (e) eighth
3. (a) Chuck (b) Amanda
   (c) 2nd, left or 4th, right (d) 4th
4. (a) first (b) fifth (c) eighth
   (d) second (e) tenth (f) sixth

Word Problems

1. (a) Andrea (b) Pete (c) Sarah
2. Blue, Red, Green, Yellow
3. 6 4. 7 5. 8

Take the Challenge!

1. 5 2. 6th or 2nd 3. 5
4. (a) 3, 4th (b) 2, 2nd
5. 4

Topic 6: Numbers to 20

1.

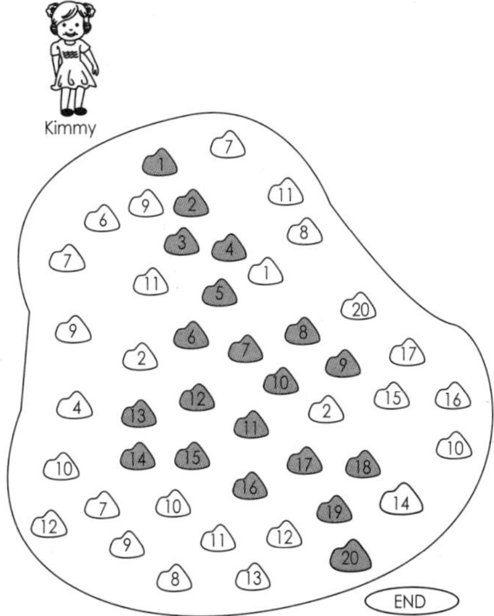

2. (a) twelve (b) eighteen
   (c) nineteen (d) thirteen
   (e) seventeen
3. (a) 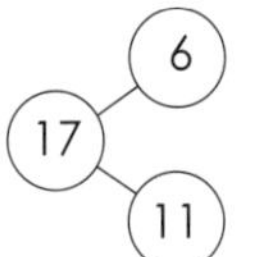 (b) 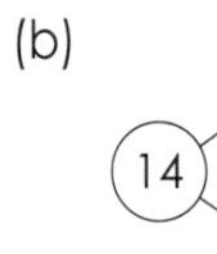
   (c) 19 — 9, 10 (d) 11 — 6, 5
   (e) 16 — 7, 9
4. Color 19
5. Color 8
6. 7, 10, 13, 16, 17
7. 19, 18, 15, 11, 6
8. (a) 12 (b) 17
   (c) 15 (d) 19
9. (a) thirteen (b) eleven
   (c) twenty (d) sixteen
10. (a) 19 (b) 17
    (c) 1, 3 (d) 3
    (e) 2, 0 or 0, 20 (f) 13
11. (a) ✓ (b) ×
    (c) ✓ (d) ×
    (e) × (f) ×
    (g) ✓ (h) ✓
    (i) × (j) ✓
12. 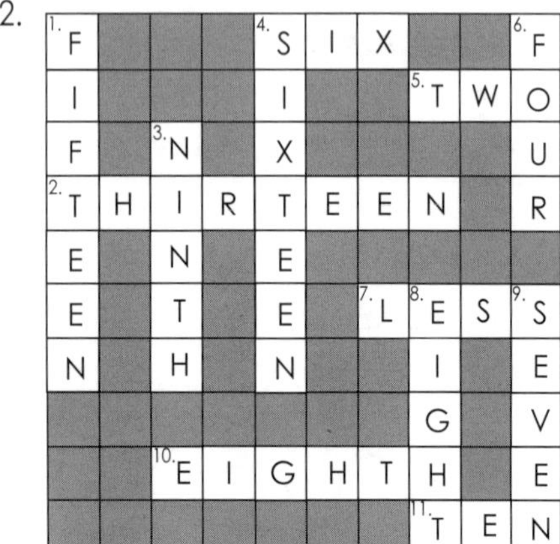

Down:
1. Fifteen
3. ninth
4. Sixteen
6. Four
8. Eight
9. seven

Across:
2. Thirteen
4. Six
5. Two
7. less
10. eighth
11. ten
13. (a) 14, 16
    (b) 15, 13, 7
    (c) 13, 17

Word Problems
1. 10, 4, 14, 14
2. 10, 7, 17, 17
3. 2, 10, 12, 12
4. 6, 10, 16, 16
5. B
6. A
7. Sean, 6
8. B, 4

Take the Challenge!
1. (a) 9, 12 (b) 10, 7 (c) 15, 20
2. 0

Topic 7: Addition and Subtraction Within 20

1. (a) 18 (b) 12 (c) 12
   (d) 18 (e) 19 (f) 19
   (g) 12 (h) 11
2. (a) 13
   (b) 1, 4, 4, 14
   (c) 4, 4, 4, 14
   (d) 2, 1, 1, 11
   (e) 2, 3, 2, 12
   (f) 1, 7, 7, 17
3. (a) 10, 4, 17
   (b) 10, 2, 16
   (c) 10, 5, 19
   (d) 1, 10, 19

(e) 10 1 , 19

(f) 10 3 , 16

(g) 6 10 , 18

(h) 10 7 , 19

(i) 10 3 , 18

(j) 1 10 , 14

4. (a) 7 (b) 10 (c) 6
   (d) 13 (e) 6
5. (a) 9 (b) 14 (c) 5
   (d) 15 (e) 8 (f) 16
   (g) 11 (h) 16
6. (a) 10 7 , 12

   (b) 10 5 , 14

   (c) 10 8 , 11

   (d) 10 9 , 11

   (e) 10 5 , 10

7. (a) 2 10 , 6

   (b) 6 10 , 7

   (c) 2 10 , 9

   (d) 1 10 , 7

   (e) 4 10 , 8

8. (a) + (b) – (c) +
   (d) + (e) – (f) –
9. (a) 12 + 4 = 16
   (b) 4 + 12 = 16
   (c) 16 – 4 = 12
   (d) 16 – 12 = 4
   (e) 16: 12, 4
10. (a) 6 + 4 = 10 (b) 13 + 2 = 15
    (c) 5 + 8 = 13 (d) 15 + 2 = 17
    (e) 12 – 4 = 8 (f) 12 – 7 = 5
    (g) 15 – 6 = 9 (h) 15 – 12 = 3
11. (a) 18 (b) 9 (c) 19
    (d) 5 (e) 8 (f) 12
    (g) 15 (h) 16 (i) 9
    (j) 7 (k) 3 (l) 7
    (m) 6 (n) 14
12. (a) 16 (b) 8 (c) 17
    (d) 12 (e) 8 (f) 13
13. (a) ✓ (b) × (c) ×
    (d) × (e) × (f) ✓
    (g) ✓ (h) ✓

Word Problems

1. 8 + 7 = 15, 15

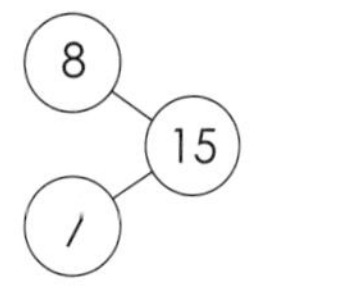

2. 17 – 9 = 8, 8

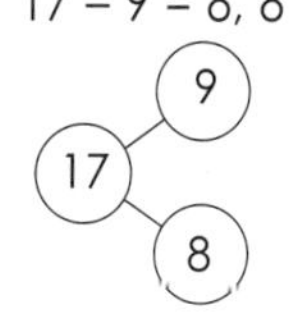

3. 11 + 7 = 18, 18

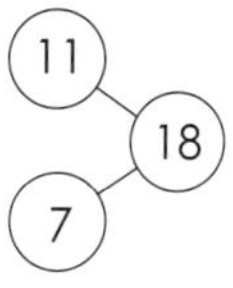

4. 19 – 6 = 13, 13

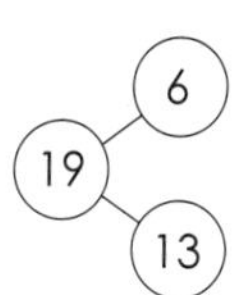

5. 16 – 9 = 7, 7

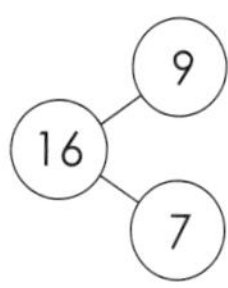

6. 9 + 5 = 14; 14 – 6 = 8; 8
7. (a) 12 + 3 = 15, 15
   (b) 15 – 4 = 11, 11
8. (a) 11 – 6 = 5, 5
   (b) 11 + 6 = 17, 17

Take the Challenge!

1. (a)

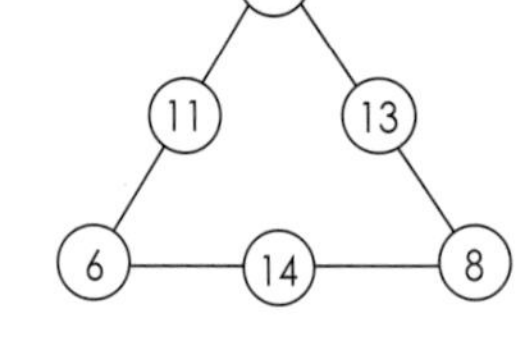

(b)

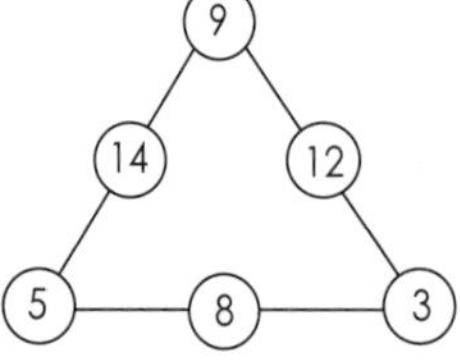

(c)

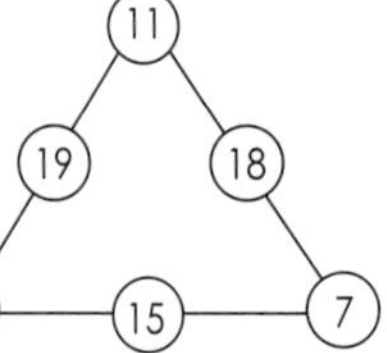

(d)

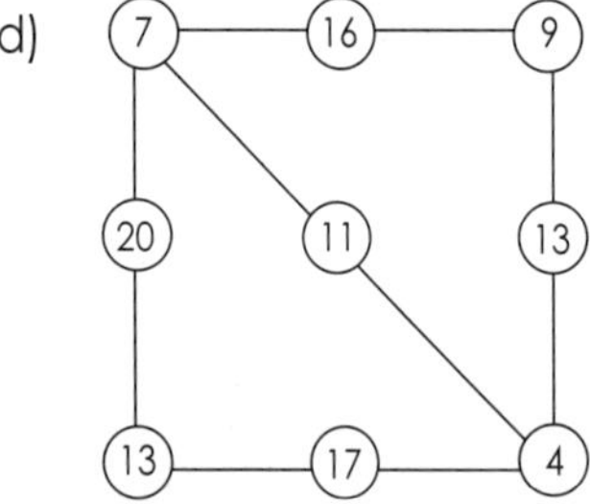

2. There are many possible ways of filling in the numbers. The answer for each part shown below is just one way.

(a)

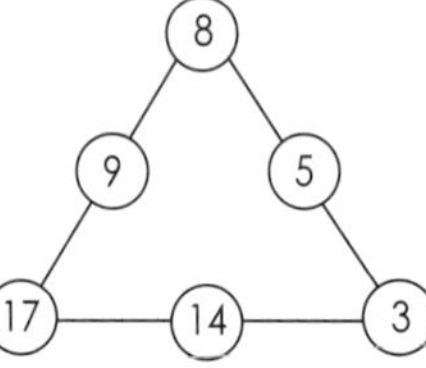

(b)

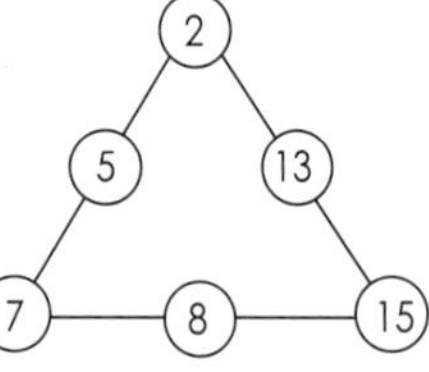

(c)

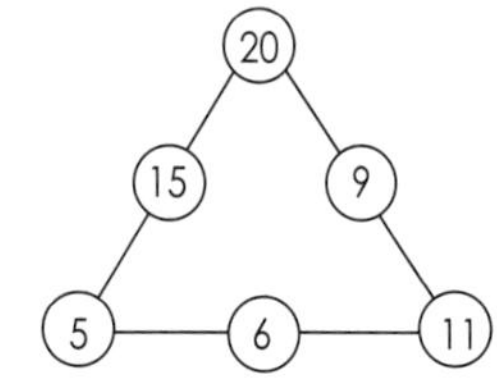

(d)

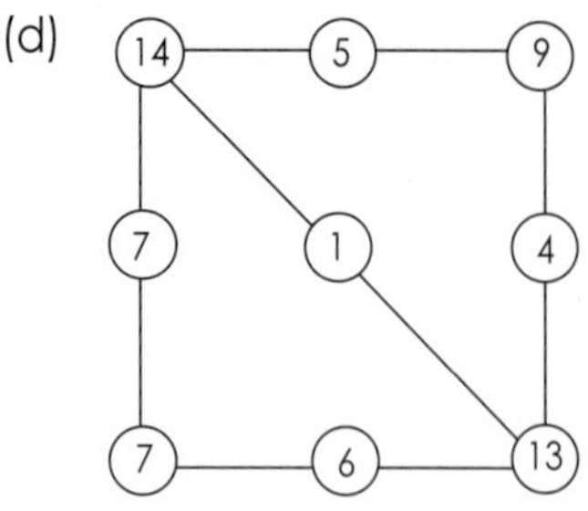

Topic 8: Shapes and Patterns

2. (a) 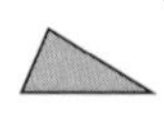     

(b) 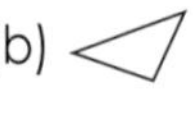 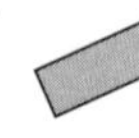   

(c)

(d) 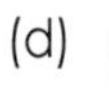    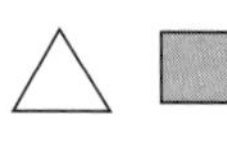

(e) 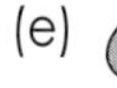 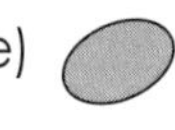 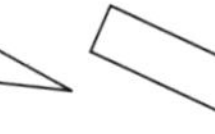 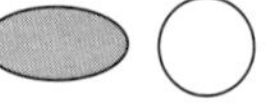

3. (a)  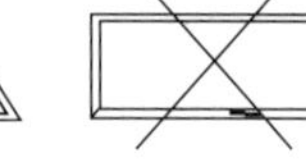 

(b) 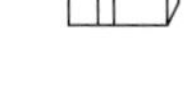 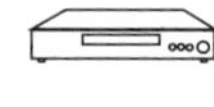  

(c)    

(d) 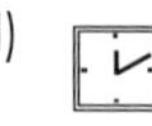   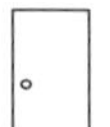 

(e) 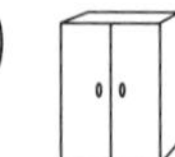   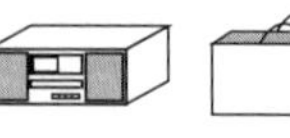

(f) 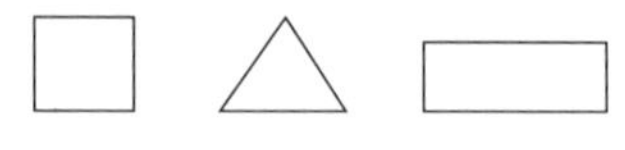 

4.  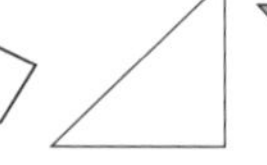 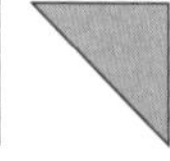

5. 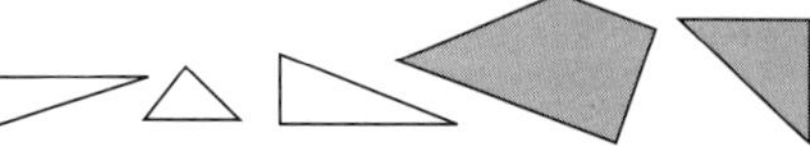

6. 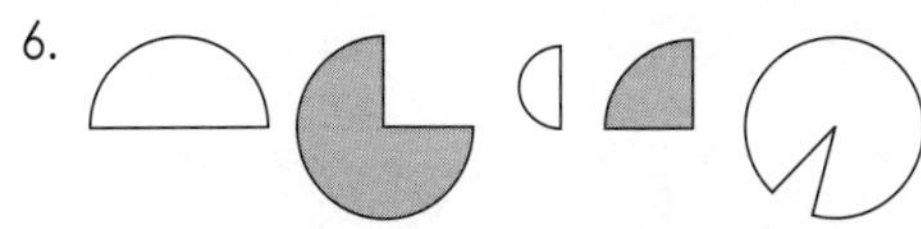

7. (a) 12, 6, triangles, squares, 6
   (b) 6, 4, 10, 2, triangles, squares

8. (a) (b) 8

9. (a) (b) 8

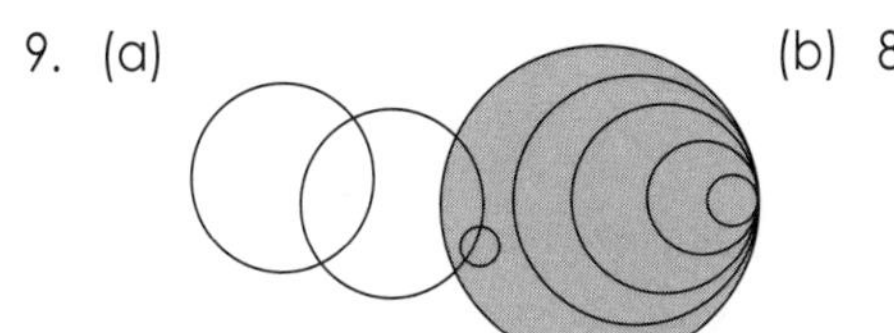

10. (a) (b) 10

11. (a) (b) medium (c)

(d) larger (e) (f)

(g)

12. (a) brown (b) brown

13. (a) pink medium (b) pink

14. (a) red (b) red

15. (a) black (b) black

Take the Challenge!

1. (a) (b) smallest size

(c) blue (d)

2. 3.

Topic 9: Length

1. (a) 12 (b) 10 (c) 6
   (d) 6 (e) 7

7.

A B C D

8.

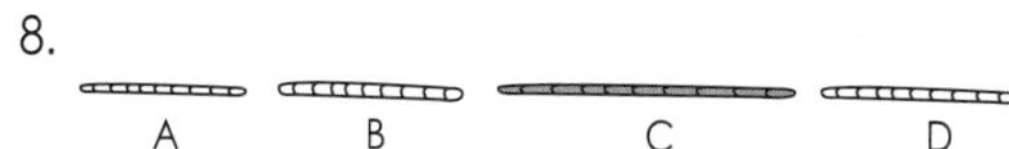

A B C D

9.

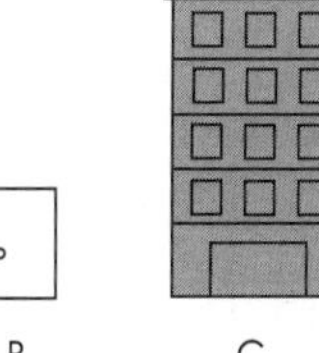

A B C D

10.

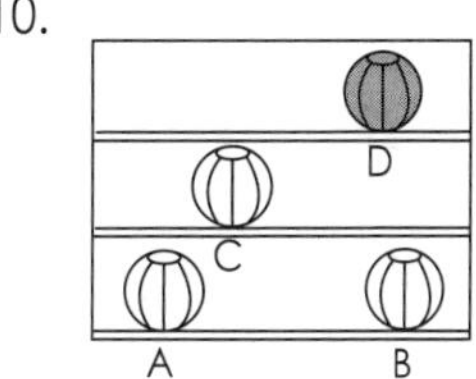

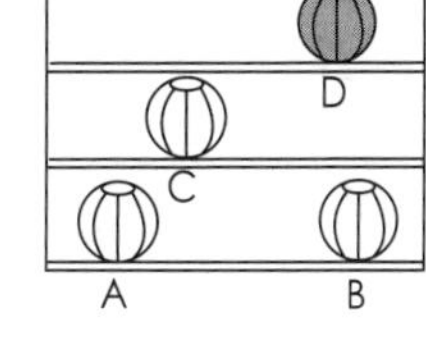

11.

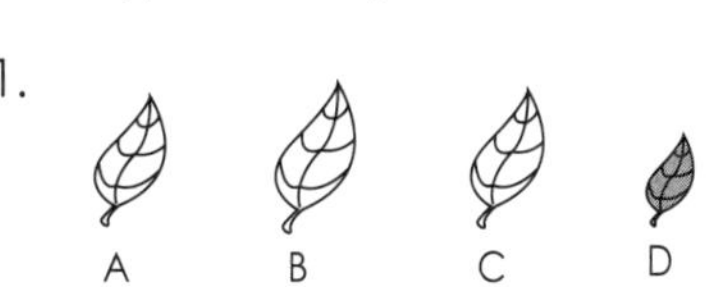

A B C D

12. love family children parents

13. HAPPINESS

14.

A B C D

15. 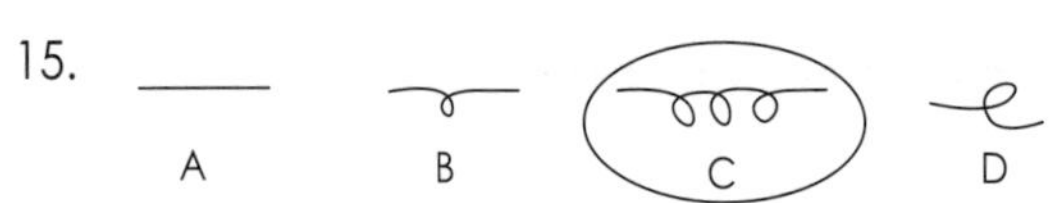

16. 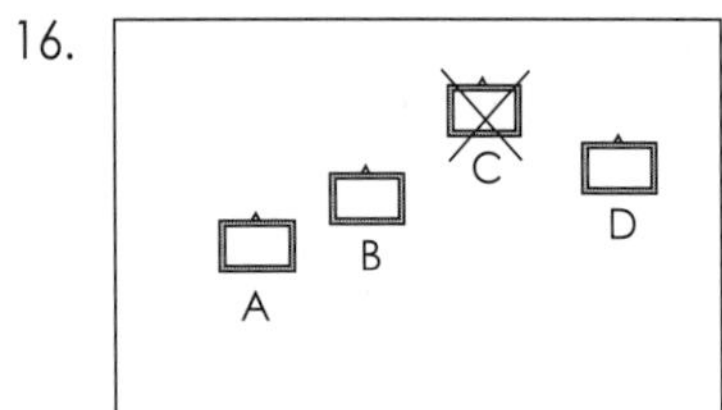

17. (a) 3 (b) 5
(c) 3 (d) 9
(e) shorter (f) longer
(g) shorter (h) B
(i) C
18. (a) 10 (b) 13
(c) 7 (d) longer
(e) shorter (f) longer
(g) C (h) B
19. (a) shortest (b) longest
(c) longer than (d) as long as
(e) longer than (f) shorter than
20. (a) 5 (b) 2
(c) taller (d) shorter
(e) Kristine (f) shorter

Word Problems

1. 7 + 8 = 15, 15
2. 6 + 5 = 11, 11
3. 9 + 4 = 13, 13
4. 11 + 7 = 18, 18
5. 5 + 5 = 10, 10
6. 7 + 9 = 16, 16
7. 5 + 5 + 5 = 15, 15
8. 4 + 5 + 7 = 16, 16

Take the Challenge!

1. (a) (b) (c) 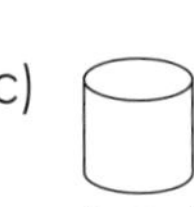
(small one)
(d) (e)
2. (a) 4 (b) 6 (c) 18

Topic 10: Weight

1. (a) 12 (b) 6
(c) 1, 12 (d) 2, 10
(e) greater
2. Color A
3. Color A
4. Color D
5. Color C
6. Color hen
7. C → D → B → A
8. E → B → C → D → A
9. A B C D
10. (a) 10 (b) 5
(c) cat (d) rat
(e)

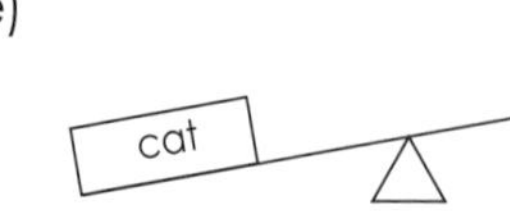

11. (a) 12 (b) 9
(c) A (d) B
(e)

Baby B
Baby A

12. (a) 7 (b) 4
(c) detergent (d) liquid soap
13. (a) 9 (b) 15
(c) clock (d) can of milk
14. (a) 10 (b) 16
(c) jam (d) candy

Word Problems

1. 5 + 3 = 8, 8
2. 15 − 8 = 7, 7
3. 9 + 2 = 11, 11
4. 12 − 6 = 6, 6
5. 7 + 4 = 11, 11
6. 4 + 9 = 13, 13
7. 8 + 7 = 15, 15
8. 5 + 7 = 12, 12
9. 11 + 7 = 18, 18
10. 8 + 5 = 13, 13
11. 6 + 8 = 14, 14
12. 3 + 9 + 3 = 15, 15

Take the Challenge!

1. (a) as heavy as (b) lighter than
(c) heavier than (d) heavier than
(e) lighter than (f) lighter than
(g) heavier than (h) lighter than
(i) heavier than (j) D
(k) E (l) lighter than
2. (a) 4 (b) 4
(c) 16

Mid-Year Review

Part 1

1. 

2. 6 + 3 = 9
3. 3

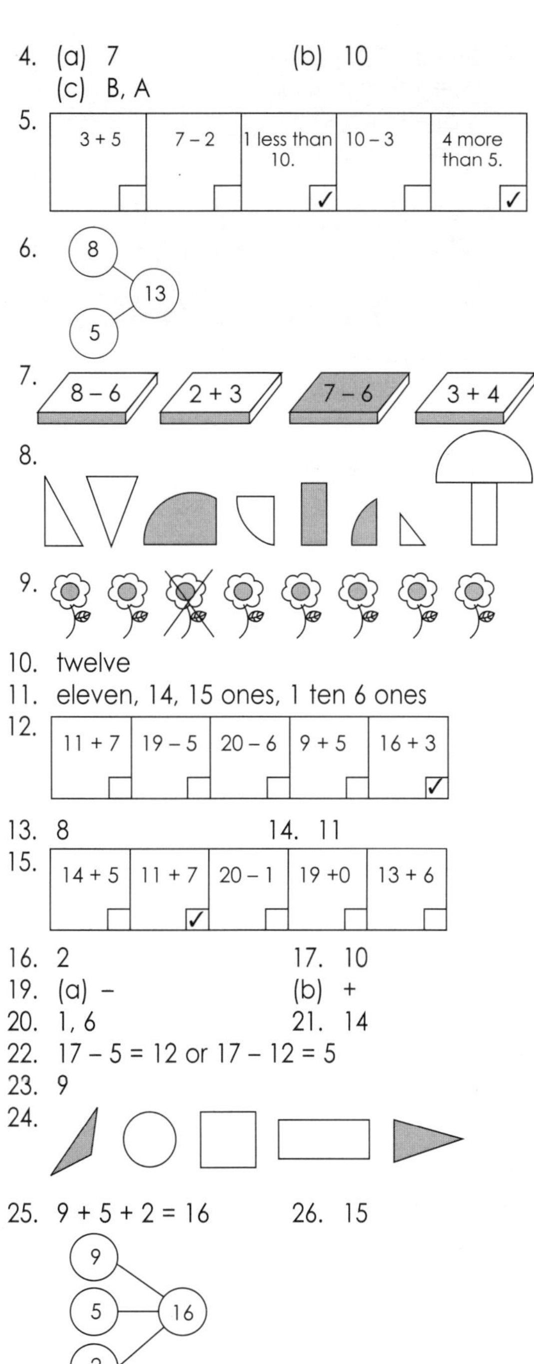

4. (a) 7 (b) 10
   (c) B, A
5. | 3 + 5 | 7 – 2 | 1 less than 10. ✓ | 10 – 3 | 4 more than 5. ✓ |
6. 8, 5 → 13
7. 8 – 6, 2 + 3, 7 – 6, 3 + 4
8.
9.
10. twelve
11. eleven, 14, 15 ones, 1 ten 6 ones
12. | 11 + 7 | 19 – 5 | 20 – 6 | 9 + 5 | 16 + 3 ✓ |
13. 8 14. 11
15. | 14 + 5 | 11 + 7 ✓ | 20 – 1 | 19 +0 | 13 + 6 |
16. 2 17. 10
19. (a) – (b) +
20. 1, 6 21. 14
22. 17 – 5 = 12 or 17 – 12 = 5
23. 9
24.
25. 9 + 5 + 2 = 16 26. 15
27. 10, 7, 0, 3, 11
28. ◯ 29. 9
30.

31. 14, 17 32. 7 + 9 = 16
33. (a) Marilyn (b) Janice
34. 4
35. (a) A (b) C (c) A
36. 14 – 5 = 9 or 37. 2
    14 – 9 = 5

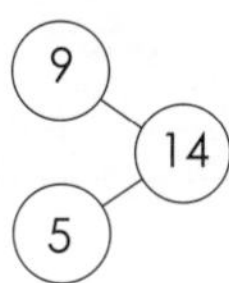

38.

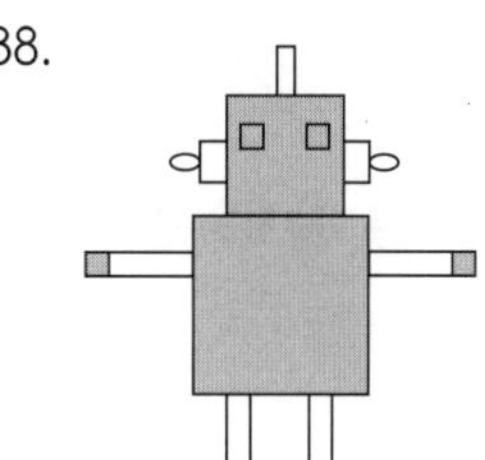

39.

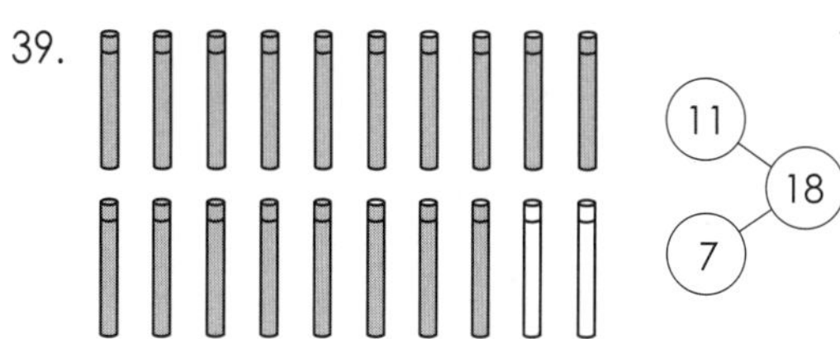

40. (a) Derick (b) Jack
    (c) Shannon (d) Jack

Part 2

41. 4 + 3 = 7, 7
42. 8 – 5 = 3, 3
43. 2 + 8 = 10, 10
44. 7 – 2 = 5, 5
45. 17 – 5 = 12, 12
46. 11 + 4 = 15, 15
47. 8
48. 19 – 3 – 8 = 8, 8
49. 6 + 7 + 4 = 17, 17
50. 7, 11

More Challenging Problems

1. 4 + 5 = 9, 8 – 1 = 7, 3 ∞ 2 = 6
2. Maria stands in the 10th position from the tallest studentl.
3. (a) 44, 52, 60 (b) 65, 60, 55
   (c) 50, 5, 60 (d) 42, 36, 30
   (e) 6, 7, 8

4. 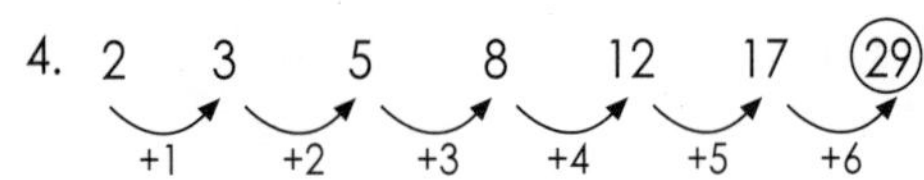

29 does not follow the pattern.
The number 29 should be 23.

5. ○ = □□
△ △ = ○○○
= □□ □□ □□
There are 6 □ in △△.

6. 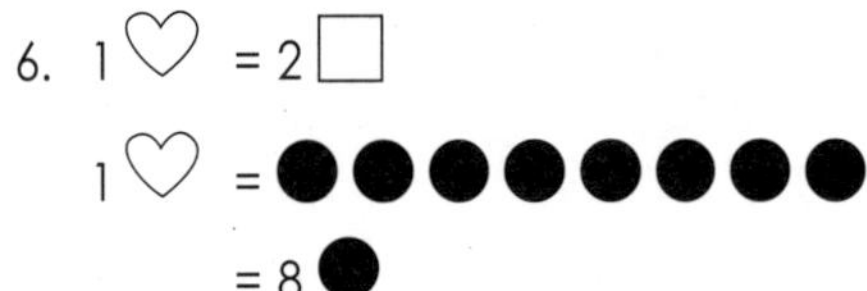

7. 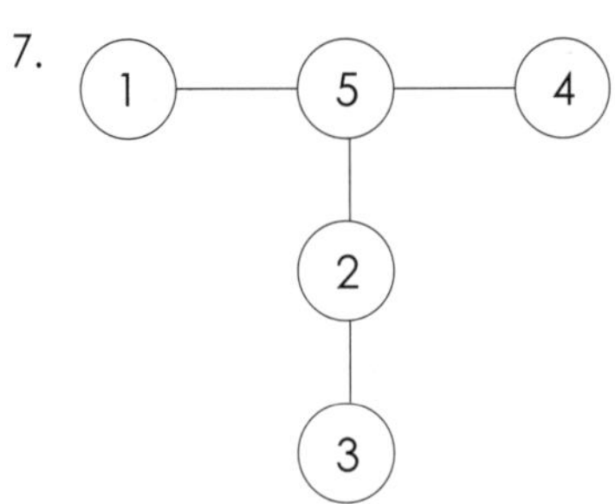

8. 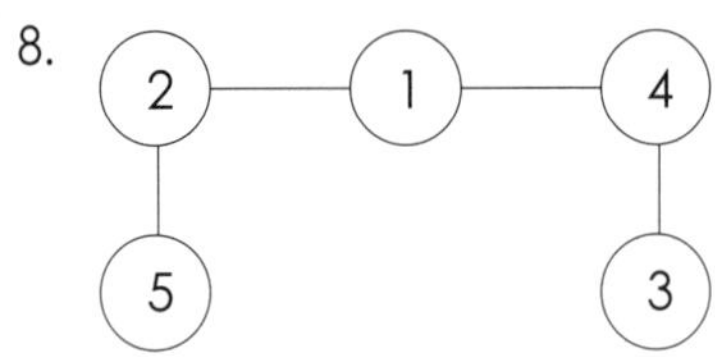

9. Position:

There are 8 people in line.

10. Anne = 3rd position
Sue = 2nd position
Pat = 4th position
Kim = 1st position

11. △ = 2
☆ = 3
○ = 12

12. □ = 8
○ = 2
△ = 5

13. 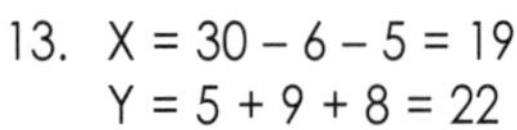
$X = 30 - 6 - 5 = 19$
$Y = 5 + 9 + 8 = 22$

14. 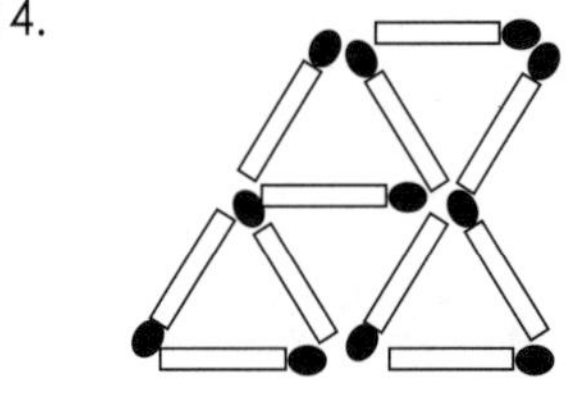

15. 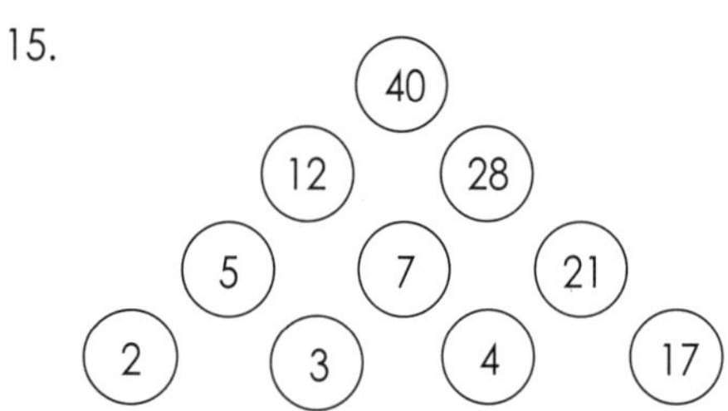

16. Each < = 10 and each ↑ = 2.
Code = 50 + 8 = 58

17. Object C is the heaviest.
Object A is the lightest.

18. mouse | rabbit | cat | dog | duckling

19. 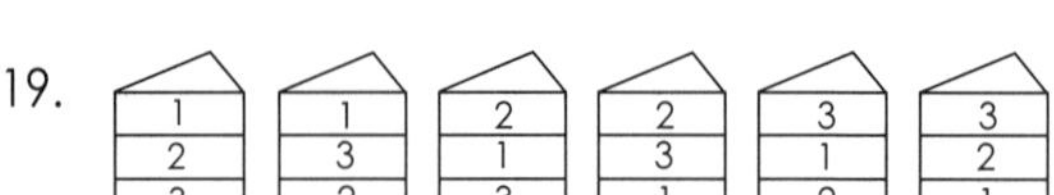